John Spencer & Co (Badger Books) Illustrated Bibliography

Volume 1: Comics, Science Fiction and Supernatural

Shane P. D. Agnew

Copyright © 2020 Shane P. D. Agnew

Cover Picture: Art by Chris Hall www.dlsreviews.com

ISBN 978-1-912578-94-8

ACKNOWLEDGEMENT

This illustrated bibliography could not have been possible without the pioneering work done by the following leading researchers of the history of the science fiction over the past several decades. In particular, thanks go to the authors of the following publications which are responsible for my interest in collecting Spencer publications and for that (I think!) I am grateful.

Mike Ashley – Fantasy Reader Guide, Cosmos Literary Agency, 1979
Steve Holland – Badger Tracks, Underworld Studio
Steve Holland & Richard Williams, British Paperback Checklist No. 23, Dragonby Press, 2005
Down the Badger Hole- Debbie Cross, Wrigley Cross Books, 1995

Special mention should also go to the following indispensable online resources

The Internet Speculative Fiction DB - http://www.isfdb.org/
Phil Stephensen-Payne's wonderful site- http://www.philsp.com/
and Brian Hunt's Fanthorpe homage site -http://peltorro.com/

John Spencer & Co. (Badger Books) Illustrated Bibliography
Volume 1: Comics, Science Fiction and Supernatural

Welcome to volume one of an intended three volume set covering the many genres of John Spencer & Co publications. This volume focuses on the Comics, Science Fiction/Fact and Supernatural. It is the accumulation of decades of collecting and has been a labour of love (and frustration) to pull together over the past few years. The book would not have been possible without the assistance of several people and the internet. The majority of the content is from my personal collection, but that owes much to previous works compiled by Mike Ashley, Steve Holland and Richard Williams. Thanks also needs to go to Chris Hall and J.R. Park for their support and encouragement. It would also be remiss of me not to thank my long-suffering wife for allowing me the time (not always begrudgingly) to spend on this project.

The series is an illustrated bibliography and checklist for reference to aid collectors and is not intended as a historical reference of Spencer publishers or their place in the British 'Mushroom Jungle' as that is well served by Messrs Ashley and Holland. However, below is a brief and potted history for any reader not familiar with John Spencer/Badger Books.

With an undertaking of this size there are undoubtedly going to be mistakes, as records are unclear and sometimes conflicting. I have had to use my judgement regarding the likeliest information and have tried to note where these conflicts exist. One of the main areas I have had to use my judgement is around the cover artist. For instance, there were two Nicholson's active around this period, John 'Nick' Nicholson (Google Andrew Darlington's excellent blog on the artist) and S. Nicholson (likely Stanley) who was responsible for cover art across the various genres. I have analysed the artwork side by side and produced the statistics and timelines for each artist which helps with defining the likely creator (my teachers always said to show your workings!).

There are also going to be omissions and there are a few unverified blanks which I believe were never produced but are referred to in other bibliographies or within adverts in previous editions. I have included these so that others may be able to confirm their existence. Accordingly, I would be very grateful to receive any additional information which you may have, or even just to feedback on the content. Please email me at agnewclan@hotmail.com.

I originally embarked on this project as a way of cataloguing my own collection, but as this became very expansive, I found it harder and harder to track down the material; mainly down to the fact that I only had snippets of information, such as a publication title or a particular story name, and ultimately, with few visual references, I didn't know exactly what I was searching for. Hopefully this book will save you many of those hours I spent trawling the internet archives and allow you (if so inclined) to build up your own collection. But be warned, it is a fine line between Collector, Completist and Obsessive.

Kindest Regards

Shane P.D Agnew

John Spencer & Co - A Brief History

Samuel Assael (1920- 1998), along with his partner Maurice Nahum (1916-1994), started John Spencer & Co publications in 1946/7 at a time, following the war, when paper was still being rationed. Working out of 24 Shepherds Bush Rd., London, W6 they began with several 32-page one-off magazines mainly covering crime (*Phantom and Dynamic Detectives Cases*) and western themes (*Ace and Thrilling Westerns*). These were priced in cents, no doubt in order to suggest they had American heritage. By the late 1940s they had started producing short Crime and Gangster novels under various house names such as Earl Ellison, Rex Marlowe, Brett Diamond and Janet Gordon etc. These were written by the likes of Sydney Bounds, N(orman). Wesley Firth and Norman Lazenby. It appears that Spencer would happily move and follow trends in the market launching books in any genre that they believed were popular. This is a theme that carried on through their 30+year publishing history.

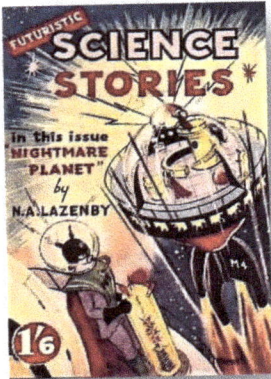

In 1950 they launched four short story digest science fiction series, which (other than the different titles) could have been one and the same series. These were *the Futuristic Science Stories, Tales of Tomorrow, Wonders of the Spaceways* and *Worlds of Fantasy*. All where adorned with 'boy's own' images of spacecrafts and space explorers (we should remember that the first manned space flight would not happen for another 11 years) and may well have been aimed at the juvenile market. These Sci-Fi digests contained short stories by a number of authors such as John F. Watts, Norman Lazenby, Leonard G. Fish, A. A. Glynn, John Glasby and Robert Lionel Fanthorpe (the latter two would feature heavily in the life of the publisher). It appears that Spencer would almost always guarantee the authors a sale regardless of the quality of the stories but paid very little for the privilege. Artists of the time such as Norman Light, Gerald Facey and Ron Turner provided most of the cover artwork. These four series came to an end in 1954 after differing numbers of editions totalling 50 digests (apart from an odd reboot in 1958 with Futuristic Science Series vol 2 no.16, which may have been intended as SF3, making it 51 editions). During 1953-54 Spencer also published several full-length science fiction stories that where not part of any particular series (although a couple of them are numbered and have cover designs that resembles the digest series). Artwork by Ray Theobald, Light and Gordon C. Davies wrapped around stories mainly by Glasby, Fanthorpe and Tom Wade.

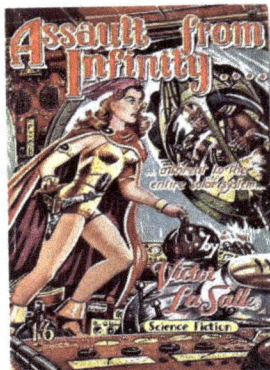

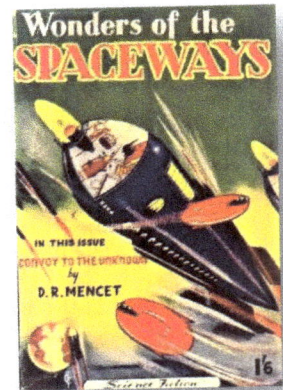

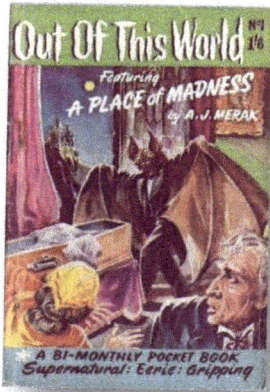

May 1954 saw the publisher launch what was to become one of their longest running series under a new imprint - Badger Books. The Out of this World/Supernatural(SN) series seems to be a possible launch of 2 different series of supernatural and fantasy works that became entwined as a single series (Out of this world #1 and #2 were produced in late 1954 but the title becomes integrated into the SN series in 1957 with SN13) . They started out as short story compilations by various authors that in reality turned out to be entirely penned by the same author under the myriad of pseudonyms of Glasby and Fanthorpe, an exception being SN9 which was short stories entirely by the famous Sci-fi writer E. C. Tubb. Later on SN29 titled *Dark Conflict* started a new approach with a full length novel by Glasby, then again a full length Fanthorpe novel appeared in SN35 and by SN40 the series began to follow a novel and short story compilation alternating pattern until it's final issue SN109 in 1967 (note there were only 108 SN titles as #108 was not produced). Early artwork as with the digest series was by Facey, Theobald, Turner et al. until the weight was taken in the late 50s by (in my opinion) one of three key individuals to work for the publication – Henry Fox (the other two being Glasby and Fanthorpe)

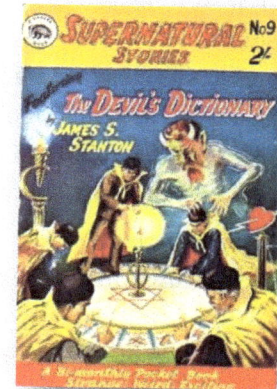

During this period John Spencer & Co relocated to 131 Brackenbury Rd., London, W6 sometime after the Autumn of 1955, a premise previously used by Hamilton & Co (and later would be also used by Grant Hughes publishers). This change seems to have had little effect in terms of type and output from the publisher, but it does allow for dating of some of the publications, especially the Spencer glamour magazines produced around this period that will be covered in a later volume.

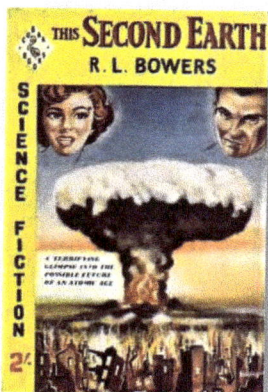

In late 1957, when the SN series was only a dozen or so editions old Spencer launched a Science Fiction Series under a new, but short lived, imprint of Cobra Books (the Cobra name had previously been used on a couple of Crime novels in the early 50s). This seems to have been a false dawn as Glasby's *This Second Earth* was the only title from what would become a long running Science Fiction series (SF) which launched again in early 1958 with Fanthorpe's *The Waiting World*. The series would go on for 117 editions until 1966 when volume number SF118 brought it to a close with Fanthorpe's *The Watching World*. Although the series was largely dominated by two prolific writers - Glasby and Fanthorpe - other authors made appearances such as W(illiam). H. Fear (who also wrote several Westerns for Spencer), Paul Charkin and R. Chetwynd-Hayes (his first novel being *The Man from the*

Bomb SF21). Algis Budrys's *Who?* also got a reprint in SF28. The cover artwork, as was typical in the early days, used a number of artists; S. Nicholson picking up the majority of the first dozen or so (I caveat this, as with a lot of the artwork, most is uncredited. However, based on other covers from around the time, along with preliminary drawings which appear to be attributed to S. Nicholson, this leads me to this conclusion). Ed Blandford, who would also produce art for the World War 2 series, contributed further artwork. However, the bulk (as would be the case across all the genres from the late 1950s onward) were created by the inexhaustible Henry Fox. The difference during 1960/61 from the SN series was the heavy reuse of American covers form the ACE and Avon series, with at least 24 covers being recycled from great artists such as Ed Emshwiller (Emsh), Ed Valigursky, Carlo Jacono and Cha'Bril (Joaquín Chacopino Fabré). This reuse of American covers is also seen heavily in the 13 Crime Series (CS) novels and occasionally in the Western series, a licensing practice that was not unusual for UK publishers at that time.

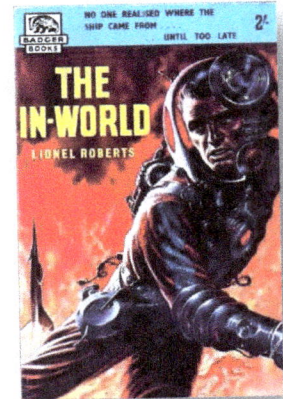

Spencer mainly produced fiction but at times did produce non-fiction books. The 4 book Science Series (SS) from 1959-62 was a series of reprints mainly around the perceived future of space travel and where humanity was heading.

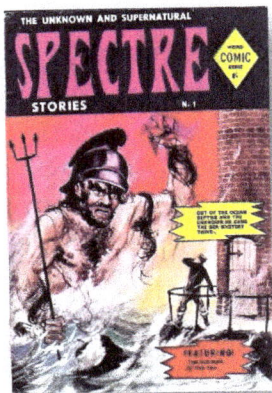

The final genre within this first volume covers the 'odd' comics produced in 1966-67 which barely lasted a year. I refer to them as odd due to the way they are constructed. Initially there were four titles, which similar to the four early sci-fi digests series (mentioned earlier) they could easily have been published under a single title. *Macabre Stories, Strange Stories, Spectre Stories* and *Fantasy Stories* were produced by Mick Anglo of MarvelMan/MiracleMan fame. It is unclear how much of these comics were drawn by Anglo personally, as he was known to have had several artists working for him. Despite this, it would be safe to say the quality of these comics was very poor.

Furthermore, the construction of the comics involved several of the covers being rehashed versions of the Sci-Fi digest, SN and SF book covers. On top of this a large proportion of the strips contained within were titles taken from their short story content. You will note there is a discrepancy in the number of comics produced under these 4 titles, with several references to 6 editions in each. I am however convinced that only 5 editions were ever produced for both *Strange* and *Spectre Stories*, the 6th edition (despite being mentioned in the other editions) having never materialised.

This was a theme throughout the publisher's history, as coming up with the titles, editions, artwork and announcing them before they have got any author/artist to pen them was the norm. At some point during this time Anglo left and artist Michael Jay was drafted in. Then when the four titles folded, Jay took up the mantel with two new titles – *The Purple Hood* and *The Adventures of Mark Tyme*. The former was a marvel character-based rip off in which our protagonist, Lee Briton, puts on a costume and becomes the Purple Hood (think Bruce Wayne and Batman). The latter involved a time traveller with a somewhat dodgy time traveling watch which meant he would randomly end up anywhere in history (a sort of early *Quantum Leap*). Both these titles ended after only two editions each, and with their demise the end of the Spencer involvement within the comic genre.

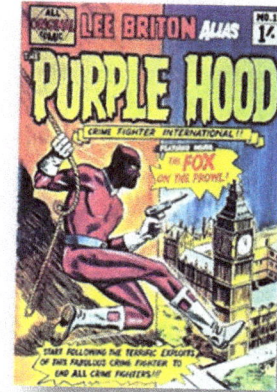

This potted history focuses on the Science Fiction/Fantasy output, but John Spencer (under Badger/Cobra imprints) produced several other series and one-off titles. The total number of publications identified is around 835 covering such genres as Crime, Spy, Magazines, Westerns, Foreign Legion, Bengal Lancers, Romance and War; which will be covered in Volume 2 and 3. To understand how John Spencer fitted into the annals of pulp publishing I highly recommend *The Mushroom Jungle - A History of Post-war British Paperback Publishing* by Steve Holland ISBN :1874113017 and *Vultures of the Void - The Legacy a History of Post War British SF* by Philip Harbottle ISBN: 9781607011491.

John Spencer & Co publications– The Stats

Covers by Artist/Year

Artists	1950	1951	1952	1953	1954	1955	1957	1958	1959	1960	1961	1962	1963	1964	1965	1966	1967	1973	1974	1978	Grand Total
Bernard Barton										1											1
Carlo Jacono										6											6
Cha'Bril										2											2
Chesley Bonestell												1									1
Curt Caesar										2											2
D.Rainey											6	2									8
Ed Blandford									1												1
Ed Emshwiller (Emsh)										8	2										10
Ed Valigursky										3											3
Eddie Jones									3	2											5
Edgar Hodges									1												1
Gerald Facey	6	5			2	2		1													16
Gordon C. Davies			1	5	3																9
Henry Fox							2	2		2	10	30	32	19	14	7	3	1			122
John Pollack							1														1
John Richards											1										1
M. D'Antonia											1										1
Michael Jay																6	4				10
Mick Anglo			5	11																	16
Norman Light																16					16
Photograph																				1	1
Ray Theobald				5	10		2	6	9												32
Richard Powers											2										2
Robert V. Engel										1											1
Ron Embleton					2	2															4
Ronald Turner		2	8	1			1	2													14
S. Nicholson								3	5	1											9
Symeon																			1		1
UNKNOWN				2	1			4	4	3	10	2		1	2	2				1	32
Grand Total	6	7	14	24	18	4	6	18	23	31	32	35	32	20	16	31	7	1	1	2	328

Stories by Actual Author/Year (Inc. Shorts and Novels)

Stories by Year Act Author	Da ▸ 1950	1951	1952	1953	1954	1955	1957	1958	1959	1960	1961	1962	1963	1964	1965	1966	1967	1973	1974	1978	Grand Total
A. A. Glynn			3	9	1																15
Alfred E. Hind		1									1		1								3
Algis Budrys			1																		1
Art Smith					1																1
Barney Ward		1																			1
C. D. Ellis		1	3																		4
Charlie Coombes									1												1
Comic Strip																					1
Dale Graham																133	12				145
E. C. Tubb			2	3	1																6
Ernest Kemp							6														13
Frederick T. Foden													1								1
Gerald Evans		1																			1
Gray Barker		1	1																		2
Harry Mansfield										1											1
Jack Lawson													2	5	5						12
John F. Watt	10	10	10	20	17				1												68
John Glasby		2	2	15	45	20	12	13	20	21	8	7	5				13				183
Laurence Sandfield																				2	4
Leonard G. Fish	1	4		1																	6
Leslie V. Heald		2	2																		6
Lionel Wright			2	3																	5
M. Vassiliev/ V. V. Dobronravov									1												1
Noel Boston										3	4	3									10
Norman Lazenby	8	2																			10
Paul Charkin									1		1										2
Peter J. Ridley		1																			1
R. Chetwynd-Hayes									1												1
R. L. Fanthorpe			3	5	9		10	31	32	28	52	58	62	43	30	16			1		381
Robert A. Wise																		1			1
Sam Merwin Jr.										1											1
Sydney J. Bounds	8																				8
Tom W. Wade		4	14	9	3			1													31
Tom W. Watt			1																		1
Victor Norwood												1									1
W. H. Fear								5													5
W. Shaw			2																		2
Will F. Jenkins										1											1
Willy Ley /Wernher Von Braun												1									1
Ernest Lister Hale(Lisle) Willis		2	2																		4
William Henry Fleming Bird		2	2		1																5
R. Brothwell		1	1	2																	4
D. F. Jameson				1																	1
UNKNOWN	3	8	2	5								1									19
Grand Total	31	35	61	79	80	20	28	50	57	57	66	71	71	48	35	149	25	1	1	2	967

Stories by Pseudonym/Year (Inc. Shorts and Novels)

Stories by Year / Psuedo Author	1950	1951	1952	1953	1954	1955	1957	1958	1959	1960	1961	1962	1963	1964	1965	1966	1967	1973	1974	1978	Grand Total
A. J. Merak			1	5	11	4	2	2	6	5	1	1	1				2			1	42
Andrew Sutton							1														2
Anthony Martin				2																	1
Art Smith					1																2
B. Ward			2																		1
Basil Sitty		1																			1
Branson D. Carter			1																		56
Bron Fane					1		1		5	5	4	9	7	10	7	4	2	1			7
Bruce Fenton			1	3	3																1
Charles Gray					1																5
Charles Grey			3	1	1																1
Clifford Wallace	1																				5
D. A. LeGraeme			2	2	1																1
D. F. Jameson			1																		3
D. J. Mencet	2	1																			1
D. R. Le Graeme				1																	7
D. R. Mencet	1	1	1	3	1																2
David Campbell			2																		3
Dean Ryan			1	2																	6
Deutero Spartacus												2	3		1						1
Earl Van Loden				1																	1
Edward Stokes		1																			1
Edward Ward		1																			3
Elton T. Neef														1	1	1					1
Elton T. Neefe																	1				1
Eric Lamont		1																			2
Erle Barton														1	1						3
Erle Van Loden				2	1																1
Everet Rigby		1																			13
Frank C. Kneller	3	1	2	5	2																1
H. J. Merak						1															1
H. K. Lennard								1													4
Hamilton Donne	3	1																			1
Hamilton Downe			1																		1
Ian Bruce					1																2
J. Austin Jackson	2																				1
J. B. Dexter									1												5
J. J. Hansby								1	1	1						2					1
J. J. Hansley								1													1
J. L. Powers											1										1
Jack Lawson			1																		2
James Elton			1							1											1
James Robertson					1																1
James Ross		1																			1
James S. Stanton/ Edward Richards								1													1
James Stanfield			1																		1
James Williams									1												1
Jerome Strickland				1																	1
John Adams											1										1
John C. Maxwell									1												1
John Crawford																	1				40
John E. Muller											1	11	15	2	2	6	2		1		1
John Ellis		1																			1
John Evans	1																				1
John F. Manders				1																	1
John Mason								1													1
John Morton											1										1
John Poole			1																		1
John R. Martin				1																	1
John Raymond					1																1
John Renolds			1																		1

Cont.…

Stories by Pseudonym/Year (Inc. Shorts and Novels) Continued

Stories by Year / Psuedo Author	1950	1951	1952	1953	1954	1955	1957	1958	1959	1960	1961	1962	1963	1964	1965	1966	1967	1973	1974	1978	Grand Total
John Robertson		1		1	2																4
John Sloan		1																			1
John Toucan			2	1	1																4
Karl Ziegfried				4	1							5	4	2	2						18
Kenneth Boyce				1																	1
Kenneth Boyea				1	4																5
L. C. Powers							1														1
L. P. Kenton											1										1
L. S. Johnson				1																	1
L. T. Bronson				1																	1
Lan Wright				1	3																4
Lawrence Smith		1																			1
Lee Barton													1								1
Leo Brett														1	4	1	2				8
Lionel Roberts							1	3	5	4	11	10	11		1						46
M. B. Stone			3	3	2			2	6	6	4	3									29
Mack James			2																		2
Mack Jones				1																	1
Martin Gulliver		1																			1
Martin L. Baker	1																				1
Max Chartair					1																1
Meryl St. John Montague				2	11	4	2			4	3	1	1	1		2					31
Michael Hamilton				2	6	4	2	2	3	3	1	1	1			2					27
Murray Leinster												1									1
Neil Balfort														1							1
Neil J. Spalding														1	1						2
Neil J. Spaulding				1																	1
Neil Thanet													1								1
Nicky Shelly													3	2					1		6
Noel Bartram																1					1
Noel Bertram										1	1										2
Oben Lerteth										2	3	3									8
Olaf Trent														1	2	1					4
Othello Baron													2	1							3
P. L. Manning							1							1							2
Paul Hammond	1																				1
Pel Torro					1																1
Peter Laynham							1	2	5	2	2	6	8	11	3	2					42
Peter O'Flinn							1	2	1	1	1	1	1			2					10
Peter O'Flynn													2	1	1						4
Phil Nobel																2					2
Phil Noble														1							1
R. Brothwell		1	2	1																	4
R. C. Kerwood			1																		1
R. G. Lomax			1																		1
R. J. Norton		1																			1
R. L. Bowers							1														1
Randall Conway				1	8	4	2	2	3	3	1	1	1			2					28
Ray Cosmic				1	3	6	4		1		2										17
Ray Mason	1	1	3	3	1																9
Raymond L. Burton								1													1
Raymond Leroyd			1																		1
Rene Rolant													1	1	1	1					4
Robert D. Ennis								1													1
Robin Tate													1	5	2	1					9
Rod Patterson				1	1					1											3
Roger Carne	1																				1
Ronald Adison		1																			1
Roy Arnold			1																		1
Stephen James		1																			1
Thomas Rochdale		1																			1
Thornton Bell														5	1						6
Trebor Thorpe				1	2		2	5	3	5	7	6	5	2	1						39
Trevor Thorpe									1												1
Uncredited	3		1																		4
Victor La Salle				1	5	2					1										9
Victor LaSalle					1																1
Vincent Robertson			1	1																	2
W. B. Clarke		1																			1
W. E. Clarkson	2																				2
Willi Deinhardt				3																	3
William Bird				1																	1
Grand Total	26	27	44	66	76	20	26	39	44	44	56	61	63	43	29	13	13	1	1	2	694

Number of Editions by Series

Series	Identifier	# of known editions
Futuristic Science Stories	FSS	16
Science Fiction Series	SF	117
Out of this World	OTW	2
Tales of Tomorrow	TT	11
Wonders of the Spaceways	WS	10
Science (Fiction) Series	S(F)S	1
Science Series	SS	4
Worlds of Fantasy	WF	14
Comics	Comics	24
Supernatural Series	SN	107

(complete list below includes publications to be covered in Vol. 2 and Vol. 3)

Lariat Western	LW	77
World War 2 Series	WW	162
Blazing Western	BW	60
Romance Series	RS	41
Non-Series (Crime/gangster)	N-S	62
Foreign Legion	FL	21
Misc.	MISC	16
Crime Series	CS	13
Science non-series	SN-S	14
Glamour Mags	GL	6
Spy	SP	6
Mystery	M	5
True War	TW	4
Bengal Lancers	Bla	4
Crime Confessions	CC	3
Private Eye	PE	3
Brad Lando	BL	2
Western Mags	West	2
Giant War	GW	2
Mystery 2nd Series	M2	1
Adventure Series	AS	2
Jungle	J	1
Mystery Crime Cases	MCC	1
Modern Humourist Mag	MH	1
Mystery Reprint	MR	1
Dynamic Detective Cases	DD	1
Phantom Detective Cases	PD	1
GGA Mag (Harem Frolics/Bohemian Tales)	GGA	2
Screen Series	SCS	1
True Adventure	TA	1
World Personality	WP	1

This book is divided into two main sections, Fiction and Non-Fiction, and subsequently further subdivided into different categories. For ease of navigation the sections and categories are colour coded. The publication titles are in alphabetical order within each category and the checklists also follow the same colour codes.

Contents

John Spencer and Co. Illustrated Bibliography Vol. 1

Fiction

Comic

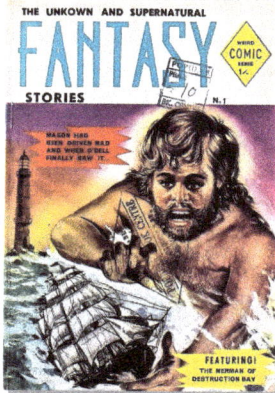

Series No/ Title Fantasy stories #1

Date 1966 **Imprint** John Spencer **Collected**

Artist Mick Anglo

Notes Cover variant from SN34.

Content The Merman of Destruction Bay-(Comic Strip), Candles of Death-(Comic Strip), The Strange One-(Comic Strip), The Thing-(Comic Strip), Forgotten Country-(Comic Strip), Midnight Ghoul-(Comic Strip)

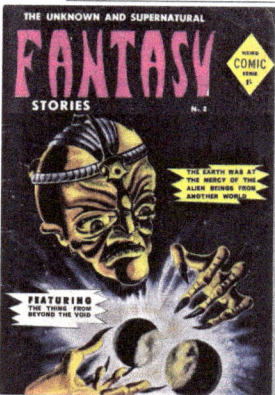

Series No/ Title Fantasy stories #2

Date 1966 **Imprint** John Spencer **Collected**

Artist Mick Anglo

Notes Cover variant from ToT11.

Content The Thing from Beyond the Void-(Comic Strip), Contract With Satan-(Comic Strip), The Isle of the Blessed-(Comic Strip), Call of the Wind-(Comic Strip), The Witch?-(Comic Strip), Secret of the Pyramid-(Comic Strip)

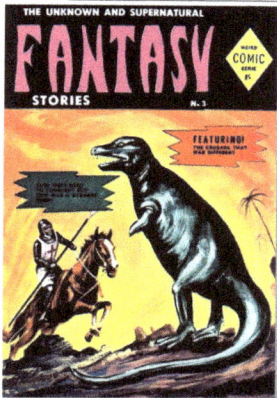

Series No/ Title Fantasy stories #3

Date 1966 **Imprint** John Spencer **Collected**

Artist Mick Anglo

Notes

Content The Crusade That Was Different-(Comic Strip), The Avenging Goddess-(Comic Strip), Voice in the Wall-(Comic Strip), A Slip in Time-(Comic Strip), In a Glass Darkly-(Comic Strip), Werewolf at Large-(Comic Strip)

Series No/ Title Fantasy stories #4

Date 1966 **Imprint** John Spencer **Collected**

Artist Mick Anglo

Notes Cover variant from ToT10.

Content The Power From Out There-(Comic Strip), The Grimoire-(Comic Strip), Tunnel of Fear-(Comic Strip), The Nine Green Men-(Comic Strip), Graveyard of the Damned-(Comic Strip), Dragon's Blood Mountain-(Comic Strip)

Comic

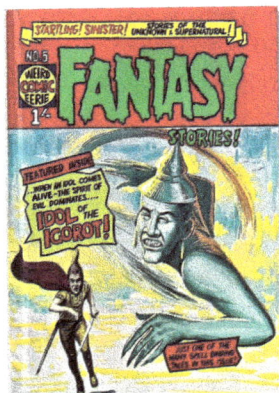

Series No/ Title Fantasy stories #5

Date 1966 **Imprint** John Spencer **Collected**

Artist Michael Jay

Notes

Content Idol of the Igorot-(Comic Strip), Stone Face-(Comic Strip), The Hag-(Comic Strip), The Green Sarcophagus-(Comic Strip), The Twisted Track-(Comic Strip), The Thing from Sheol-(Comic Strip)

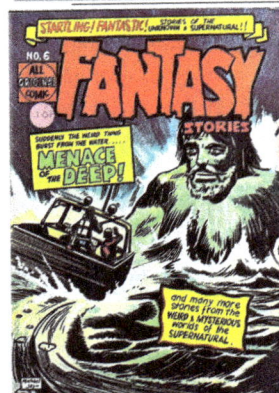

Series No/ Title Fantasy stories #6

Date 1966 **Imprint** John Spencer **Collected**

Artist Michael Jay

Notes

Content Menace of the Deep-(Comic Strip), Witches Brew-(Comic Strip), The Stone Tablets-(Comic Strip), Night Walkers-(Comic Strip), Weird Castle-(Comic Strip), Something at the Door-(Comic Strip)

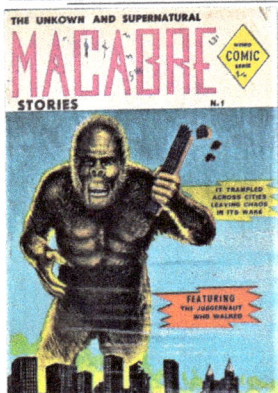

Series No/ Title Macabre Stories #1

Date 1966 **Imprint** John Spencer **Collected**

Artist Mick Anglo

Notes Cover variant from SF105.

Content The Juggernaut Who Walked-(Comic Strip), The Coffin-(Comic Strip), The Parrot-(Comic Strip), Power Mad-Nicky Shelly(Comic Strip), The Tartars-(Comic Strip), The Ghost-(Comic Strip), The Dreamer-(Comic Strip)

Series No/ Title Macabre Stories #2

Date 1966 **Imprint** John Spencer **Collected**

Artist Mick Anglo

Notes Cover variant from SF51.

Content Resting Place-(Comic Strip), The Sleeper-(Comic Strip), Night Cry-(Comic Strip), Guest of Honour-(Comic Strip), Day of the Beasts-(Comic Strip), Strange Country-(Comic Strip)

Comic

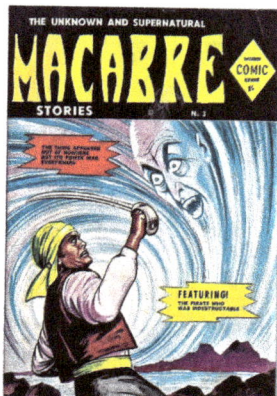

Series No/ Title   Macabre Stories #3

Date   1966   Imprint   John Spencer   Collected

Artist   Mick Anglo

Notes

Content   The Pirate Who Was Indestructible-(Comic Strip), Bitter Reflection-(Comic Strip), The Kraken-(Comic Strip), Dark Staircase-(Comic Strip), The Midnight Museum-(Comic Strip), The Golden Warrior-(Comic Strip)

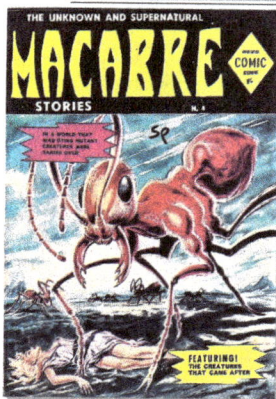

Series No/ Title   Macabre Stories #4

Date   1966   Imprint   John Spencer   Collected

Artist   Mick Anglo

Notes   Cover variant from SF22.

Content   The Creatures That Came After-(Comic Strip), Zombie-(Comic Strip), Moon Wolf!-(Comic Strip), Suddenly…at Twilight-(Comic Strip), The Hand of Gehenna-(Comic Strip), The Loch Ness Terror-(Comic Strip)

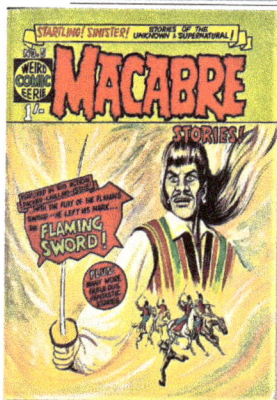

Series No/ Title   Macabre Stories #5

Date   1966   Imprint   John Spencer   Collected

Artist   Michael Jay

Notes

Content   The Flaming Sword-(Comic Strip), Wolfman's Vengeance-(Comic Strip), Sands of Eternity-(Comic Strip), Before the Beginning-(Comic Strip), Voodoo Vengeance-(Comic Strip), The Bow and the Bugle-(Comic Strip)

Series No/ Title   Macabre Stories #6

Date   1966   Imprint   John Spencer   Collected

Artist   Michael Jay

Notes

Content   Lord of the Crag-(Comic Strip), 4 Dimensional Beam-(Comic Strip), Grip of Fear-(Comic Strip), The Evil One!-(Comic Strip), Strange Door-(Comic Strip), All in the Mind-(Comic Strip)

Comic

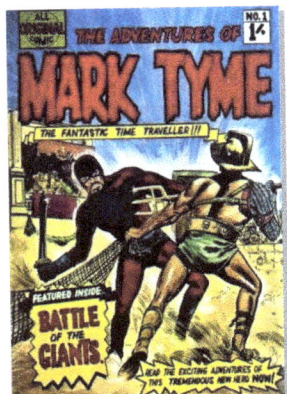

Series No/ Title Mark Tyme #1

Date 1967   **Imprint** John Spencer   **Collected**

Artist Michael Jay

Notes

Content Battle of the Giants!-(Comic Strip), Stone Age Menace!-(Comic Strip), Island of Fear-(Comic Strip)

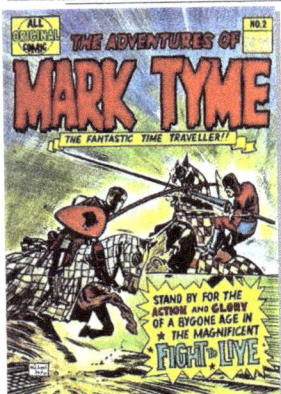

Series No/ Title Mark Tyme #2

Date 1967   **Imprint** John Spencer   **Collected**

Artist Michael Jay

Notes

Content Fight For Life-(Comic Strip), Planet of Fear-(Comic Strip), To Tame a Tyrant-(Comic Strip)

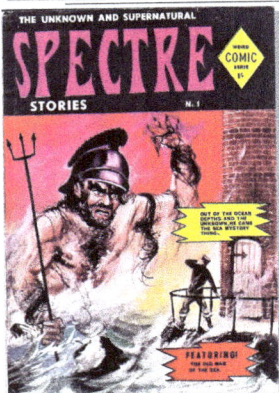

Series No/ Title Spectre Stories #1

Date 1966   **Imprint** John Spencer   **Collected**

Artist Mick Anglo

Notes Cover variant from SN3.

Content The Old Man of the Sea-(Comic Strip), The Challenge-(Comic Strip), The Web of Cerian-(Comic Strip), The Tiny World…-(Comic Strip), Dead or Alive?-(Comic Strip), The World of the Sun-(Comic Strip)

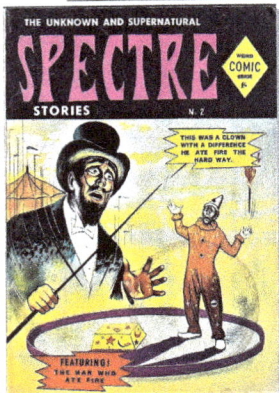

Series No/ Title Spectre Stories #2

Date 1966   **Imprint** John Spencer   **Collected**

Artist Mick Anglo

Notes

Content The Man Who Ate Fire-(Comic Strip), The Power-(Comic Strip), The Walking Dead-(Comic Strip), Vengeance of Thor-(Comic Strip), Time Out of Mind-(Comic Strip), Night of the Ghoul-(Comic Strip)

Comic

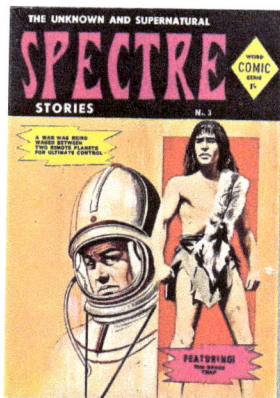

Series No/ Title	Spectre Stories #3
Date	1966
Imprint	John Spencer
Collected	
Artist	Mick Anglo
Notes	Cover variant from SF98.
Content	The Space Trap-(Comic Strip), The Family-(Comic Strip), Strange Land-(Comic Strip), Ghost Rider-(Comic Strip), The Werewolf-(Comic Strip), The Manhattan Warlock-(Comic Strip)

Series No/ Title	Spectre Stories #4
Date	1966
Imprint	John Spencer
Collected	
Artist	Mick Anglo
Notes	
Content	Power of the Phantom Genie-(Comic Strip), Out of the Vault-(Comic Strip), House of Despair-(Comic Strip), Valley of the Kings-(Comic Strip), Voodoo Hell Drums-(Comic Strip), Land of the Living Dead-(Comic Strip)

Series No/ Title	Spectre Stories #5
Date	1966
Imprint	John Spencer
Collected	
Artist	Michael Jay
Notes	
Content	Valley of the Shadow-(Comic Strip), Death-Note!-(Comic Strip), Ice Tomb-(Comic Strip), Face in the Dark!-(Comic Strip), Moonlight Island-(Comic Strip), Black Abyss-(Comic Strip)

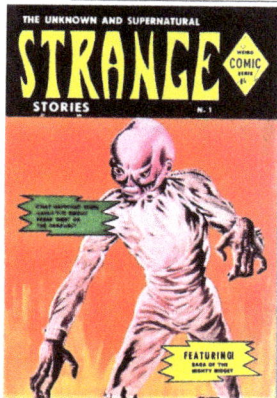

Series No/ Title	Strange Stories #1
Date	1966
Imprint	John Spencer
Collected	
Artist	Mick Anglo
Notes	Cover variant from SF19.
Content	The Saga of the Mighty Midget-(Comic Strip), The Zuku Plant-(Comic Strip), Back From the Dead-(Comic Strip), The Robots-(Comic Strip), Adventure on the High Seas-(Comic Strip), The Space Warp-(Comic Strip)

Comic

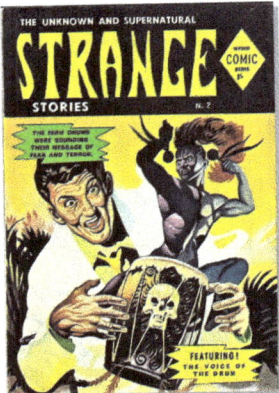

Series No/ Title	Strange Stories #2
Date	1966	Imprint	John Spencer	Collected
Artist	Mick Anglo
Notes	Cover variant from SN6.
Content	The Drud-(Comic Strip), Voice of the Drum-(Comic Strip), Twilight Ancestor-(Comic Strip), The Shrouded Abbot-(Comic Strip), The Hypnotist-(Comic Strip), Mermaid Reef-(Comic Strip)

Series No/ Title	Strange Stories #3
Date	1966	Imprint	John Spencer	Collected
Artist	Mick Anglo
Notes	Cover variant from SF68.
Content	Hexere!-(Comic Strip), The Man Who Conquered Time-(Comic Strip), The Warlock-(Comic Strip), The Serpent Ring-(Comic Strip), The Abbot's Ring-(Comic Strip), Nightmare on Ice-(Comic Strip)

Series No/ Title	Strange Stories #4
Date	1966	Imprint	John Spencer	Collected
Artist	Mick Anglo
Notes	
Content	Legend of the Lost World-(Comic Strip), Phantom Crusader-(Comic Strip), The Vampire-(Comic Strip), Slave God of the Norsu-(Comic Strip), Whirlwind of Death-(Comic Strip), The Reluctant Corpse-(Comic Strip)

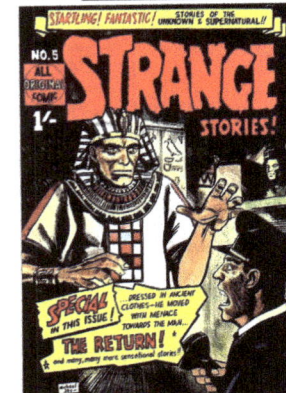

Series No/ Title	Strange Stories #5
Date	1966	Imprint	John Spencer	Collected
Artist	Michael Jay
Notes	
Content	The Joker!-(Comic Strip), Jaws of Steel-(Comic Strip), The Mountain Thing!-(Comic Strip), The Return-(Comic Strip), They Flew by Night-(Comic Strip), The Secret of Dr. Stark-(Comic Strip)

Comic

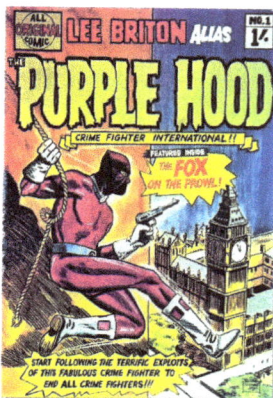

Series No/ Title **The Purple Hood #1**

Date **1967**   Imprint **John Spencer**   Collected

Artist **Michael Jay**

Notes

Content **The Fox on the Prowl-(Comic Strip), The Rocket Caper!-(Comic Strip), Desert Fury!-(Comic Strip)**

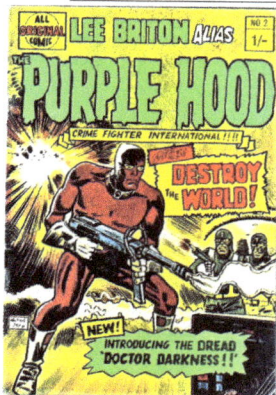

Series No/ Title **The Purple Hood #2**

Date **1967**   Imprint **John Spencer**   Collected

Artist **Michael Jay**

Notes

Content **Destroy the World!-(Comic Strip), Deep Danger-(Comic Strip), Escape or Die-(Comic Strip)**

Futuristic Science Stories

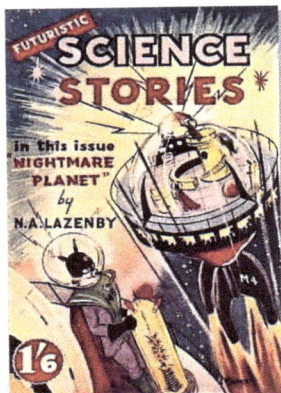

Series No/ Title Futuristic Science Stories #01

Date 1950 Imprint John Spencer Collected

Artist Gerald Facey

Notes April.

Content Worlds of Fear-J. Austin Jackson(Norman Lazenby), The Worm of Venus-Martin Gulliver(Norman Lazenby), The Green Ray-Ray Mason(John F. Watt), 1982, Nightmare Planet-(Norman Lazenby), Stanhope's Moon-(Frederick T. Foden)

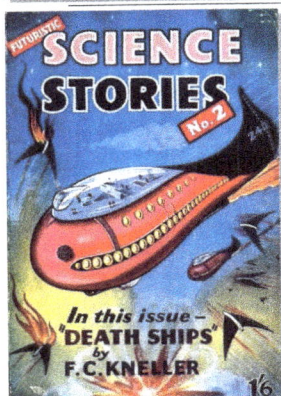

Series No/ Title Futuristic Science Stories #02

Date 1950 Imprint John Spencer Collected

Artist Gerald Facey

Notes August. Signature unclear but looks like AEG.

Content The Fire Goddess-D. J. Mencet(John F. Watt), Death Ships-Frank C. Kneller(John F. Watt), One Million Years Ago-Hamilton Donne(John F. Watt), Plasma Men Bring Death-(Norman Lazenby), Vultures of the Void-Clifford Wallace(Sydney J. Bounds)

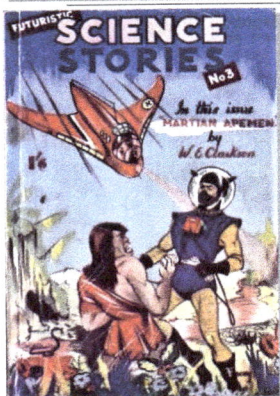

Series No/ Title Futuristic Science Stories #03

Date 1950 Imprint John Spencer Collected

Artist Gerald Facey

Notes December.

Content Prison Planet-Roger Carne(Sydney J. Bounds), Martian Apemen-W. E. Clarkson(Sydney J. Bounds), Menace from the Atom-W. E. Clarkson(Sydney J. Bounds), The Mechans of Muah-(Norman Lazenby), Treasure in Space-Uncredited()

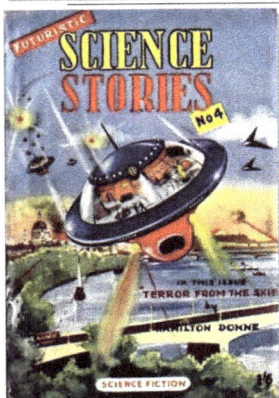

Series No/ Title Futuristic Science Stories #04

Date 1951 Imprint John Spencer Collected

Artist Gerald Facey

Notes February.

Content Spawn of the Void-Edward Stokes(John F. Watt), Terror From the Skies-Hamilton Downe(John F. Watt), Space Trader-(R. Brothwell), The Problem Ship-David Campbell(Leonard G. Fish), Beast Men of Mars-M. B. Stone()

Futuristic Science Stories

Series No/ Title   Futuristic Science Stories #05

Date 1951   **Imprint** John Spencer   **Collected**

Artist   Ronald Turner

Notes   December. Artist possibly Facey.

Content   The Irreparable Sunset-(Tom W. Wade), Re-Creation-(Gerald Evans), The Alien-(Leonard G. Fish), Space Patrol-Jack Lawson(Jack Lawson), Station Neptune-John Poole()

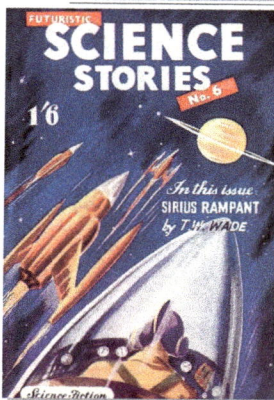

Series No/ Title   Futuristic Science Stories #06

Date 1952   **Imprint** John Spencer   **Collected**

Artist   Ronald Turner

Notes   April. Artist possibly Facey.

Content   Sirius Rampant-(Tom W. Wade), Out of the Past-(Leslie V. Heald), Worlds Without End-Lionel Roberts(R. L. Fanthorpe), The Legacy-Jerome Strickland(Lionel Wright), Heritage-Lan Wright(Lionel Wright)

Series No/ Title   Futuristic Science Stories #07

Date 1952   **Imprint** John Spencer   **Collected**

Artist   Ronald Turner

Notes   July.

Content   Rebels of Venus-Frank C. Kneller(John F. Watt), Perseus-(A. A. Glynn), Cano Sapiens-Roy Arnold(Tom W. Watt), Discovery-Lionel Roberts(R. L. Fanthorpe), The Pirates of the Black Moon-B. Ward(Barney Ward)

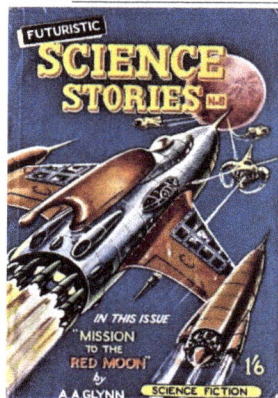

Series No/ Title   Futuristic Science Stories #08

Date 1952   **Imprint** John Spencer   **Collected**

Artist   Norman Light

Notes   October.

Content   Minerals From Mars-(Tom W. Wade), Last Throw From Ganymede-John R. Martin(Tom W. Wade), Mission to the Red Moon-(A. A. Glynn), Moondust-A. J. Merak(John Glasby), The Manipulators-(W. Shaw)

Futuristic Science Stories

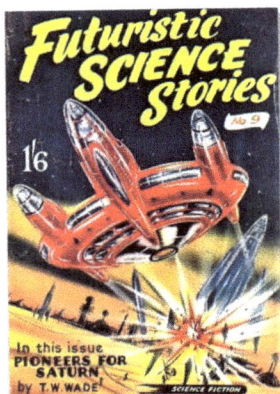

Series No/ Title	Futuristic Science Stories #09
Date	1953
Imprint	John Spencer
Collected	
Artist	Norman Light
Notes	January. Artist possibly Davies.
Content	Pioneers For Saturn-(Tom W. Wade), Slaves of Space-Bruce Fenton(John F. Watt), Journey into Tomorrow-Frank C. Kneller(John F. Watt), Power Politics-(R. Brothwell)

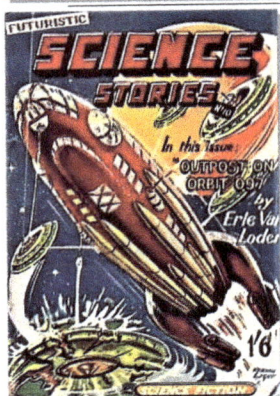

Series No/ Title	Futuristic Science Stories #10
Date	1953
Imprint	John Spencer
Collected	
Artist	Norman Light
Notes	April.
Content	Crimson Terror-Rod Patterson(John F. Watt), Time Pit-Michael Hamilton(John Glasby), Cosmic Conception-Dean Ryan(), Outpost on Orbit 097-Erle Van Loden(Ernest Lister Hale(Lisle) Willis)

Series No/ Title	Futuristic Science Stories #11
Date	1953
Imprint	John Spencer
Collected	
Artist	Norman Light
Notes	May.
Content	Planetoid of Peril-(A. A. Glynn), Veiled Planet-A. J. Merak(John Glasby), Mad Heritage-Willi Deinhardt(), The Clipper Ships of Space-(R. L. Fanthorpe), Raw Material-Lionel Roberts(R. L. Fanthorpe)

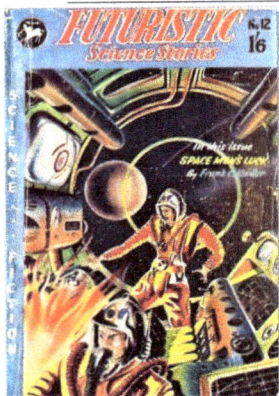

Series No/ Title	Futuristic Science Stories #12
Date	1953
Imprint	John Spencer
Collected	
Artist	Gordon C. Davies
Notes	August.
Content	World of Fear-D. R. Mencet(John F. Watt), Spacemen's Luck-Frank C. Kneller(John F. Watt), Demon Dimension-(A. A. Glynn), Critical Age-William Bird(William Henry Fleming Bird), Honour Bright-Charles Grey(E. C. Tubb)

Futuristic Science Stories

Series No/ Title	Futuristic Science Stories #13
Date	1953
Imprint	John Spencer
Collected	
Artist	Ron Embleton
Notes	October.
Content	The Indigenous Revolt-(Tom W. Wade), Lost in Space-D. R. Mencet(John F. Watt), The Devil's Weed-Ray Mason(John F. Watt), Time Triangle-Lionel Roberts(R. L. Fanthorpe), The Long Trek-Lan Wright(Lionel Wright)

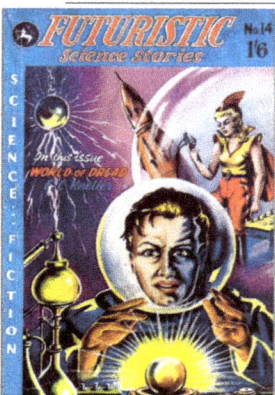

Series No/ Title	Futuristic Science Stories #14
Date	1954
Imprint	John Spencer
Collected	
Artist	Ron Embleton
Notes	January. Artist possibly Theobald.
Content	World of Dread-Frank C. Kneller(John F. Watt), Traitors of the Void-D. R. Mencet(John F. Watt), No Tomorrow-Kenneth Boyea(John F. Watt), Death From the Swamps-Ian Bruce(John F. Watt), Visiting Celebrity-Charles Grey(E. C. Tubb), Saucers From Space-Trebor Thorpe(R. L. Fanthorpe)

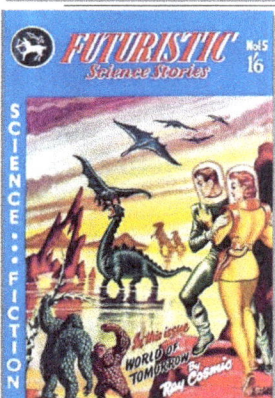

Series No/ Title	Futuristic Science Stories #15
Date	1954
Imprint	John Spencer
Collected	
Artist	Ron Embleton
Notes	April.
Content	Such Worlds Are Dangerous-A. J. Merak(John Glasby), The Aphesian Riddle-Randall Conway(John Glasby), World of Tomorrow-Ray Cosmic(John Glasby), Museum Piece-Charles Gray(E. C. Tubb), The Green Hell of Venus-Pel Torro(R. L. Fanthorpe)

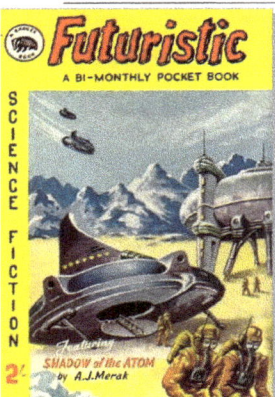

Series No/ Title	Futuristic Science Stories Vol 2 #16
Date	1958
Imprint	Badger
Collected	
Artist	Ray Theobald
Notes	February. Appearance and date suggests it was intended to be part of the SF series. Issued as SF16 but date would put is as possibly SF3 or the missing SF2.
Content	Shadow of the Atom-A. J. Merak(John Glasby), The Entropists-Randall Conway(John Glasby), Final Answer-Ray Cosmic(John Glasby), Pyramid Problem-Michael Hamilton(John Glasby), The Things That are Mars-Peter Laynham(John Glasby)

Science Fiction Series

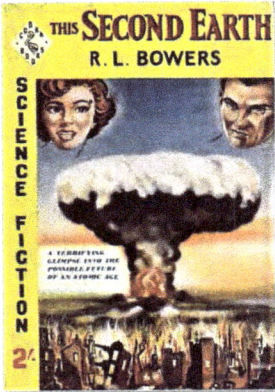

Series No/ Title	Science (Fiction) Series #1		
Date	1957	Imprint	Cobra	Collected
Artist	S. Nicholson		
Notes	November. Appears to have been a false start on a new Sci-fi series.		
Content	This Second Earth-R. L. Bowers(John Glasby)		

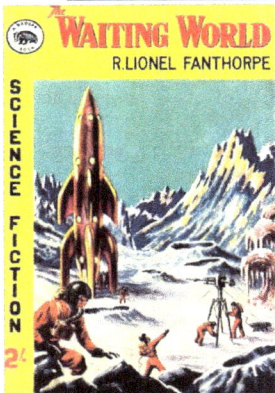

Series No/ Title	Science Fiction Series #001		
Date	1958	Imprint	Badger	Collected
Artist			
Notes	January.		
Content	The Waiting World-(R. L. Fanthorpe)		

Not Issued

Series No/ Title	Science Fiction Series #002		
Date	1958	Imprint		Collected
Artist			
Notes	It appears this number was not used/produced. Likely that 'The World Makers' should have been SF2 and that FFS #16 should have been SF3		
Content	Not Produced-()		

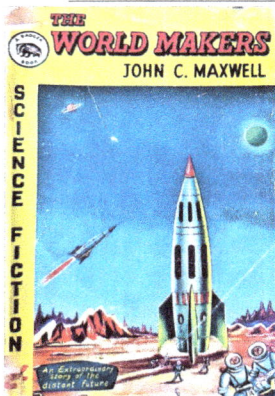

Series No/ Title	Science Fiction Series #003		
Date	1958	Imprint	Badger	Collected
Artist	S. Nicholson		
Notes	January. Duplicate SF3 issued. Probably should have been SF2		
Content	The World Makers-John C. Maxwell(John Glasby)		

Science Fiction Series

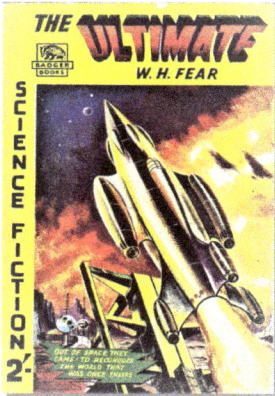

Series No/ Title	Science Fiction Series #003
Date	1958
Imprint	Badger
Collected	
Artist	Gerald Facey
Notes	July. Duplicate SF3 issued. Likely intended to be the missing SF8
Content	The Ultimate-(W. H. Fear)

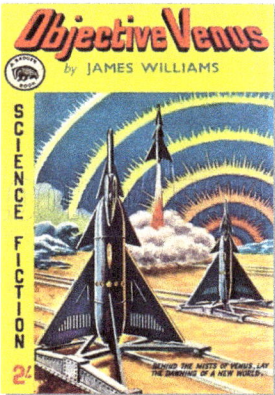

Series No/ Title	Science Fiction Series #004
Date	1958
Imprint	Badger
Collected	
Artist	S. Nicholson
Notes	February.
Content	Objective Venus-James Williams(Tom W. Wade)

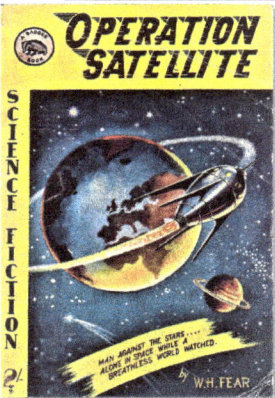

Series No/ Title	Science Fiction Series #005
Date	1958
Imprint	Badger
Collected	
Artist	S. Nicholson
Notes	March.
Content	Operation Satellite-(W. H. Fear)

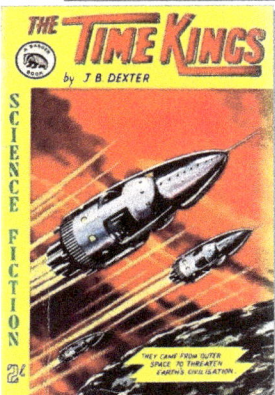

Series No/ Title	Science Fiction Series #006
Date	1958
Imprint	Badger
Collected	
Artist	
Notes	March.
Content	The Time Kings-J. B. Dexter(John Glasby)

Science Fiction Series

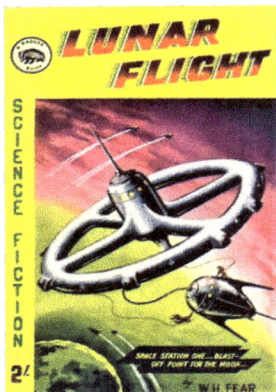

Series No/ Title	Science Fiction Series #007		
Date	1958	Imprint **Badger**	Collected
Artist			
Notes	May.		
Content	Lunar Flight-(W. H. Fear)		

Not Issued

Series No/ Title	Science Fiction Series #008		
Date	1958	Imprint	Collected
Artist			
Notes	It appears this number was not used/produced. Likely it should have been 'The Ultimate' which was a second SF3		
Content	Not Produced-()		

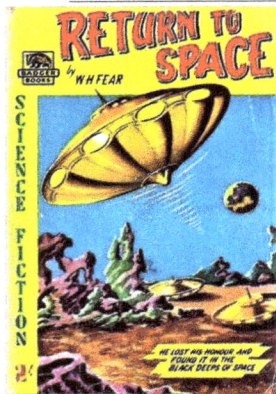

Series No/ Title	Science Fiction Series #009		
Date	1958	Imprint **Badger**	Collected
Artist			
Notes	September.		
Content	Return from Space-(W. H. Fear)		

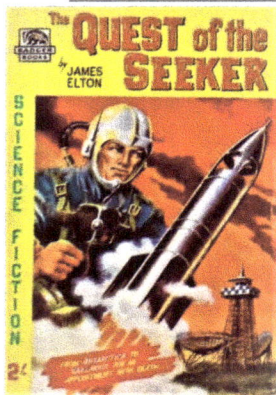

Series No/ Title	Science Fiction Series #010		
Date	1958	Imprint **Badger**	Collected
Artist	S. Nicholson		
Notes	October.		
Content	The Quest of the Seeker-James Elton(W. H. Fear)		

Science Fiction Series

Series No/ Title   Science Fiction Series #011

Date   **1958**   Imprint   **Badger**   Collected

Artist   S. Nicholson

Notes   November.

Content   The Destroyers-P. L. Manning(John Glasby)

Series No/ Title   Science Fiction Series #012

Date   1959   Imprint   **Badger**   Collected

Artist   S. Nicholson

Notes   January.

Content   Light of Mars-(Paul Charkin)

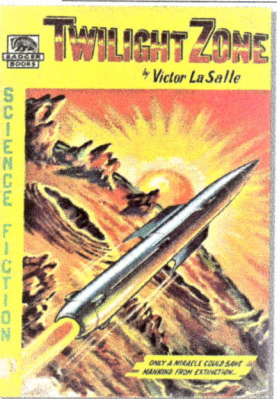

Series No/ Title   Science Fiction Series #013

Date   1959   Imprint   **Badger**   Collected

Artist   S. Nicholson

Notes   March. Reprint of 'Twilight Zone' non-series.

Content   Twilight Zone-Victor La Salle(John Glasby), Point of No Return-Max Chartair(John Glasby)

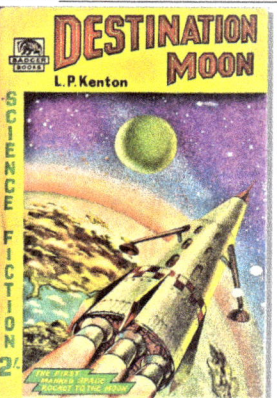

Series No/ Title   Science Fiction Series #014

Date   1959   Imprint   **Badger**   Collected

Artist   S. Nicholson

Notes   April.

Content   Destination Moon-L. P. Kenton(R. L. Fanthorpe)

Science Fiction Series

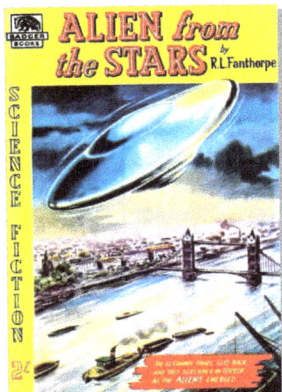

Series No/ Title	Science Fiction Series #015
Date	1959
Imprint	Badger
Collected	
Artist	
Notes	April.
Content	Alien From the Stars-(R. L. Fanthorpe)

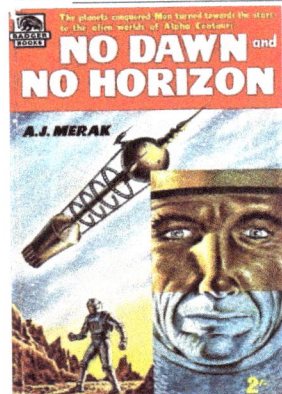

Series No/ Title	Science Fiction Series #016
Date	1959
Imprint	Badger
Collected	
Artist	Ed Blandford
Notes	May.
Content	No Dawn and No Horizon-A. J. Merak(John Glasby)

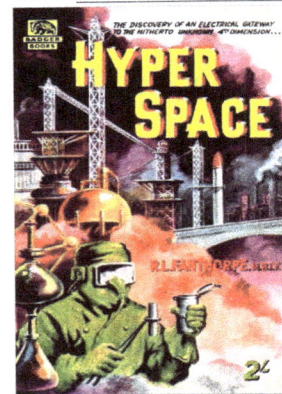

Series No/ Title	Science Fiction Series #017
Date	1959
Imprint	Badger
Collected	
Artist	
Notes	May.
Content	Hyper Space-(R. L. Fanthorpe)

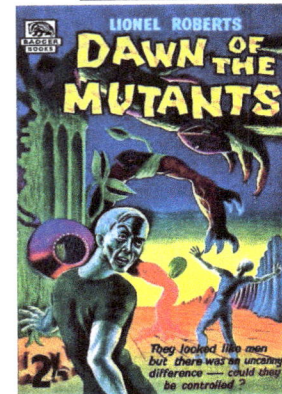

Series No/ Title	Science Fiction Series #018
Date	1959
Imprint	Badger
Collected	
Artist	
Notes	July.
Content	Dawn of the Mutants-Lionel Roberts(R. L. Fanthorpe)

Science Fiction Series

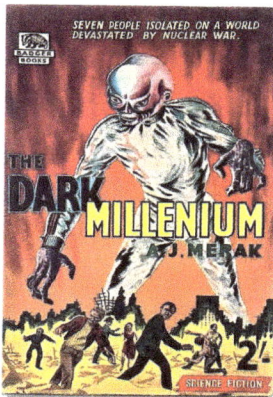

Series No/ Title Science Fiction Series #019

Date 1959   **Imprint** Badger   Collected

Artist

Notes August.

Content The Dark Millenium-A. J. Merak(John Glasby)

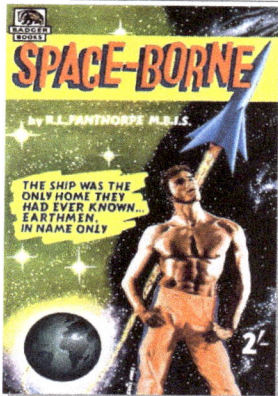

Series No/ Title Science Fiction Series #020

Date 1959   **Imprint** Badger   Collected

Artist Eddie Jones

Notes August.

Content Space-Borne-(R. L. Fanthorpe), Destination - Infinity-Rod Patterson(John F. Watt)

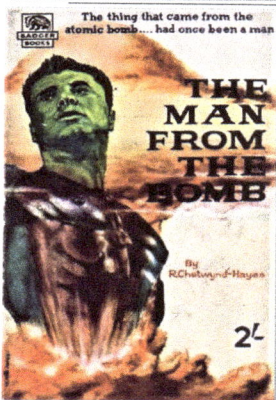

Series No/ Title Science Fiction Series #021

Date 1959   **Imprint** Badger   Collected

Artist Eddie Jones

Notes October.

Content The Man From The Bomb-(R. Chetwynd-Hayes)

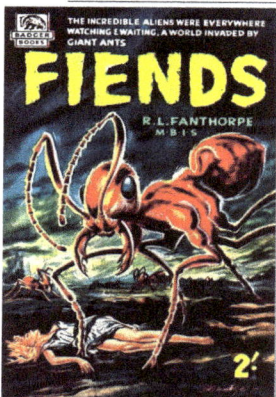

Series No/ Title Science Fiction Series #022

Date 1959   **Imprint** Badger   Collected

Artist Edgar Hodges

Notes November.

Content Fiends-(R. L. Fanthorpe)

Science Fiction Series

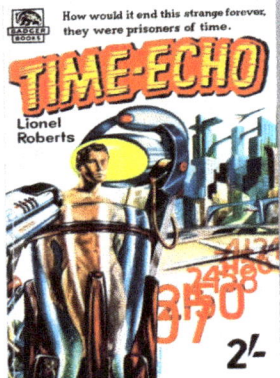

How would it end this strange forever, they were prisoners of time.

TIME-ECHO
Lionel Roberts

2/-

Series No/ Title — Science Fiction Series #023

Date — 1959 — Imprint — Badger — Collected

Artist — Eddie Jones

Notes — November.

Content — Time Echo-Lionel Roberts(R. L. Fanthorpe)

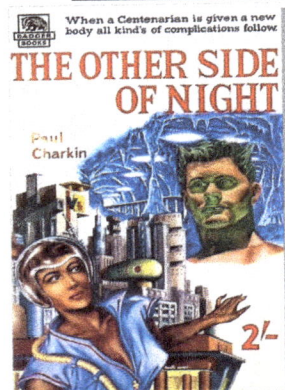

When a Centenarian is given a new body all kind's of complications follow.

THE OTHER SIDE OF NIGHT
Paul Charkin

2/-

Series No/ Title — Science Fiction Series #024

Date — 1960 — Imprint — Badger — Collected

Artist — Eddie Jones

Notes — January.

Content — The Other Side of Night-(Paul Charkin)

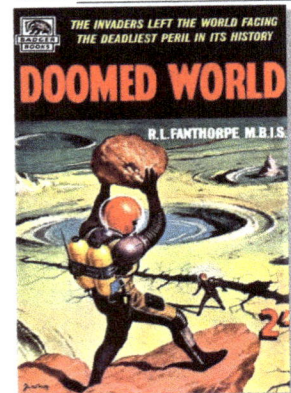

THE INVADERS LEFT THE WORLD FACING THE DEADLIEST PERIL IN ITS HISTORY

DOOMED WORLD
R.L.FANTHORPE M.B.I.S.

Series No/ Title — Science Fiction Series #025

Date — 1960 — Imprint — Badger — Collected

Artist — Carlo Jacono

Notes — January. Reused cover from Urania #193. However it looks to be a Jacono copy of a Ace D-103 cover credited to Ed Valigursky

Content — Doomed World-(R. L. Fanthorpe)

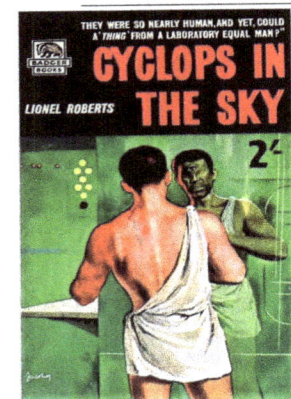

THEY WERE SO NEARLY HUMAN, AND YET, COULD A 'THING' FROM A LABORATORY EQUAL MAN ?

CYCLOPS IN THE SKY
LIONEL ROBERTS

2/-

Series No/ Title — Science Fiction Series #026

Date — 1960 — Imprint — Badger — Collected

Artist — Carlo Jacono

Notes — February. Reused cover from Urania #186

Content — Cyclops In the Sky-Lionel Roberts(R. L. Fanthorpe)

Science Fiction Series

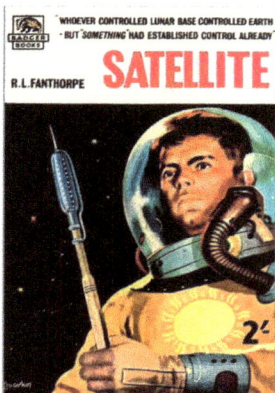

Series No/ Title	Science Fiction Series #027		
Date	1960	Imprint	Badger	Collected
Artist	Carlo Jacono		
Notes	February. Reused cover from Urania #183		
Content	Satellite-(R. L. Fanthorpe)		

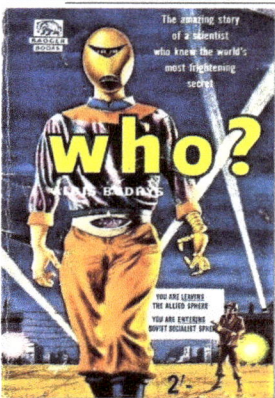

Series No/ Title	Science Fiction Series #028		
Date	1960	Imprint	Badger	Collected
Artist	Robert V. Engel		
Notes	March. Reprint of the 1958 Pyramid novel		
Content	Who?-(Algis Budrys)		

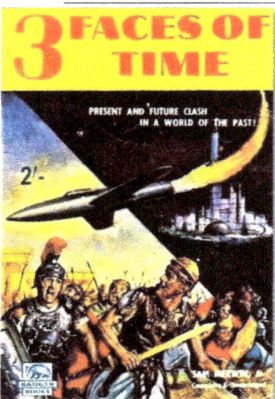

Series No/ Title	Science Fiction Series #029		
Date	1960	Imprint	Badger	Collected
Artist	Ed Emshwiller (Emsh)		
Notes	March. An expanded version of 'Journey to Misenum' published in 'Startling Stories' Aug. 1953. Reused cover from Ace D-121		
Content	3 Faces of Time-(Sam Merwin Jr.)		

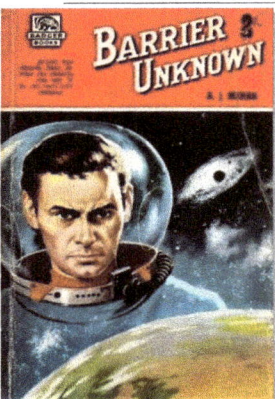

Series No/ Title	Science Fiction Series #030		
Date	1960	Imprint	Badger	Collected
Artist	Carlo Jacono		
Notes	May. Reused cover from Urania #205		
Content	Barrier Unknown-A. J. Merak(John Glasby)		

Science Fiction Series

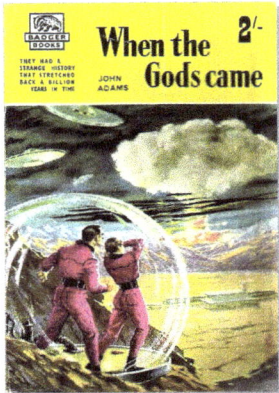

Series No/ Title	Science Fiction Series #031
Date	1960 Imprint **Badger** Collected
Artist	M. D'Antonia
Notes	May. Reused cover from Urania #213
Content	When The Gods Came-John Adams(John Glasby)

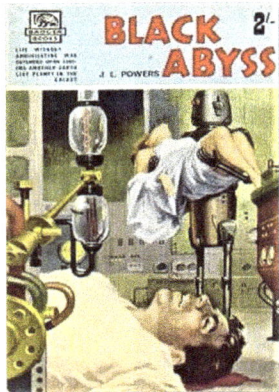

Series No/ Title	Science Fiction Series #032
Date	1960 Imprint **Badger** Collected
Artist	Carlo Jacono
Notes	May. Reused cover from Urania #161
Content	Black Abyss-J. L. Powers(John Glasby)

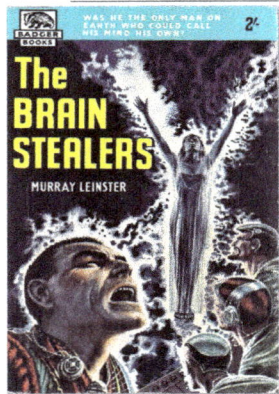

Series No/ Title	Science Fiction Series #033
Date	1960 Imprint **Badger** Collected
Artist	Ed Emshwiller (Emsh)
Notes	June. Reprint of ACE D-79 ,1954 novel that had originally appeared in "Startling Stories" Magazine. Reused cover from Ace D-413
Content	The Brain Stealers-Murray Leinster(Will F. Jenkins)

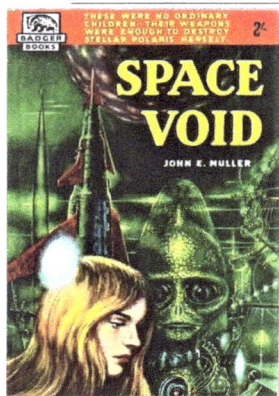

Series No/ Title	Science Fiction Series #034
Date	1960 Imprint **Badger** Collected
Artist	Ed Emshwiller (Emsh)
Notes	June. Reprint of "Dawn of the Half-Gods". Reused cover from Ace D-422
Content	Space Void-John E. Muller(John Glasby)

Science Fiction Series

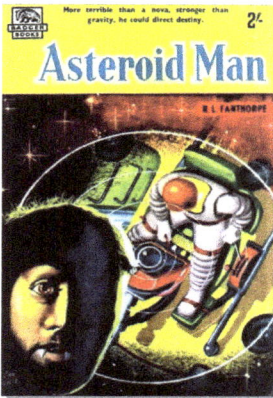

Series No/ Title	Science Fiction Series #035
Date	1960
Imprint	Badger
Collected	
Artist	Cha' Bril
Notes	July. Cover signed Cha' Bril (believed to be Joaquín Chacopino Fabré). Reused from Toray(Spanish) No.71
Content	Asteroid Man-(R. L. Fanthorpe)

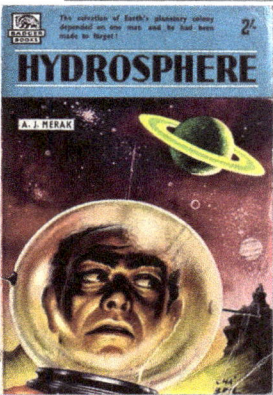

Series No/ Title	Science Fiction Series #036
Date	1960
Imprint	Badger
Collected	
Artist	Cha' Bril
Notes	July. Cover signed Cha' Bril (believed to be Joaquín Chacopino Fabré). Reused from Toray(Spanish) no.86
Content	Hydrosphere-A. J. Merak(John Glasby)

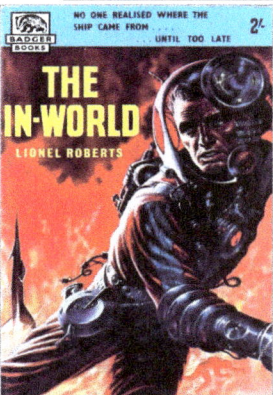

Series No/ Title	Science Fiction Series #037
Date	1960
Imprint	Badger
Collected	
Artist	Ed Emshwiller (Emsh)
Notes	August. Reused cover from Ace D-199
Content	The In-World-Lionel Roberts(R. L. Fanthorpe)

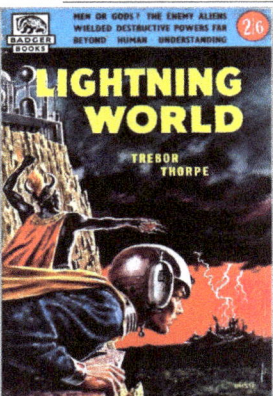

Series No/ Title	Science Fiction Series #038
Date	1960
Imprint	Badger
Collected	
Artist	Ed Emshwiller (Emsh)
Notes	August. Reused cover from Ace D-345
Content	Lightning World-Trebor Thorpe(R. L. Fanthorpe)

Science Fiction Series

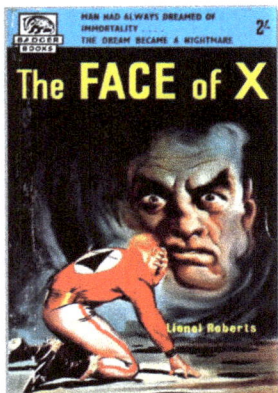

Series No/ Title   Science Fiction Series #039

Date   1960   Imprint   Badger   Collected

Artist   Ed Emshwiller (Emsh)

Notes   August. Reused cover from Ace D-237

Content   The Face of X-Lionel Roberts(R. L. Fanthorpe)

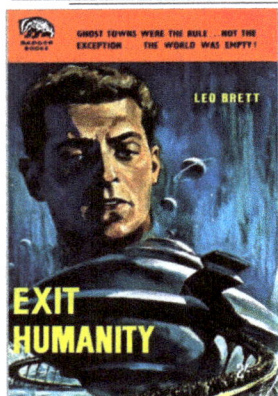

Series No/ Title   Science Fiction Series #040

Date   1960   Imprint   Badger   Collected

Artist   UNKNOWN

Notes   October. Reused cover from Ace D-391. Artist likely to be Ed Valigursky

Content   Exit Humanity-Leo Brett(R. L. Fanthorpe)

Series No/ Title   Science Fiction Series #041

Date   1960   Imprint   Badger   Collected

Artist   Ed Emshwiller (Emsh)

Notes   October. Reused cover from Ace D-335

Content   Juggernaut-Bron Fane(R. L. Fanthorpe)

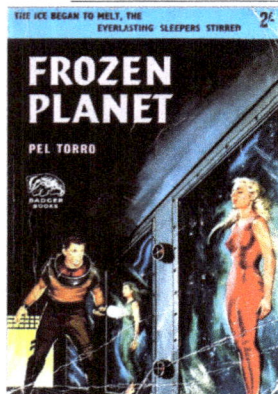

Series No/ Title   Science Fiction Series #042

Date   1960   Imprint   Badger   Collected

Artist   Ed Valigursky

Notes   October. Reused cover from Ace D-291

Content   Frozen Planet-Pel Torro(R. L. Fanthorpe)

Science Fiction Series

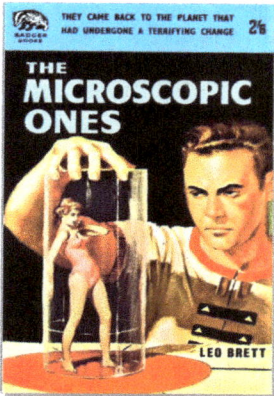

Series No/ Title	Science Fiction Series #043
Date	1960
Imprint	Badger
Collected	
Artist	Ed Valigursky
Notes	November. Reused cover from Ace D-249
Content	The Microscopic Ones-Leo Brett(R. L. Fanthorpe)

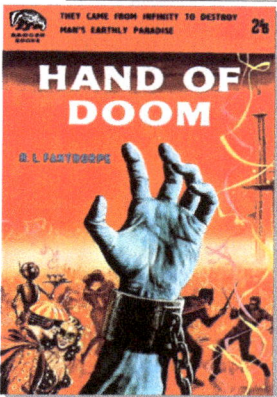

Series No/ Title	Science Fiction Series #044
Date	1960
Imprint	Badger
Collected	
Artist	Ed Emshwiller (Emsh)
Notes	November. Reused cover from Ace D-421
Content	Hand of Doom-(R. L. Fanthorpe)

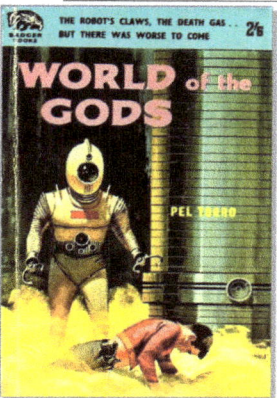

Series No/ Title	Science Fiction Series #045
Date	1960
Imprint	Badger
Collected	
Artist	Ed Valigursky
Notes	November. Reused cover from Ace D-381
Content	World of the Gods-Pel Torro(R. L. Fanthorpe)

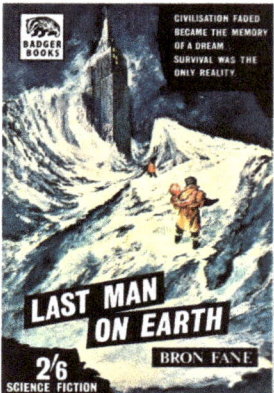

Series No/ Title	Science Fiction Series #046
Date	1961
Imprint	Badger
Collected	
Artist	UNKNOWN
Notes	January. Reused cover from Avon T-360
Content	Last Man on Earth-Bron Fane(R. L. Fanthorpe)

Science Fiction Series

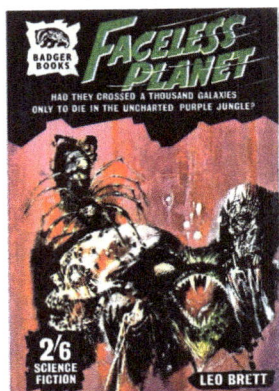

Series No/ Title	Science Fiction Series #047		
Date	1961	Imprint Badger	Collected
Artist	Richard Powers		
Notes	January. Reused cover from Avon T-289		
Content	Faceless Planet-Leo Brett(R. L. Fanthorpe)		

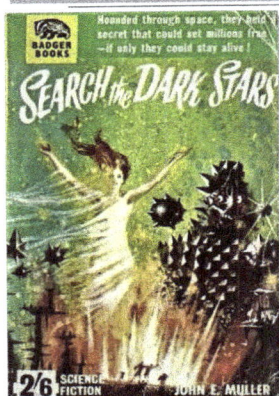

Series No/ Title	Science Fiction Series #048		
Date	1961	Imprint Badger	Collected
Artist	Richard Powers		
Notes	February. Reused cover from Avon T-172		
Content	Search the Dark Stars-John E. Muller(A. A. Glynn)		

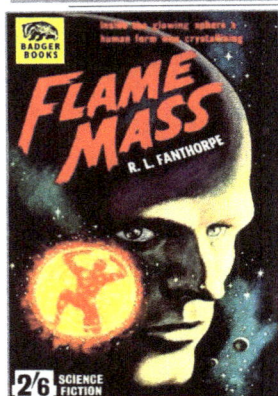

Series No/ Title	Science Fiction Series #049		
Date	1961	Imprint Badger	Collected
Artist	Ed Emshwiller (Emsh)		
Notes	February. Reused cover from Ace D-455		
Content	Flamemass-(R. L. Fanthorpe)		

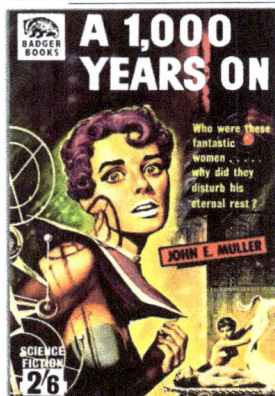

Series No/ Title	Science Fiction Series #050		
Date	1961	Imprint Badger	Collected
Artist	Ed Emshwiller (Emsh)		
Notes	February. Reused cover from Ace D-274		
Content	A 1000 Years On-John E. Muller(R. L. Fanthorpe)		

Science Fiction Series

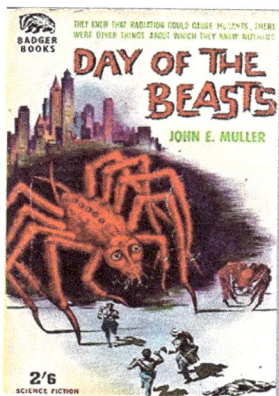

Series No/ Title   Science Fiction Series #051

Date   1961   Imprint   Badger   Collected

Artist

Notes   March.

Content   Day of the Beasts-John E. Muller(John Glasby)

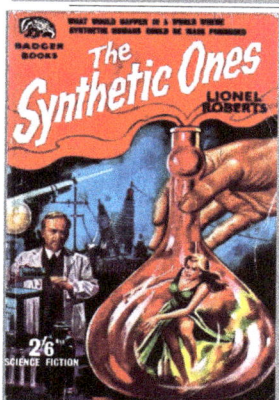

Series No/ Title   Science Fiction Series #052

Date   1961   Imprint   Badger   Collected

Artist

Notes   March.

Content   The Synthetic Ones-Lionel Roberts(R. L. Fanthorpe)

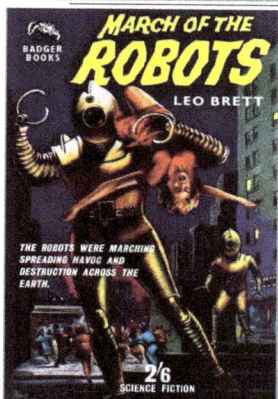

Series No/ Title   Science Fiction Series #053

Date   1961   Imprint   Badger   Collected

Artist   Henry Fox

Notes   March.

Content   March of The Robots-Leo Brett(R. L. Fanthorpe)

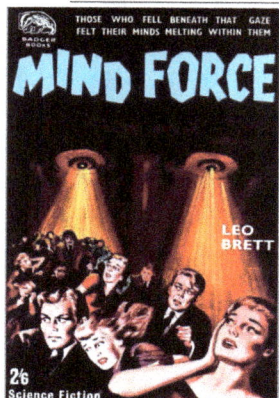

Series No/ Title   Science Fiction Series #054

Date   1961   Imprint   Badger   Collected

Artist

Notes   May.

Content   Mind Force-Leo Brett(R. L. Fanthorpe)

Science Fiction Series

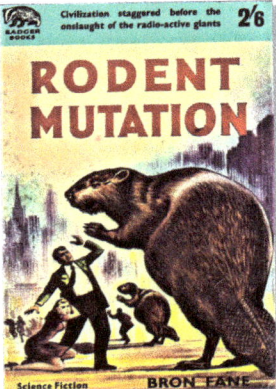

Series No/ Title   Science Fiction Series #055

Date   1961   Imprint   Badger   Collected

Artist

Notes   May.

Content   Rodent Mutation-Bron Fane(R. L. Fanthorpe)

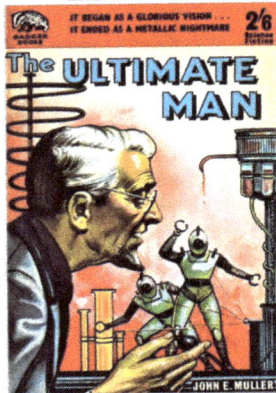

Series No/ Title   Science Fiction Series #056

Date   1961   Imprint   Badger   Collected

Artist

Notes   May.

Content   Ultimate Man-John E. Muller(R. L. Fanthorpe)

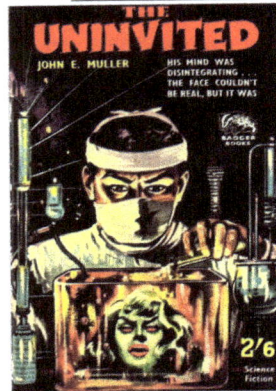

Series No/ Title   Science Fiction Series #057

Date   1961   Imprint   Badger   Collected

Artist   Henry Fox

Notes   June.

Content   The Uninvited-John E. Muller(R. L. Fanthorpe)

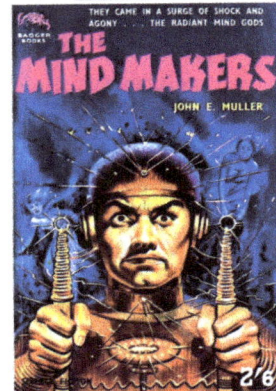

Series No/ Title   Science Fiction Series #058

Date   1961   Imprint   Badger   Collected

Artist   Henry Fox

Notes   August.

Content   The Mind Makers-John E. Muller(R. L. Fanthorpe)

Science Fiction Series

Series No/ Title   Science Fiction Series #059

Date   1961   Imprint   Badger   Collected

Artist

Notes   August. Book based on the 1960 American film of the same name

Content   12 To the Moon-(Robert A. Wise)

Series No/ Title   Science Fiction Series #060

Date   1961   Imprint   Badger   Collected

Artist   John Richards

Notes   October.

Content   Crimson Planet-John E. Muller(R. L. Fanthorpe)

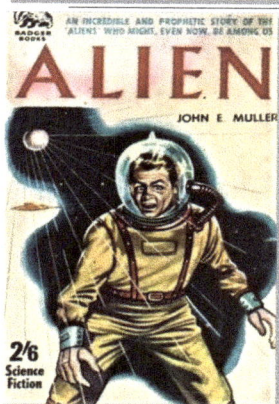

Series No/ Title   Science Fiction Series #061

Date   1961   Imprint   Badger   Collected

Artist

Notes   October.

Content   Alien-John E. Muller(John Glasby)

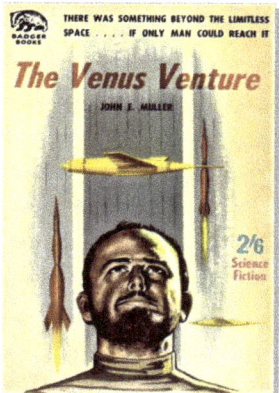

Series No/ Title   Science Fiction Series #062

Date   1961   Imprint   Badger   Collected

Artist   Henry Fox

Notes   November.

Content   The Venus Venture-John E. Muller(R. L. Fanthorpe)

Science Fiction Series

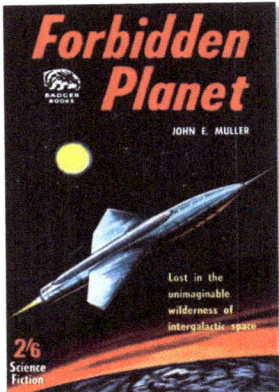

Series No/ Title	Science Fiction Series #063
Date	1961	Imprint	Badger	Collected
Artist	
Notes	November.
Content	Forbidden Planet-John E. Muller(R. L. Fanthorpe)

Series No/ Title	Science Fiction Series #064
Date	1962	Imprint	Badger	Collected
Artist	Henry Fox
Notes	January.
Content	Night of the Black Horror-(Victor Norwood)

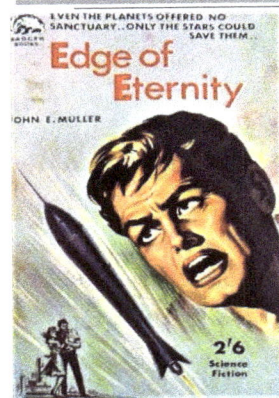

Series No/ Title	Science Fiction Series #065
Date	1962	Imprint	Badger	Collected
Artist	Henry Fox
Notes	January.
Content	Edge of Eternity-John E. Muller(John Glasby)

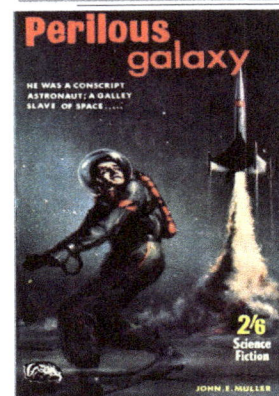

Series No/ Title	Science Fiction Series #066
Date	1962	Imprint	Badger	Collected
Artist	
Notes	March.
Content	Perilous Galaxy-John E. Muller(R. L. Fanthorpe)

Science Fiction Series

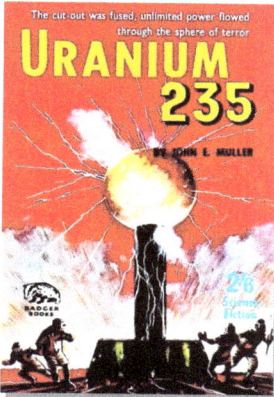

Series No/ Title	Science Fiction Series #067
Date	1962
Imprint	Badger
Collected	
Artist	Henry Fox
Notes	March.
Content	Uranium 235-John E. Muller(R. L. Fanthorpe)

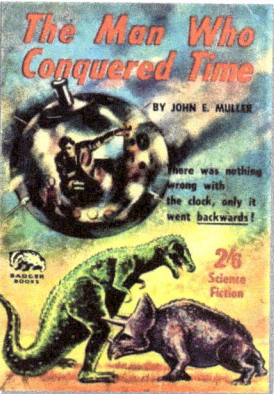

Series No/ Title	Science Fiction Series #068
Date	1962
Imprint	Badger
Collected	
Artist	Henry Fox
Notes	April.
Content	The Man Who Conquered Time-John E. Muller(R. L. Fanthorpe)

Series No/ Title	Science Fiction Series #069
Date	1962
Imprint	Badger
Collected	
Artist	Henry Fox
Notes	April.
Content	Orbit One-John E. Muller(R. L. Fanthorpe)

Series No/ Title	Science Fiction Series #070
Date	1962
Imprint	Badger
Collected	
Artist	Henry Fox
Notes	June.
Content	Micro Infinity-John E. Muller(R. L. Fanthorpe)

Science Fiction Series

Series No/ Title	Science Fiction Series #071		
Date	1962	Imprint	Badger	Collected
Artist	Henry Fox		
Notes	June.		
Content	Beyond Time-John E. Muller(R. L. Fanthorpe)		

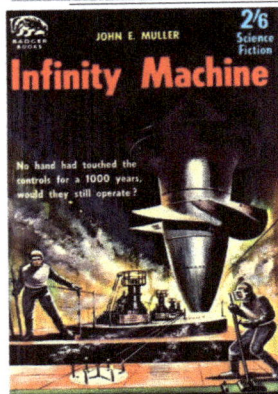

Series No/ Title	Science Fiction Series #072		
Date	1962	Imprint	Badger	Collected
Artist			
Notes	July.		
Content	Infinity Machine-John E. Muller(R. L. Fanthorpe)		

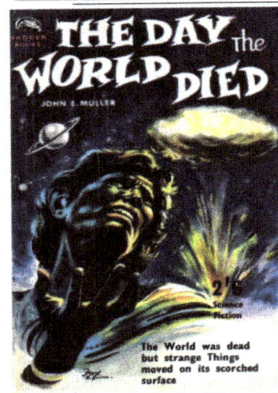

Series No/ Title	Science Fiction Series #073		
Date	1962	Imprint	Badger	Collected
Artist	Henry Fox		
Notes	July.		
Content	The Day the World Died-John E. Muller(R. L. Fanthorpe)		

Series No/ Title	Science Fiction Series #074		
Date	1962	Imprint	Badger	Collected
Artist	Henry Fox		
Notes	September.		
Content	X-Machine-John E. Muller(R. L. Fanthorpe)		

Science Fiction Series

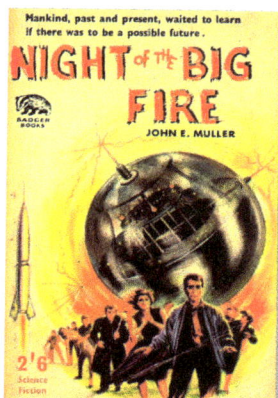

Series No/ Title **Science Fiction Series #075**

Date **1962**   Imprint **Badger**   Collected

Artist **Henry Fox**

Notes **September.**

Content **Night of The Big Fire-John E. Muller(John Glasby)**

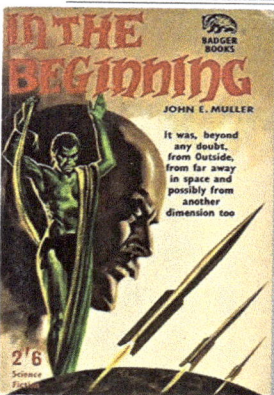

Series No/ Title **Science Fiction Series #076**

Date **1962**   Imprint **Badger**   Collected

Artist **Henry Fox**

Notes **September.**

Content **In The Beginning-John E. Muller()**

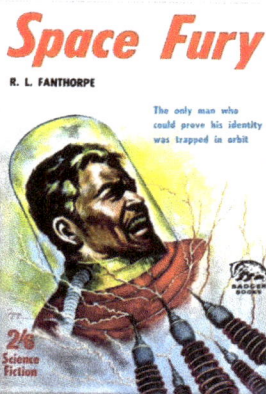

Series No/ Title **Science Fiction Series #077**

Date **1962**   Imprint **Badger**   Collected

Artist **Henry Fox**

Notes **October.**

Content **Space Fury-(R. L. Fanthorpe)**

Series No/ Title **Science Fiction Series #078**

Date **1962**   Imprint **Badger**   Collected

Artist **Henry Fox**

Notes **October.**

Content **Walk Through Tomorrow-Karl Ziegfried(R. L. Fanthorpe)**

Science Fiction Series

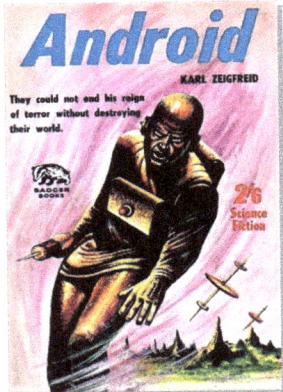

Series No/ Title	Science Fiction Series #079
Date	1962
Imprint	Badger
Collected	
Artist	Henry Fox
Notes	October.
Content	Android-Karl Ziegfried(R. L. Fanthorpe)

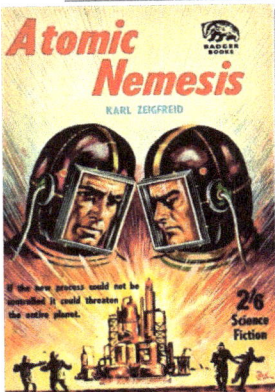

Series No/ Title	Science Fiction Series #080
Date	1962
Imprint	Badger
Collected	
Artist	Henry Fox
Notes	November.
Content	Atomic Nemesis-Karl Ziegfried(R. L. Fanthorpe)

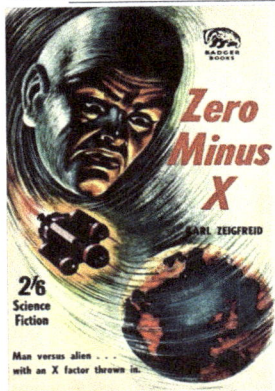

Series No/ Title	Science Fiction Series #081
Date	1962
Imprint	Badger
Collected	
Artist	Henry Fox
Notes	November.
Content	Zero Minus-Karl Ziegfried(R. L. Fanthorpe)

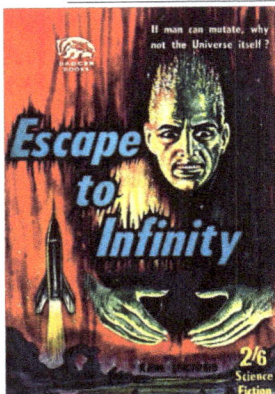

Series No/ Title	Science Fiction Series #082
Date	1963
Imprint	Badger
Collected	
Artist	Henry Fox
Notes	January.
Content	Escape To Infinity-Karl Ziegfried(R. L. Fanthorpe)

Science Fiction Series

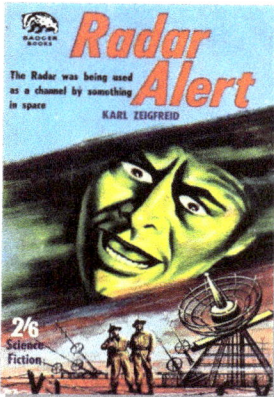

Series No/ Title	Science Fiction Series #083
Date	1963
Imprint	Badger
Collected	
Artist	Henry Fox
Notes	January.
Content	Radar Alert-Karl Ziegfried(R. L. Fanthorpe)

Series No/ Title	Science Fiction Series #084
Date	1963
Imprint	Badger
Collected	
Artist	Henry Fox
Notes	March.
Content	World of Tomorrow-Karl Ziegfried(R. L. Fanthorpe)

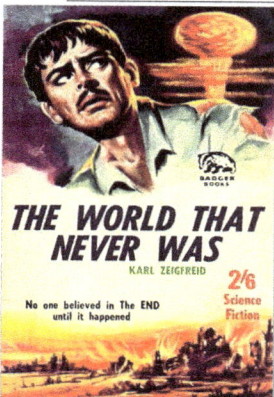

Series No/ Title	Science Fiction Series #085
Date	1963
Imprint	Badger
Collected	
Artist	Henry Fox
Notes	March.
Content	The World That Never Was-Karl Ziegfried(R. L. Fanthorpe)

Series No/ Title	Science Fiction Series #086
Date	1963
Imprint	Badger
Collected	
Artist	Henry Fox
Notes	April.
Content	Galaxy 666-Pel Torro(R. L. Fanthorpe)

Science Fiction Series

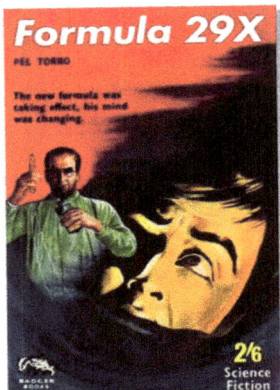

Series No/ Title	Science Fiction Series #087
Date	1963
Imprint	Badger
Collected	
Artist	Henry Fox
Notes	April.
Content	Formula 29X-Pel Torro(R. L. Fanthorpe)

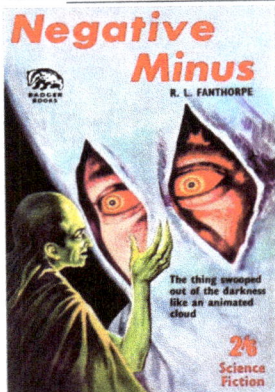

Series No/ Title	Science Fiction Series #088
Date	1963
Imprint	Badger
Collected	
Artist	Henry Fox
Notes	May.
Content	Negative Minus-(R. L. Fanthorpe)

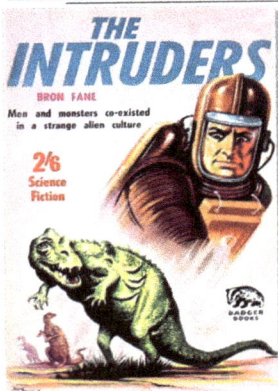

Series No/ Title	Science Fiction Series #089
Date	1963
Imprint	Badger
Collected	
Artist	Henry Fox
Notes	May.
Content	The Intruders-Bron Fane(R. L. Fanthorpe)

Series No/ Title	Science Fiction Series #090
Date	1963
Imprint	Badger
Collected	
Artist	Henry Fox
Notes	June.
Content	Plan for Conquest-(A. A. Glynn)

Science Fiction Series

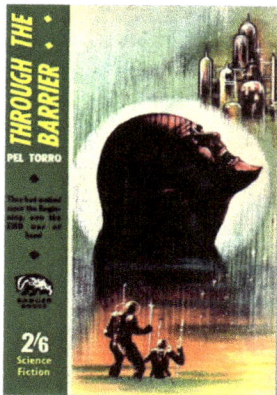

Series No/ Title   Science Fiction Series #091

Date   1963   Imprint   Badger   Collected

Artist   Henry Fox

Notes   June.

Content   Through The Barrier-Pel Torro(R. L. Fanthorpe)

Series No/ Title   Science Fiction Series #092

Date   1963   Imprint   Badger   Collected

Artist   Henry Fox

Notes   July.

Content   Somewhere Out There-Bron Fane(R. L. Fanthorpe)

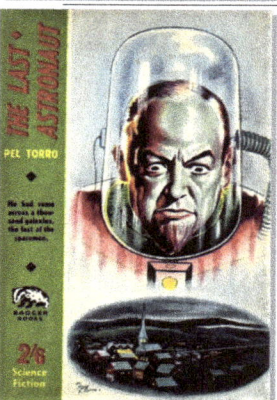

Series No/ Title   Science Fiction Series #093

Date   1963   Imprint   Badger   Collected

Artist   Henry Fox

Notes   July.

Content   The Last Astronaut-Pel Torro(R. L. Fanthorpe)

Series No/ Title   Science Fiction Series #094

Date   1963   Imprint   Badger   Collected

Artist   Henry Fox

Notes   September.

Content   The Alien Ones-Leo Brett(R. L. Fanthorpe)

Science Fiction Series

Series No/ Title	Science Fiction Series #095
Date	1963
Imprint	Badger
Collected	
Artist	Henry Fox
Notes	September.
Content	Power Sphere-Leo Brett(R. L. Fanthorpe)

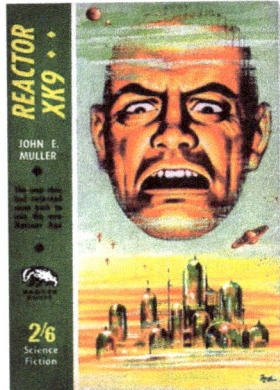

Series No/ Title	Science Fiction Series #096
Date	1963
Imprint	Badger
Collected	
Artist	Henry Fox
Notes	October.
Content	Reactor Xk9-John E. Muller(R. L. Fanthorpe)

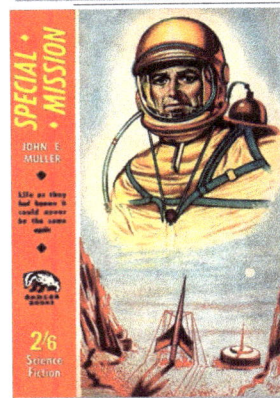

Series No/ Title	Science Fiction Series #097
Date	1963
Imprint	Badger
Collected	
Artist	Henry Fox
Notes	October.
Content	Special Mission-John E. Muller(R. L. Fanthorpe)

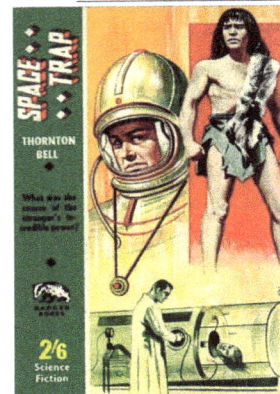

Series No/ Title	Science Fiction Series #098
Date	1964
Imprint	Badger
Collected	
Artist	Henry Fox
Notes	January.
Content	Space Trap-Thornton Bell(R. L. Fanthorpe)

Science Fiction Series

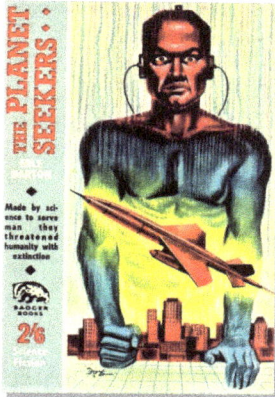

Series No/ Title	Science Fiction Series #099			Collected
Date	1964	Imprint	Badger	
Artist	Henry Fox			
Notes	January.			
Content	The Planet Seekers-Erle Barton(R. L. Fanthorpe)			

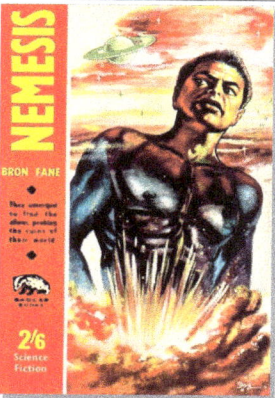

Series No/ Title	Science Fiction Series #100			Collected
Date	1964	Imprint	Badger	
Artist	Henry Fox			
Notes	March.			
Content	Nemesis-Bron Fane(R. L. Fanthorpe)			

Series No/ Title	Science Fiction Series #101			Collected
Date	1964	Imprint	Badger	
Artist	Henry Fox			
Notes	March.			
Content	The Return-Pel Torro(R. L. Fanthorpe)			

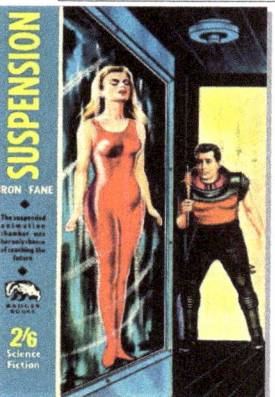

Series No/ Title	Science Fiction Series #102			Collected
Date	1964	Imprint	Badger	
Artist	Henry Fox			
Notes	May.			
Content	Suspension-Bron Fane(R. L. Fanthorpe)			

Science Fiction Series

Series No/ Title	Science Fiction Series #103
Date	1964
Imprint	Badger
Collected	
Artist	Henry Fox
Notes	May.
Content	Projection Infinity-Karl Ziegfried(R. L. Fanthorpe)

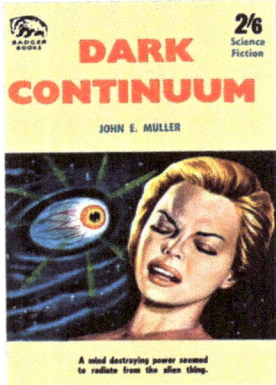

Series No/ Title	Science Fiction Series #104
Date	1964
Imprint	Badger
Collected	
Artist	Henry Fox
Notes	July.
Content	Dark Continuum-John E. Muller(R. L. Fanthorpe)

Series No/ Title	Science Fiction Series #105
Date	1964
Imprint	Badger
Collected	
Artist	
Notes	July.
Content	Mark of The Beast-John E. Muller(R. L. Fanthorpe)

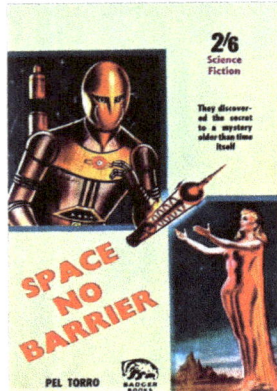

Series No/ Title	Science Fiction Series #106
Date	1964
Imprint	Badger
Collected	
Artist	Henry Fox
Notes	October.
Content	Space No Barrier-Pel Torro(R. L. Fanthorpe)

Science Fiction Series

Series No/ Title	Science Fiction Series #107
Date	1964 Imprint Badger Collected
Artist	Henry Fox
Notes	October.
Content	No Way Back-Karl Ziegfried(R. L. Fanthorpe)

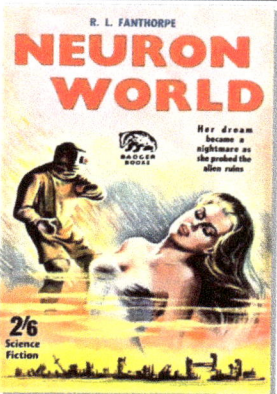

Series No/ Title	Science Fiction Series #108
Date	1965 Imprint Badger Collected
Artist	Henry Fox
Notes	January.
Content	Neuron World-(R. L. Fanthorpe)

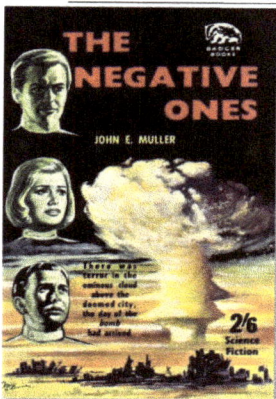

Series No/ Title	Science Fiction Series #109
Date	1965 Imprint Badger Collected
Artist	Henry Fox
Notes	January.
Content	Negative Ones-John E. Muller(R. L. Fanthorpe)

Series No/ Title	Science Fiction Series #110
Date	1965 Imprint Badger Collected
Artist	Henry Fox
Notes	March.
Content	Force 97X-Pel Torro(R. L. Fanthorpe)

Science Fiction Series

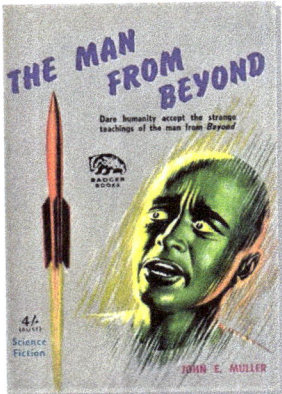

Series No/ Title	Science Fiction Series #111
Date	1965
Imprint	Badger
Collected	
Artist	Henry Fox
Notes	March.
Content	The Man From Beyond-John E. Muller(R. L. Fanthorpe)

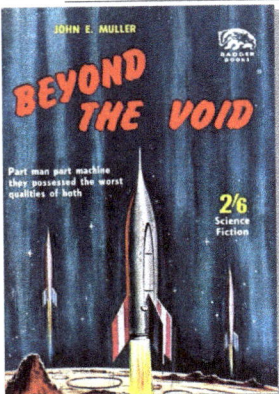

Series No/ Title	Science Fiction Series #112
Date	1965
Imprint	Badger
Collected	
Artist	
Notes	August.
Content	Beyond the Void-John E. Muller(R. L. Fanthorpe)

Series No/ Title	Science Fiction Series #113
Date	1965
Imprint	Badger
Collected	
Artist	
Notes	August.
Content	Barrier 346-Karl Ziegfried(R. L. Fanthorpe)

Series No/ Title	Science Fiction Series #114
Date	1965
Imprint	Badger
Collected	
Artist	Henry Fox
Notes	December.
Content	Girl From Tomorrow-Karl Ziegfried(R. L. Fanthorpe)

Science Fiction Series

Series No/ Title	Science Fiction Series #115
Date	1965 Imprint Badger Collected
Artist	Henry Fox
Notes	December.
Content	U.F.O 517-Bron Fane(R. L. Fanthorpe)

Series No/ Title	Science Fiction Series #116
Date	1966 Imprint Badger Collected
Artist	Henry Fox
Notes	March.
Content	Phenomena X-John E. Muller(R. L. Fanthorpe)

Series No/ Title	Science Fiction Series #117
Date	1966 Imprint Badger Collected
Artist	Henry Fox
Notes	March.
Content	Survival Project-John E. Muller(R. L. Fanthorpe)

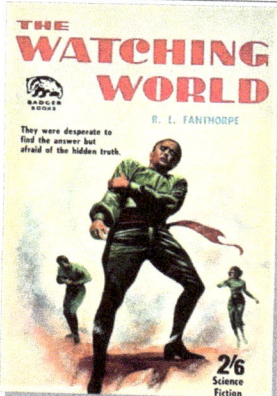

Series No/ Title	Science Fiction Series #118
Date	1966 Imprint Badger Collected
Artist	Henry Fox
Notes	March.
Content	The Watching World-(R. L. Fanthorpe)

Science Fiction Series

Series No/ Title Science Fiction Series #115

Date 1965   Imprint Badger   Collected

Artist Henry Fox

Notes December.

Content U.F.O 517-Bron Fane(R. L. Fanthorpe)

Series No/ Title Science Fiction Series #116

Date 1966   Imprint Badger   Collected

Artist Henry Fox

Notes March.

Content Phenomena X-John E. Muller(R. L. Fanthorpe)

Series No/ Title Science Fiction Series #117

Date 1966   Imprint Badger   Collected

Artist Henry Fox

Notes March.

Content Survival Project-John E. Muller(R. L. Fanthorpe)

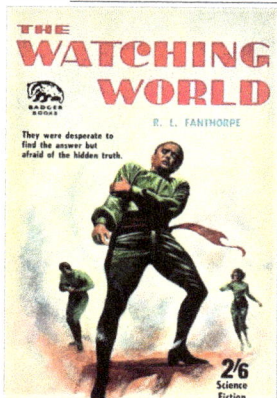

Series No/ Title Science Fiction Series #118

Date 1966   Imprint Badger   Collected

Artist Henry Fox

Notes March.

Content The Watching World-(R. L. Fanthorpe)

Science Non-Series

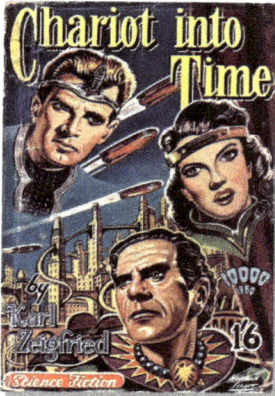

Series No/ Title	Chariot Into Time
Date	1953
Imprint	John Spencer
Collected	
Artist	Norman Light
Notes	May.
Content	Chariot Into Time-Karl Ziegfried(Tom W. Wade)

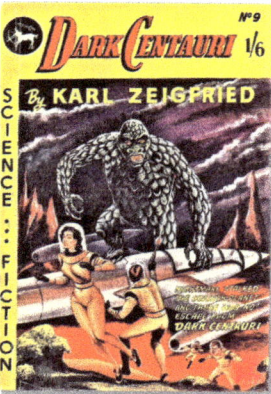

Series No/ Title	Dark Centauri
Date	1954
Imprint	John Spencer
Collected	
Artist	Ray Theobald
Notes	April.
Content	Dark Centauri-Karl Ziegfried(John Glasby)

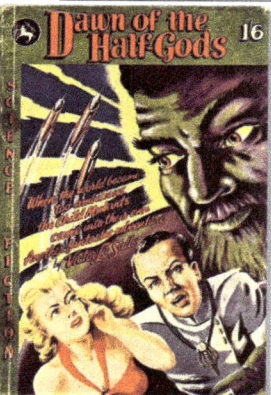

Series No/ Title	Dawn Of The Half-Gods
Date	1953
Imprint	John Spencer
Collected	
Artist	Ray Theobald
Notes	October.
Content	Dawn of the Half-Gods-Victor La Salle(John Glasby)

Series No/ Title	Menace From Mercury
Date	1954
Imprint	John Spencer
Collected	
Artist	Ray Theobald
Notes	March.
Content	Menace From Mercury-Victor La Salle(R. L. Fanthorpe), More Than Mortal-Victor LaSalle(Tom W. Wade)

Science Non-Series

Series No/ Title   Suns In Duo

Date	1953	Imprint	John Spencer	Collected

Artist   Gordon C. Davies

Notes   January.

Content   Suns in Duo-Victor La Salle(Tom W. Wade)

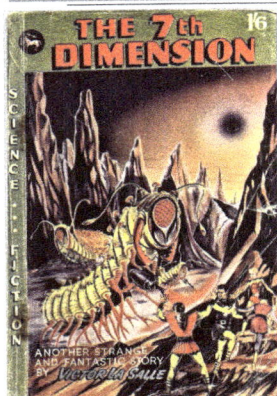

Series No/ Title   The 7th Dimension

Date	1953	Imprint	John Spencer	Collected

Artist   Ray Theobald

Notes   July.

Content   The 7th Dimension-Victor La Salle(Tom W. Wade)

Series No/ Title   The Black Sphere

Date	1952	Imprint	John Spencer	Collected

Artist   Norman Light

Notes   October.

Content   The Black Sphere-Victor La Salle(Gerald Evans)

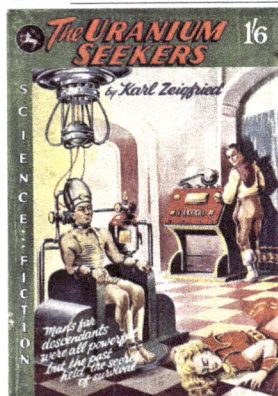

Series No/ Title   The Uranium Seekers

Date	1953	Imprint	John Spencer	Collected

Artist   Ray Theobald

Notes   December.

Content   The Uranium Seekers-Karl Ziegfried(John Glasby)

Science Non-Series

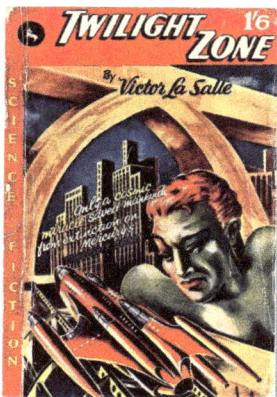

Series No/ Title	Twilight Zone
Date	1954
Imprint	John Spencer
Collected	
Artist	Ray Theobald
Notes	February.
Content	Twilight Zone-Victor La Salle(John Glasby)

Tales of Tomorrow

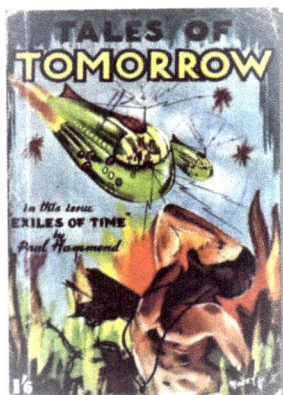

Series No/ Title	Tales of Tomorrow #01
Date	1950
Imprint	John Spencer
Collected	
Artist	Gerald Facey
Notes	September.
Content	Dangerous Moon-John Evans(), Exiles in Time-Paul Hammond(Sydney J. Bounds), Invaders From the Stars-James Ross(Sydney J. Bounds), The Last Ten Men on Earth-Basil Sitty(Norman Lazenby), The Forgotten days-Uncredited()

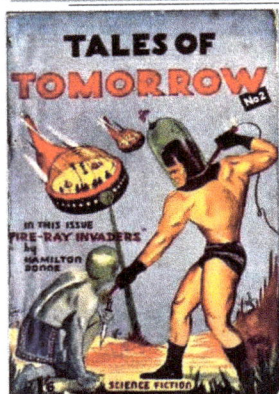

Series No/ Title	Tales of Tomorrow #02
Date	1951
Imprint	John Spencer
Collected	
Artist	Gerald Facey
Notes	January.
Content	Fire-Ray Invaders-Hamilton Donne(John F. Watt), The Star Ship-Eric Lamont(), Soldiers of Space-R. J. Norton(), Black Pirate-John Renolds(), Aftermath-Edward Ward(Barney Ward)

Series No/ Title	Tales of Tomorrow #03
Date	1951
Imprint	John Spencer
Collected	
Artist	Ronald Turner
Notes	March.
Content	The Encompassed Globe-James Stanfield(Tom W. Wade), Forgotten World-John Ellis(John F. Watt), Expedition Eternity-David Campbell(Leonard G. Fish), Hell Planet-(Leonard G. Fish), Reaction-Thomas Rochdale(Alfred E. Hind)

Series No/ Title	Tales of Tomorrow #04
Date	1952
Imprint	John Spencer
Collected	
Artist	Ronald Turner
Notes	July.
Content	Slave Ships-Ray Mason(John F. Watt), Threat from Space-Bruce Fenton(John F. Watt), Suicide Mission-Mack James(John F. Watt), Sargasso of Space-(A. A. Glynn)

Tales of Tomorrow

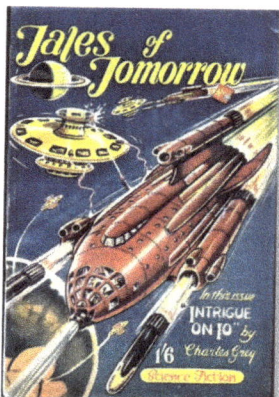

Series No/ Title	Tales of Tomorrow #05
Date	1952
Imprint	John Spencer
Collected	
Artist	Norman Light
Notes	September.

Content: The Incredible Scourge-(Tom W. Wade), The Crystalline World-Vincent Robertson(Tom W. Wade), Intrigue on Io-Charles Grey(E. C. Tubb), War Potential-John Toucan(William Henry Fleming Bird)

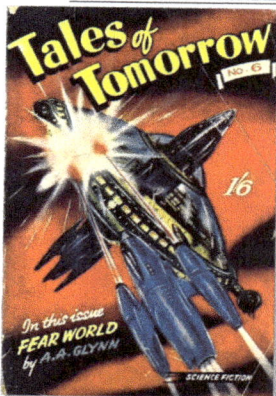

Series No/ Title	Tales of Tomorrow #06
Date	1953
Imprint	John Spencer
Collected	
Artist	Ronald Turner
Notes	January.

Content: The Thought Machine-Ray Mason(John F. Watt), Fear World-(A. A. Glynn), Point of No Return-Max Chartair(John Glasby), Galactic Interlude-Willi Deinhardt(), Safari on Venus-D. A. LeGraeme(Dale Graham)

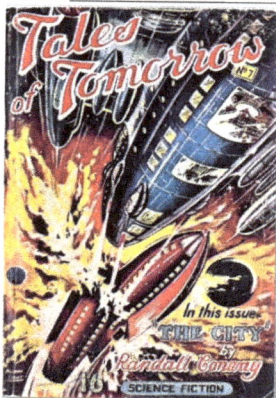

Series No/ Title	Tales of Tomorrow #07
Date	1953
Imprint	John Spencer
Collected	
Artist	Norman Light
Notes	May. ed. Samuel(Sol) Assael, Maurice Nahum.

Content: Bifurcation-A. J. Merak(John Glasby), The City-Randall Conway(John Glasby), Laughing Gas-Willi Deinhardt(), Interplanetary Zoo-Earl Van Loden(Ernest Lister Hale(Lisle) Willis)

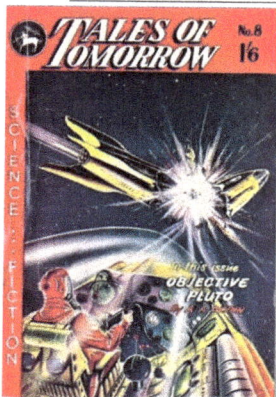

Series No/ Title	Tales of Tomorrow #08
Date	1953
Imprint	John Spencer
Collected	
Artist	Gordon C. Davies
Notes	August.

Content: Project Survival-Kenneth Boyea(John F. Watt), Satellite Peril-Bruce Fenton(John F. Watt), Dungeon of Time-Anthony Martin(A. A. Glynn), Objective Pluto-(A. A. Glynn), Repercussions-John Toucan(William Henry Fleming Bird)

Tales of Tomorrow

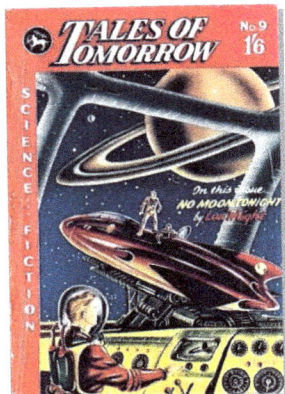

Series No/ Title   Tales of Tomorrow #09

Date   1953   **Imprint**   John Spencer   **Collected**

Artist   Gordon C. Davies

Notes   October.

Content   Globe of Dread-(Tom W. Wade), The Moment in Time-Vincent Robertson(Tom W. Wade), Danger Out of Space-Frank C. Kneller(John F. Watt), A Matter of Concealment-Ray Cosmic(John Glasby), No Moon Tonight-Lan Wright(Lionel Wright)

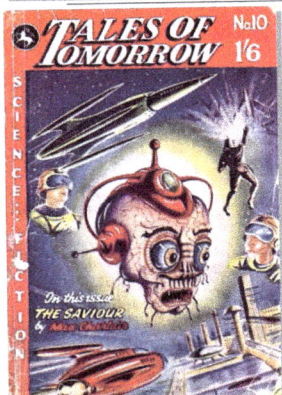

Series No/ Title   Tales of Tomorrow #10

Date   1954   **Imprint**   John Spencer   **Collected**

Artist   Gordon C. Davies

Notes   April.

Content   Alien Threat-Mack Jones(John F. Watt), The Fugitive-Bruce Fenton(John F. Watt), Stowaway-A. J. Merak(John Glasby), The Saviour-Max Chartair(John Glasby), The Big Slowdown-Art Smith(Art Smith)

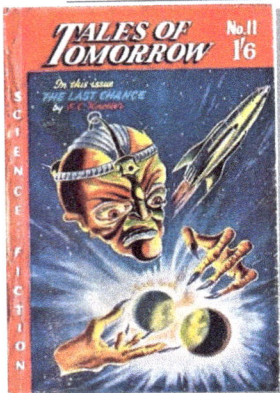

Series No/ Title   Tales of Tomorrow #11

Date   1954   **Imprint**   John Spencer   **Collected**

Artist   Ray Theobald

Notes   June. Artist possibly Davies.

Content   The Lethal Mist-Kenneth Boyea(John F. Watt), The Last Chance-Frank C. Kneller(John F. Watt), Planet of Desire-A. J. Merak(John Glasby), The Road to Anywhere-Max Chartair(John Glasby), Computer insane-Michael Hamilton(John Glasby)

Wonders of the Spaceways Series

Series No/ Title Wonders of the Spaceways #01

Date 1951 **Imprint** John Spencer **Collected**

Artist Gerald Facey

Notes February.

Content The Peril from the Moon-(Tom W. Wade), Convoy to the Unknown-D. R. Mencet(John F. Watt), Lust for conquest-Frank C. Kneller(John F. Watt), The Green Cloud-John Robertson(John F. Watt), The Purple Flower-Stephen James(), Rake's Progress-Peter J. Ridley(Peter J. Ridley)

Series No/ Title Wonders of the Spaceways #02

Date 1952 **Imprint** John Spencer **Collected**

Artist Ronald Turner

Notes January. Artist possibly Facey.

Content The Minacious Termites-(Tom W. Wade), Struggle For Calisto-L. S. Johnson(Tom W. Wade), The Isolationists-(R. Brothwell), The Monument-(Leslie V. Heald)

Series No/ Title Wonders of the Spaceways #03

Date 1952 **Imprint** John Spencer **Collected**

Artist Ronald Turner

Notes May.

Content The Menace of the Discoids-R. G. Lomax(Tom W. Wade), Scourge of Space-D. R. Mencet(John F. Watt), Martian Outcast-Neil J. Spalding(John F. Watt), The Lighter-D. A. LeGraeme(Dale Graham), Synthesis of Knowledge-Erle Van Loden(Ernest Lister Hale(Lisle) Willis)

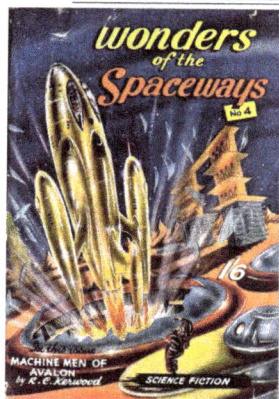

Series No/ Title Wonders of the Spaceways #04

Date 1952 **Imprint** John Spencer **Collected**

Artist Ronald Turner

Notes September. Artist possibly Davies.

Content Assignment in Venus-(Tom W. Wade), Anno Mundi-Branson D. Carter(Tom W. Wade), Jovian Flypaper-D. F. Jameson(D. F. Jameson), Machine-Men of Avaion-R. C. Kerwood()

Wonders of the Spaceways Series

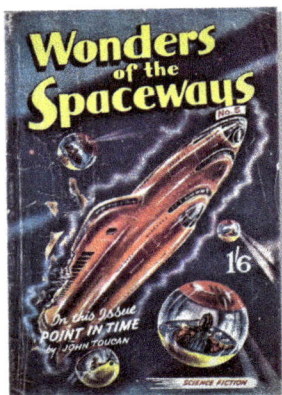

Series No/ Title Wonders of the Spaceways #05

Date	1952	Imprint	John Spencer		Collected	

Artist Gordon C. Davies

Notes November.

Content Mistakes Do Happen-(Tom W. Wade), Helping Hand-Charles Grey(E. C. Tubb), Buried in Space-Dean Ryan(), Point in Time-John Toucan(William Henry Fleming Bird), Demons of Daavol-Erle Van Loden(Ernest Lister Hale(Lisle) Willis)

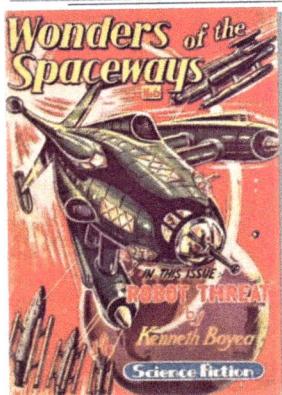

Series No/ Title Wonders of the Spaceways #06

Date	1953	Imprint	John Spencer		Collected	

Artist Norman Light

Notes January.

Content Robot Threat-Kenneth Boyce(John F. Watt), Prisoners of Mars-D. R. Mencet(John F. Watt), Space Warning-James Robertson(John F. Watt), The Golden Hibiscus-A. J. Merak(John Glasby)

Series No/ Title Wonders of the Spaceways #07

Date	1953	Imprint	John Spencer		Collected	

Artist Norman Light

Notes July.

Content Spawn of Space-Ray Mason(John F. Watt), Sillisian Menace-Frank C. Kneller(John F. Watt), Void Warp-Ray Cosmic(John Glasby), Mission Venus-Meryl St. John Montague(Laurence Sandfield), Lambda Point-D. A. LeGraeme(Dale Graham)

Series No/ Title Wonders of the Spaceways #08

Date	1953	Imprint	John Spencer		Collected	

Artist Ray Theobald

Notes October.

Content The Purple Sun-John Robertson(John F. Watt), Unrecorded Incident-(A. A. Glynn), Moon King-A. J. Merak(John Glasby), Star's End-Max Chartair(John Glasby), Allomorph-Ray Cosmic(John Glasby)

Wonders of the Spaceways Series

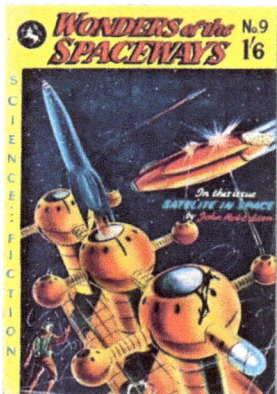

Series No/ Title Wonders of the Spaceways #09

Date 1954   **Imprint** John Spencer   **Collected**

Artist Ray Theobald

Notes January.

Content Integral Menace-(Tom W. Wade), Satellite in Space-John Robertson(John F. Watt), Mischa-A. J. Merak(John Glasby), The Laughter of Space-Michael Hamilton(John Glasby), Chronolel-Max Chartair(John Glasby)

Series No/ Title Wonders of the Spaceways #10

Date 1954   **Imprint** John Spencer   **Collected**

Artist Ray Theobald

Notes April.

Content The Final Threat-John Robertson(John F. Watt), Captives of Vesta-Ray Mason(John F. Watt), Renegades of the Void-Kenneth Boyea(John F. Watt), Destination - Infinity-Rod Patterson(John F. Watt), Marauders of the Void-Lionel Roberts(R. L. Fanthorpe)

Worlds of Fantasy Series

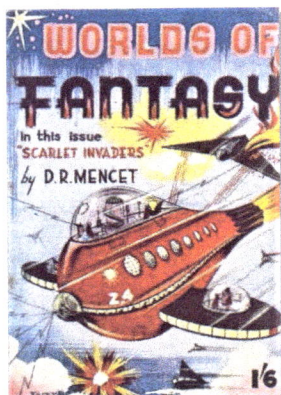

Series No/ Title	Worlds of Fantasy #01			
Date	1950	Imprint	John Spencer	Collected
Artist	Gerald Facey			
Notes	June.			
Content	Scarlet Invaders-D. R. Mencet(John F. Watt), Vandal of the Void-Frank C. Kneller(John F. Watt), Martian Terror-Hamilton Donne(John F. Watt), Conquerors of the Moon-J. Austin Jackson(Norman Lazenby), Gods of Helle-(Norman Lazenby)			

Series No/ Title	Worlds of Fantasy #02			
Date	1950	Imprint	John Spencer	Collected
Artist	Gerald Facey			
Notes	November.			
Content	Lunar Revolt-Frank C. Kneller(John F. Watt), Plan for Conquest-D. J. Mencet(John F. Watt), The Planeteer-Martin L. Baker(Sydney J. Bounds), Space Pirates-Hamilton Donne(John F. Watt), The Outlaw of Space-Lawrence Smith(Sydney J. Bounds), The Visitors-Uncredited(Leonard G. Fish)			

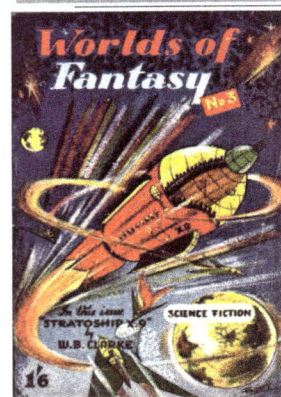

Series No/ Title	Worlds of Fantasy #03			
Date	1951	Imprint	John Spencer	Collected
Artist	Gerald Facey			
Notes	January.			
Content	The Elder Race-John Sloan(Tom W. Wade), Revolt!-Ronald Adison(), Stratoship X9-W. B. Clarke(Norman Lazenby), Moons of fear-(Norman Lazenby), Treachery From Venus-Everet Rigby()			

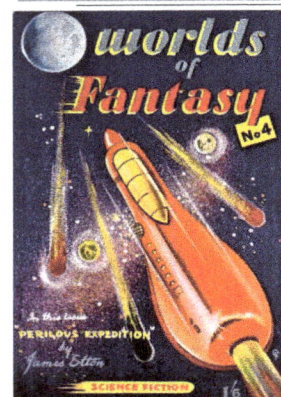

Series No/ Title	Worlds of Fantasy #04			
Date	1951	Imprint	John Spencer	Collected
Artist	Gerald Facey			
Notes	November.			
Content	Perilous Expedition-James Elton(John F. Watt), The Death Planet-D. J. Mencet(John F. Watt), Doomed World-Ray Mason(John F. Watt), World of the Ancients-(C. D. Ellis)			

Worlds of Fantasy Series

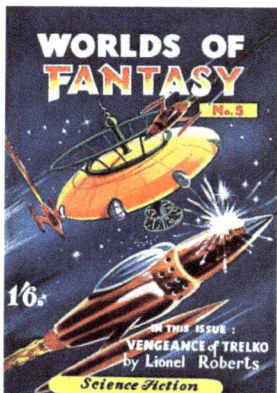

Series No/ Title	Worlds of Fantasy #05
Date	1952 Imprint	John Spencer Collected
Artist	Ronald Turner
Notes	April. Artist possibly Facey.
Content	The Impending Heritage-(Tom W. Wade), The Aquatic Piracy-Raymond Leroyd(Tom W. Wade), Agent of Earth-(R. Brothwell), Vengeance of Trelko-Lionel Roberts(R. L. Fanthorpe)

Series No/ Title	Worlds of Fantasy #06
Date	1952 Imprint	John Spencer Collected
Artist	Norman Light
Notes	August.
Content	Wreckers of Space-Mack James(John F. Watt), Threat from Mars-Frank C. Kneller(John F. Watt), Death From the Swamps-Ray Mason(John F. Watt), Adaptability-D. A. LeGraeme(Dale Graham), Colonist-John F. Manders(Laurence Sandfield), Mightier Weapon-(Laurence Sandfield)

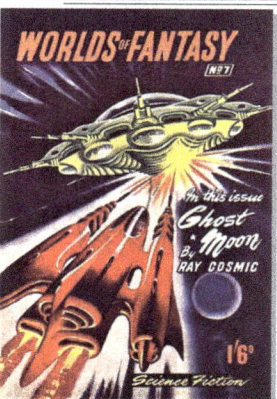

Series No/ Title	Worlds of Fantasy #07
Date	1952 Imprint	John Spencer Collected
Artist	Ronald Turner
Notes	September.
Content	First Effort-L. T. Bronson(E. C. Tubb), Ghost Moon-Ray Cosmic(John Glasby), There's No Tomorrow-Charles Grey(E. C. Tubb), Out of the Blue-(Alfred E. Hind), Quietus-(W. Shaw)

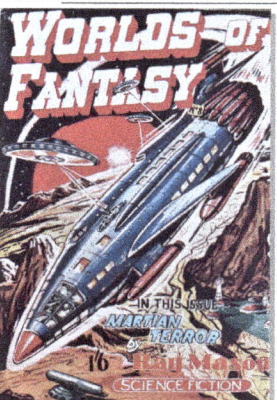

Series No/ Title	Worlds of Fantasy #08
Date	1952 Imprint	John Spencer Collected
Artist	Norman Light
Notes	December.
Content	Journey to the Dawn-(Tom W. Wade), Martian Terror-Ray Mason(John F. Watt), Weird Plant-B. Ward(Barney Ward), Space Adventurer-Uncredited(Barney Ward)

Worlds of Fantasy Series

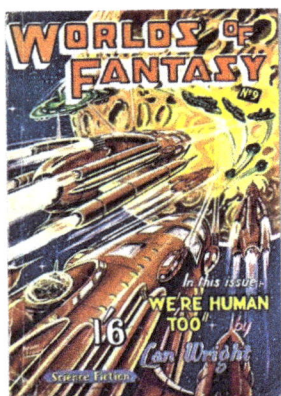

Series No/ Title   Worlds of Fantasy #09

Date	1953	Imprint	John Spencer	Collected	

Artist   Norman Light

Notes   April.

Content   Realm of Danger-(A. A. Glynn), Rogue Ship-(Alfred E. Hind), We're Human Too-Lan Wright(Lionel Wright)

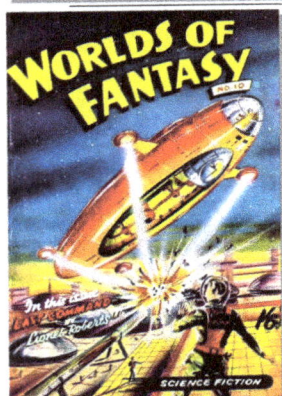

Series No/ Title   Worlds of Fantasy #10

Date	1953	Imprint	John Spencer	Collected	

Artist   Gordon C. Davies

Notes   June.

Content   Tables Turned-(A. A. Glynn), The Expanding Bacillus-D. R. Le Graeme(Dale Graham), Last Command-Lionel Roberts(R. L. Fanthorpe), Tomorrow is Also a Day-Dean Ryan(), Emergency-(Laurence Sandfield), Princess in a Bubble-Trebor Thorpe(R. L. Fanthorpe)

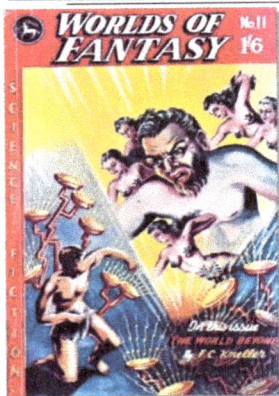

Series No/ Title   Worlds of Fantasy #11

Date	1953	Imprint	John Spencer	Collected	

Artist   Ray Theobald

Notes   September.

Content   Marooned on Venus-Bruce Fenton(John F. Watt), The World Beyond-Frank C. Kneller(John F. Watt), Backtrack-Anthony Martin(A. A. Glynn), The Storm Movers-A. J. Merak(John Glasby), Zerzuran Plague-Michael Hamilton(John Glasby)

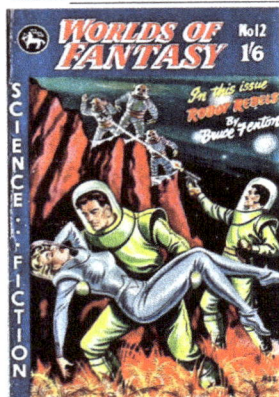

Series No/ Title   Worlds of Fantasy #12

Date	1954	Imprint	John Spencer	Collected	

Artist   Gordon C. Davies

Notes   February. Artist possibly Embleton.

Content   There is No Future-(Tom W. Wade), Last Survivor-Neil J. Spaulding(John F. Watt), Robot Rebels-Bruce Fenton(John F. Watt), Riddle of the Robots-Kenneth Boyea(John F. Watt), Martian Bonanza-Lionel Roberts(R. L. Fanthorpe)

Worlds of Fantasy Series

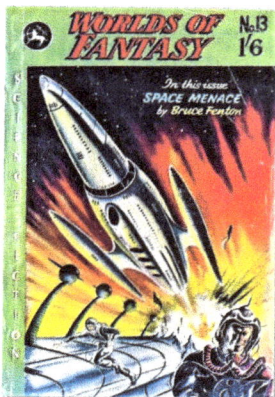

Series No/ Title	Worlds of Fantasy #13
Date	1954
Imprint	John Spencer
Collected	
Artist	Gordon C. Davies
Notes	April.
Content	Space Menace-Bruce Fenton(John F. Watt), The Byarkil Eaters-A. J. Merak(John Glasby), Paradise Planet-Max Chartair(John Glasby), Time Trouble-Randall Conway(John Glasby), Time Warp-D. A. LeGraeme(Dale Graham), Genesis-John Toucan(William Henry Fleming Bird)

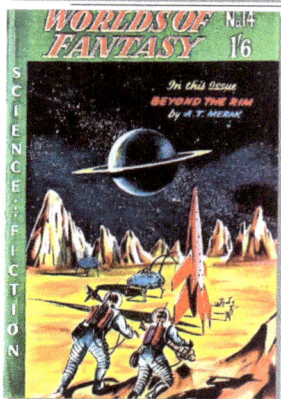

Series No/ Title	Worlds of Fantasy #14
Date	1954
Imprint	John Spencer
Collected	
Artist	Ray Theobald
Notes	June. Artist possibly Davies.
Content	Beyond the Rim-A. J. Merak(John Glasby), Edge of Darkness-Max Chartair(John Glasby), Conquest-Bron Fane(R. L. Fanthorpe), Galactic Twin-Trebor Thorpe(R. L. Fanthorpe)

Supernatural/Out of this World Series

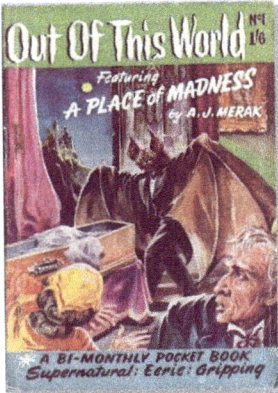

Series No/ Title	Out of this World #1
Date	1954	Imprint	John Spencer	Collected
Artist	Ray Theobald
Notes	October.
Content	A Place of Madness-A. J. Merak(John Glasby), The Nightmare Road-Ray Cosmic(John Glasby), Angel of the Bottomless Pit-Michael Hamilton(John Glasby), The Seventh Image-Randall Conway(John Glasby), The Devil at My Elbow-Max Chartair(John Glasby)

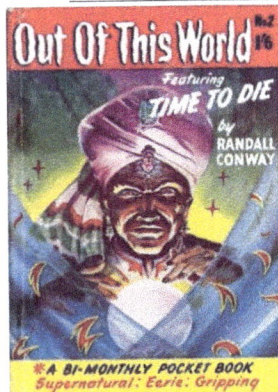

Series No/ Title	Out of this World #2
Date	1954	Imprint	John Spencer	Collected
Artist	Ronald Turner
Notes	December.
Content	Time To Die-Randall Conway(John Glasby), Coven of Thirteen-Michael Hamilton(John Glasby), A little Devil Dancing-Max Chartair(John Glasby), The Stairway-Ray Cosmic(John Glasby), The Unseen-A. J. Merak(John Glasby)

Series No/ Title	Supernatural Series #001
Date	1954	Imprint	John Spencer	Collected
Artist	Ray Theobald
Notes	May. ed. John S. Manning (Assael)
Content	The Gods of Fear-Randall Conway(John Glasby), Lycanthrope-Ray Cosmic(John Glasby), Vengeance of Set-Michael Hamilton(John Glasby), The Cloak of Darkness-Max Chartair(John Glasby), The Devil's Canvas-A. J. Merak(John Glasby)

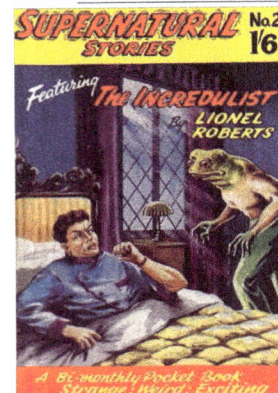

Series No/ Title	Supernatural Series #002
Date	1954	Imprint	John Spencer	Collected
Artist	Ray Theobald
Notes	July. ed. John S. Manning (Assael)
Content	The Incredulist-John Raymond(R. L. Fanthorpe), Frog-Max Chartair(John Glasby), Things of the Dark-A. J. Merak(John Glasby), Hunter's Moon-Randall Conway(John Glasby), And Very Few Get Out-(R. L. Fanthorpe)

Supernatural/Out of this World Series

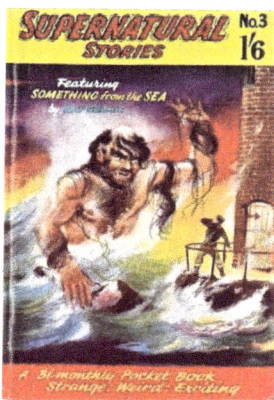

Series No/ Title Supernatural Series #003

Date 1954 **Imprint** John Spencer **Collected**

Artist Gerald Facey

Notes September. ed. John S. Manning (Assael)

Content Something from the Sea-Ray Cosmic(John Glasby), The Crystal Skull-A. J. Merak(John Glasby), Haunt of the Vampire-Max Chartair(John Glasby), The Other Séance-Michael Hamilton(John Glasby), Will O' the Wisp-Randall Conway(John Glasby)

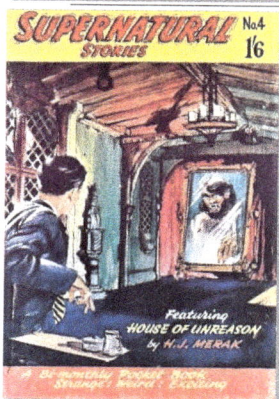

Series No/ Title Supernatural Series #004

Date 1954 **Imprint** John Spencer **Collected**

Artist Gerald Facey

Notes November. ed. John S. Manning (Assael)

Content House of Unreason-H. J. Merak(John Glasby), The Weird Lovers-(A. A. Glynn), The Zegrembi Bracelet-Max Chartair(John Glasby), They Fly by Night-Randall Conway(John Glasby), The Chair-Ray Cosmic(John Glasby)

Series No/ Title Supernatural Series #005

Date 1955 **Imprint** John Spencer **Collected**

Artist Gerald Facey

Notes January. ed. John S. Manning (Assael)

Content My Name Is Satan-A. J. Merak(John Glasby), Lurani-Max Chartair(John Glasby), The Whisper of the Wind-Randall Conway(John Glasby), The Dark Ones-Ray Cosmic(John Glasby), Somewhere in the Moonlight-Michael Hamilton(John Glasby)

Series No/ Title Supernatural Series #006

Date 1955 **Imprint** John Spencer **Collected**

Artist Ronald Turner

Notes March. ed. John S. Manning (Assael)

Content Voice of the Drum-Michael Hamilton(John Glasby), The Supernaturalist-A. J. Merak(John Glasby), Without a Shadow of a Doubt-Max Chartair(John Glasby), The Hungry House-Randall Conway(John Glasby), Lorelei-Ray Cosmic(John Glasby)

Supernatural/Out of this World Series

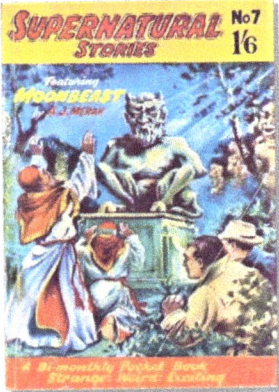

Series No/ Title Supernatural Series #007

Date 1955   Imprint John Spencer   Collected

Artist Gerald Facey

Notes May. ed. John S. Manning (Assael)

Content Moonbeast-A. J. Merak(John Glasby), Mask of Asmodeus-Max Chartair(John Glasby), The Hungry Gods-Randall Conway(John Glasby), Shadow Over Endor-Ray Cosmic(John Glasby), The Crystal Fear-Michael Hamilton(John Glasby)

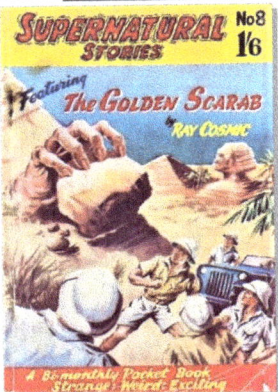

Series No/ Title Supernatural Series #008

Date 1955   Imprint John Spencer   Collected

Artist Ronald Turner

Notes August. ed. John S. Manning (Assael)

Content The Golden Scarab-Ray Cosmic(John Glasby), The Reincarnate-A. J. Merak(John Glasby), The Ugly Ones-Max Chartair(John Glasby), The Man Who Lost Thursday-Randall Conway(John Glasby), A Place of Meeting-Michael Hamilton(John Glasby)

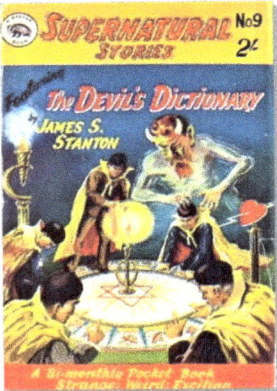

Series No/ Title Supernatural Series #009

Date 1957   Imprint Badger   Collected

Artist Ray Theobald

Notes May. ed. John S. Manning (Assael)

Content The Dolmen-Raymond L. Burton(E. C. Tubb), The Artist's Model-Robert D. Ennis(E. C. Tubb), The Devil's Dictionary-James S. Stanton/ Edward Richards(E. C. Tubb), The Ancient Alchemist-John Mason(E. C. Tubb), The Witch of Peronia-L. C. Powers(E. C. Tubb), Snake Vengeance-Andrew Sutton(E. C. Tubb)

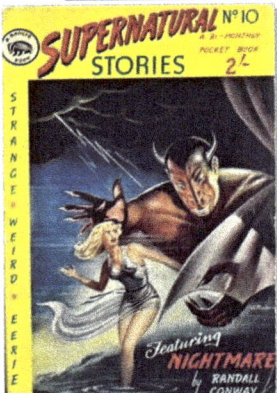

Series No/ Title Supernatural Series #010

Date 1957   Imprint Badger   Collected

Artist John Pollack

Notes June. ed. John S. Manning (Assael)

Content Nightmare-Randall Conway(John Glasby), The Three Green Sisters-A. J. Merak(John Glasby), Witch-Water-Max Chartair(John Glasby), The Midnight Walkers-Michael Hamilton(John Glasby), Mr Pilkington's Ghost-J. J. Hansby(John Glasby), The Cloak of Darkness-H. K. Lennard(John Glasby)

Supernatural/Out of this World Series

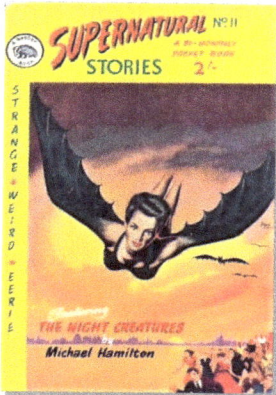

Series No/ Title Supernatural Series #011

Date 1957 **Imprint** Badger **Collected**

Artist Henry Fox

Notes September.

Content The Night Creatures-Michael Hamilton(John Glasby), The Haunter-A. J. Merak(John Glasby), Lord of the Necromancers-Max Chartair(John Glasby), It Came by Appointment-Randall Conway(John Glasby), The Lonely Things-Peter Laynham(John Glasby)

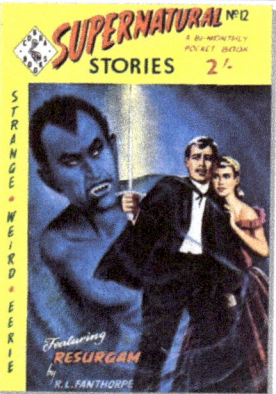

Series No/ Title Supernatural Series #012

Date 1957 **Imprint** Cobra **Collected**

Artist Henry Fox

Notes October. ed. John S. Manning (Assael)

Content Resurgam-(R. L. Fanthorpe), I've Been Here Before-Leo Brett(R. L. Fanthorpe), The Uncanny Affair at Greycove-Lionel Roberts(R. L. Fanthorpe), The Sorcerer's Cave-Trebor Thorpe(R. L. Fanthorpe), Fang-Pel Torro(R. L. Fanthorpe)

Series No/ Title Supernatural Series #013

Date 1957 **Imprint** Cobra **Collected**

Artist Ray Theobald

Notes December. ed. John S. Manning (Assael)

Content Secret of the Snows-(R. L. Fanthorpe), Sky Herd-Bron Fane(R. L. Fanthorpe), The Spectre of the Tower-Lionel Roberts(R. L. Fanthorpe), Ghost Ship-Trebor Thorpe(R. L. Fanthorpe), The Black Hound-Pel Torro(R. L. Fanthorpe)

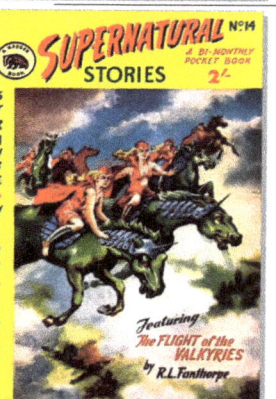

Series No/ Title Supernatural Series #014

Date 1958 **Imprint** Badger **Collected**

Artist Ray Theobald

Notes January. ed. John S. Manning (Assael)

Content The Flight of The Valkyries-(R. L. Fanthorpe), The Séance-Bron Fane(R. L. Fanthorpe), The Old House-Lionel Roberts(R. L. Fanthorpe), Song of the Banshee-Trebor Thorpe(R. L. Fanthorpe), The Creature-Pel Torro(R. L. Fanthorpe)

Supernatural/Out of this World Series

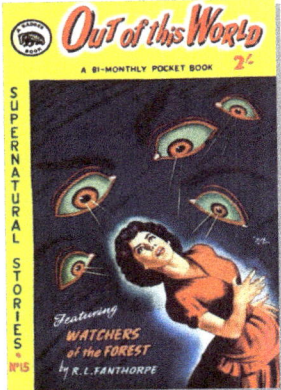

Series No/ Title Supernatural Series #015

Date	1958	Imprint	Badger	Collected

Artist Henry Fox

Notes April. ed. John S. Manning (Assael)

Content Watchers of the Forest-(R. L. Fanthorpe), Out of the Vault-Lionel Roberts(R. L. Fanthorpe), The Earthen Vessel-Trebor Thorpe(R. L. Fanthorpe), Black River Mill-Pel Torro(R. L. Fanthorpe), Voodoo Vengeance-Bron Fane(R. L. Fanthorpe)

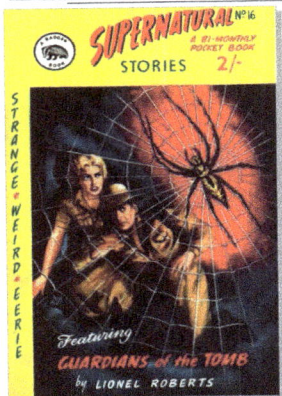

Series No/ Title Supernatural Series #016

Date	1958	Imprint	Badger	Collected

Artist Henry Fox

Notes June. ed. John S. Manning (Assael)

Content Guardians of the Tomb-Lionel Roberts(R. L. Fanthorpe), The Effigy-Leo Brett(R. L. Fanthorpe), The Creatures from Below-(R. L. Fanthorpe), The Iron Oven-Trebor Thorpe(R. L. Fanthorpe), Last Bus to Llangery-Pel Torro(R. L. Fanthorpe)

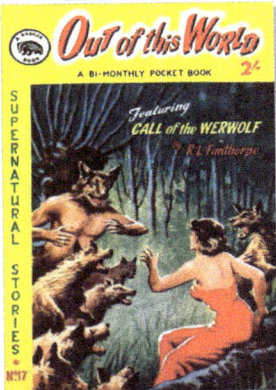

Series No/ Title Supernatural Series #017

Date	1958	Imprint	Badger	Collected

Artist Ray Theobald

Notes August. ed. John S. Manning (Assael)

Content Call of the Werewolf-(R. L. Fanthorpe), The Secret Room-Bron Fane(R. L. Fanthorpe), The Dancing Wraiths-Lionel Roberts(R. L. Fanthorpe), The Phantom Hand-Trebor Thorpe(R. L. Fanthorpe), The Screaming Skull-Pel Torro(R. L. Fanthorpe)

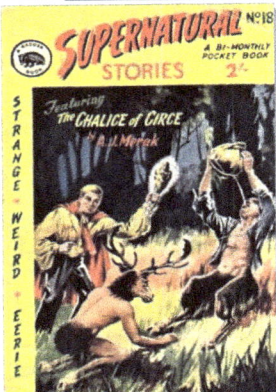

Series No/ Title Supernatural Series #018

Date	1958	Imprint	Badger	Collected

Artist Ray Theobald

Notes October. ed. John S. Manning (Assael)

Content The Chalice of Circe-A. J. Merak(John Glasby), Something About Gargoyles-Randall Conway(John Glasby), The Hungry Ones-Michael Hamilton(John Glasby), The Tunnel of Fear-J. J. Hansby(John Glasby), Dark Kith and Kin-Peter Laynham(John Glasby)

Supernatural/Out of this World Series

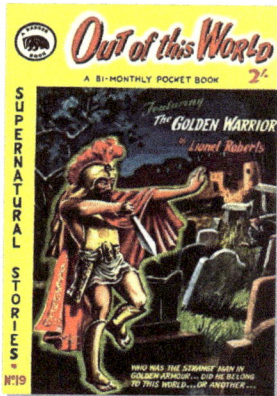

Series No/ Title	Supernatural Series #019
Date	1958 Imprint **Badger** Collected
Artist	Ray Theobald
Notes	November. ed. John S. Manning (Assael)
Content	The Golden Warrior-Lionel Roberts(R. L. Fanthorpe), The Kraken-Leo Brett(R. L. Fanthorpe), Invisible Witness-(R. L. Fanthorpe), Night of the Ghoul-Bron Fane(R. L. Fanthorpe), The Phantom of the Goodwins-Trebor Thorpe(R. L. Fanthorpe)

Series No/ Title	Supernatural Series #020
Date	1958 Imprint **Badger** Collected
Artist	Ray Theobald
Notes	December. ed. John S. Manning (Assael)
Content	The Death Note-(R. L. Fanthorpe), The Spawn of Satan-Leo Brett(R. L. Fanthorpe), The Valley of the Vampire-Bron Fane(R. L. Fanthorpe), Sinister Stranger-Lionel Roberts(R. L. Fanthorpe), The Other Driver-Pel Torro(R. L. Fanthorpe)

Series No/ Title	Supernatural Series #021
Date	1959 Imprint **Badger** Collected
Artist	Ray Theobald
Notes	January. ed. John S. Manning (Assael)
Content	The Haunted Pool-Trevor Thorpe(R. L. Fanthorpe), The Lamia-Leo Brett(R. L. Fanthorpe), The Stone Crusader-(R. L. Fanthorpe), The Silent Stranger-Bron Fane(R. L. Fanthorpe), Unknown Realm-Lionel Roberts(R. L. Fanthorpe)

Series No/ Title	Supernatural Series #022
Date	1959 Imprint **Badger** Collected
Artist	Ray Theobald
Notes	February. ed. John S. Manning (Assael)
Content	Out of The Shadows-Randall Conway(John Glasby), Take the Last Train-A. J. Merak(John Glasby), The Serpent Ring-Max Chartair(John Glasby), Hexerei-Michael Hamilton(John Glasby), Somewhere the Devil Hides-Peter Laynham(John Glasby)

Supernatural/Out of this World Series

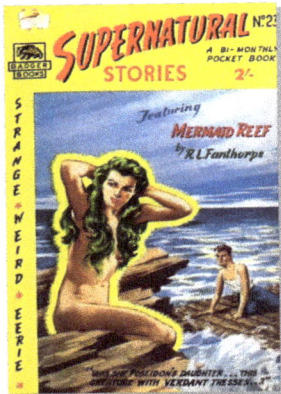

Series No/ Title   Supernatural Series #023

Date	1959	Imprint **Badger**	Collected

Artist   Ray Theobald

Notes   March. ed. John S. Manning (Assael)

Content   Mermaid Reef-(R. L. Fanthorpe), The Unrealistic Theatre-Leo Brett(R. L. Fanthorpe), The Other Line-Bron Fane(R. L. Fanthorpe), The Swan Mea-Lionel Roberts(R. L. Fanthorpe), The Clock That Struck Thirteen-Trebor Thorpe(R. L. Fanthorpe)

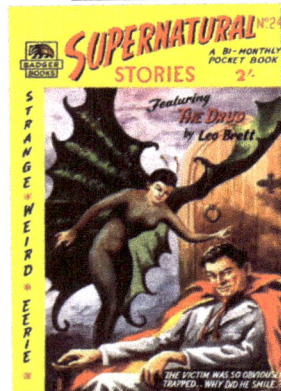

Series No/ Title   Supernatural Series #024

Date	1959	Imprint **Badger**	Collected

Artist   Ray Theobald

Notes   April. ed. John S. Manning (Assael)

Content   The Drud-Leo Brett(R. L. Fanthorpe), Quest for Atlantis-(R. L. Fanthorpe), The Green Cloud-Bron Fane(R. L. Fanthorpe), The Hypnotist-Lionel Roberts(R. L. Fanthorpe), The Poltergeist-Pel Torro(R. L. Fanthorpe)

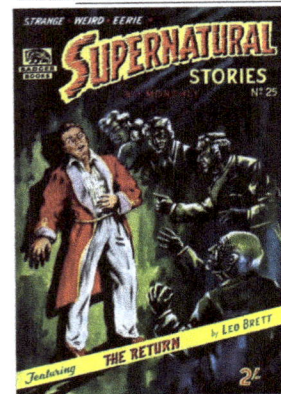

Series No/ Title   Supernatural Series #025

Date	1959	Imprint **Badger**	Collected

Artist   Ray Theobald

Notes   May. ed. John S. Manning (Assael)

Content   The Return-Leo Brett(R. L. Fanthorpe), The Guide and the God-(R. L. Fanthorpe), Pursuit-Bron Fane(R. L. Fanthorpe), The Man Within-Trebor Thorpe(R. L. Fanthorpe), Charlatan-Pel Torro(R. L. Fanthorpe)

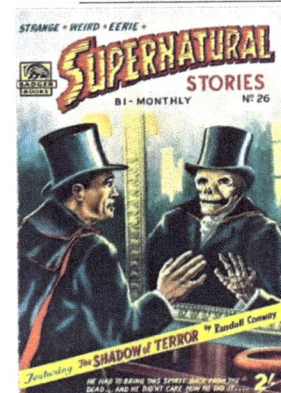

Series No/ Title   Supernatural Series #026

Date	1959	Imprint **Badger**	Collected

Artist   Ray Theobald

Notes   June. ed. John S. Manning (Assael)

Content   The Shadow of Terror-Randall Conway(John Glasby), Doorway to Darkness-A. J. Merak(John Glasby), Ebb Tide-Max Chartair(John Glasby), The Dark Possessed-Michael Hamilton(John Glasby), The Crimson Evil-J. J. Hansley(John Glasby)

Supernatural/Out of this World Series

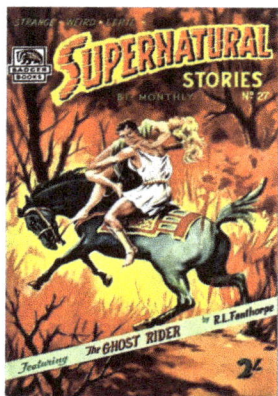

Series No/ Title	Supernatural Series #027
Date	1959
Imprint	Badger
Collected	
Artist	Ray Theobald
Notes	July. ed. John S. Manning (Assael)
Content	The Ghost Rider-(R. L. Fanthorpe), White Wolf-Leo Brett(R. L. Fanthorpe), Jungle of Death-Bron Fane(R. L. Fanthorpe), Gestalt-Lionel Roberts(R. L. Fanthorpe), The Man Who Was Nothing-Trebor Thorpe(R. L. Fanthorpe)

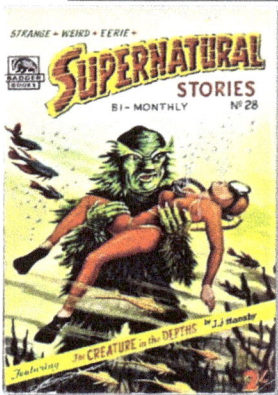

Series No/ Title	Supernatural Series #028
Date	1959
Imprint	Badger
Collected	
Artist	Ray Theobald
Notes	September. ed. John S. Manning (Assael)
Content	The Creature in the Depths-J. J. Hansby(John Glasby), A Pattern of Evil-A. J. Merak(John Glasby), The Lady Labyrinth-Max Chartair(John Glasby), Dark of the Dawn-Randall Conway(John Glasby), The Pipes of Pan-Michael Hamilton(John Glasby)

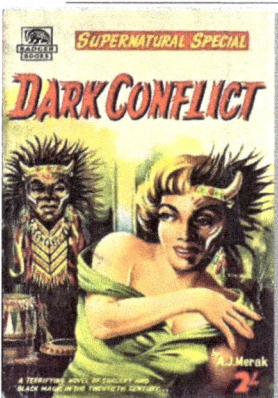

Series No/ Title	Supernatural Series #029
Date	1959
Imprint	Badger
Collected	
Artist	Ray Theobald
Notes	November.
Content	Dark Conflict-A. J. Merak(John Glasby)

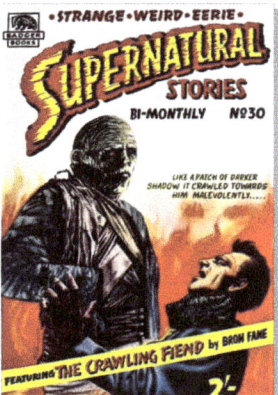

Series No/ Title	Supernatural Series #030
Date	1960
Imprint	Badger
Collected	
Artist	Eddie Jones
Notes	January. ed. John S. Manning (Assael)
Content	The Crawling Fiend-Bron Fane(R. L. Fanthorpe), Right Through My Hair-Noel Bertram(Noel Boston), Whence? Wither?-(R. L. Fanthorpe), Vault of Terror-Lionel Roberts(R. L. Fanthorpe), Excalibur-Trebor Thorpe(R. L. Fanthorpe)

Supernatural/Out of this World Series

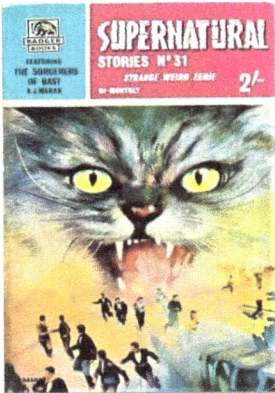

Series No/ Title	Supernatural Series #031
Date 1960	**Imprint** Badger Collected
Artist	Curt Caesar
Notes	March. ed. John S. Manning (Assael)
Content	The Sorcerers of Bast-A. J. Merak(John Glasby), The Phantom Wakes-Max Chartair(John Glasby), Strange Company-Randall Conway(John Glasby), Never Look Behind You-Michael Hamilton(John Glasby), Something Old-Peter Laynham(John Glasby)

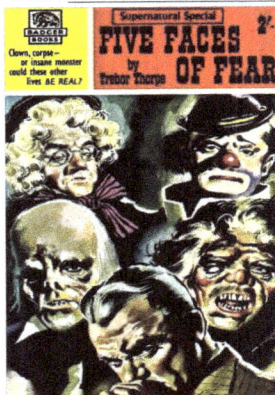

Series No/ Title	Supernatural Series #032
Date 1960	**Imprint** Badger Collected
Artist	Symeon
Notes	March. ed. John S. Manning (Assael)
Content	Five Faces of Fear-Trebor Thorpe(R. L. Fanthorpe)

Series No/ Title	Supernatural Series #033
Date 1960	**Imprint** Badger Collected
Artist	Carlo Jacono
Notes	May. Reused Cover from Urania #150.
Content	The Man Who Could not Die-(R. L. Fanthorpe), The Audit Chamber-Noel Bertram(Noel Boston), The Midnight Museum-Leo Brett(R. L. Fanthorpe), Curtain Up-Bron Fane(R. L. Fanthorpe), The Sinister Circle-Trebor Thorpe(R. L. Fanthorpe)

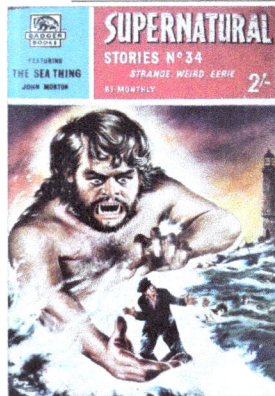

Series No/ Title	Supernatural Series #034
Date 1960	**Imprint** Badger Collected
Artist	Henry Fox
Notes	June. ed. John S. Manning (Assael)
Content	A Place of Madness-A. J. Merak(John Glasby), The Sea Thing-John Morton(John Glasby), The Nightmare Road-Ray Cosmic(John Glasby), Angel of the Bottomless Pit-Michael Hamilton(John Glasby), The Seventh Image-Randall Conway(John Glasby), The Devil at My Elbow-Max Chartair(John Glasby)

Supernatural/Out of this World Series

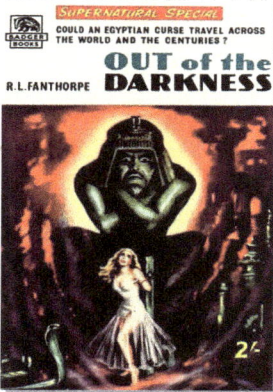

Series No/ Title	Supernatural Series #035		
Date	1960	Imprint	Badger	Collected
Artist	Henry Fox		
Notes	July. ed. John S. Manning (Assael)		
Content	Out of the Darkness-(R. L. Fanthorpe)		

Series No/ Title	Supernatural Series #036		
Date	1960	Imprint	Badger	Collected
Artist	Bernard Barton		
Notes	August. ed. John S. Manning (Assael)		
Content	Time To Die-Randall Conway(John Glasby), Face of Evil-(R. L. Fanthorpe), Coven of Thirteen-Michael Hamilton(John Glasby), A little Devil Dancing-Max Chartair(John Glasby), The Stairway-Ray Cosmic(John Glasby), The Unseen-A. J. Merak(John Glasby)		

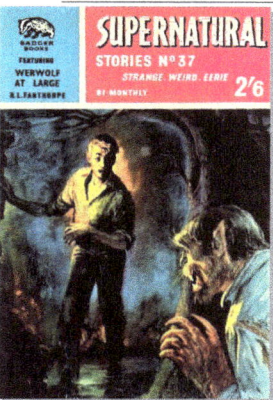

Series No/ Title	Supernatural Series #037		
Date	1960	Imprint	Badger	Collected
Artist			
Notes	November. Reused cover from Ace D-309		
Content	Werewolf at Large-(R. L. Fanthorpe), From Realms Beyond-Leo Brett(R. L. Fanthorpe), Bump in the Night-Noel Bartram(Noel Boston), The Secret of the Lake-Bron Fane(R. L. Fanthorpe), Bardell's Wild Talent-Trebor Thorpe(R. L. Fanthorpe)		

Series No/ Title	Supernatural Series #038		
Date	1961	Imprint	Badger	Collected
Artist	Henry Fox		
Notes	January. ed. John S. Manning (Assael)		
Content	Whirlwind of Death-(R. L. Fanthorpe), The Carnival Horror-Leo Brett(R. L. Fanthorpe), Black Marsh Mill-Trebor Thorpe(R. L. Fanthorpe), The Face of Stone-Pel Torro(R. L. Fanthorpe), The Loch Ness Terror-Bron Fane(R. L. Fanthorpe)		

Supernatural/Out of this World Series

Series No/ Title	Supernatural Series #039
Date	1961 Imprint **Badger** Collected
Artist	
Notes	February. Reused cover from Avon 623
Content	Voodoo Hell Drums-Trebor Thorpe(R. L. Fanthorpe), Land of the Living Dead-Leo Brett(R. L. Fanthorpe), The Magician Sleeps-(R. L. Fanthorpe), The Deathless Wings-Bron Fane(R. L. Fanthorpe), Wolf Man's Vengeance-Pel Torro(R. L. Fanthorpe)

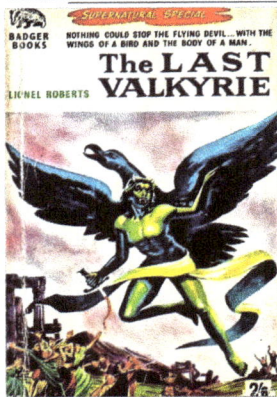

Series No/ Title	Supernatural Series #040
Date	1961 Imprint **Badger** Collected
Artist	D.Rainey
Notes	February.
Content	The Last Valkyrie-Lionel Roberts(R. L. Fanthorpe)

Series No/ Title	Supernatural Series #041
Date	1961 Imprint **Badger** Collected
Artist	Henry Fox
Notes	March.
Content	Fingers Of Darkness-(R. L. Fanthorpe), The Bellarmine Jars-Noel Bertram(Noel Boston), Before the Beginning-Leo Brett(R. L. Fanthorpe), The Green Sarcophagus-Bron Fane(R. L. Fanthorpe), Lost Land of Lemuria-Trebor Thorpe(R. L. Fanthorpe)

Series No/ Title	Supernatural Series #042
Date	1961 Imprint **Badger** Collected
Artist	Henry Fox
Notes	March.
Content	The Unpossessed-John E. Muller(John Glasby)

Supernatural/Out of this World Series

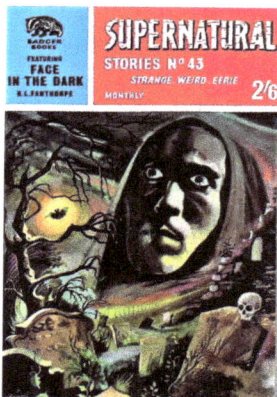

Series No/ Title	Supernatural Series #043
Date	1961 Imprint **Badger** Collected
Artist	D.Rainey
Notes	May.
Content	Face In the Dark-(R. L. Fanthorpe), The Face at the Window-Noel Bertram(Noel Boston), They Flew by Night-Leo Brett(R. L. Fanthorpe), Black Abyss-Bron Fane(R. L. Fanthorpe), Swamp Thing-Trebor Thorpe(R. L. Fanthorpe)

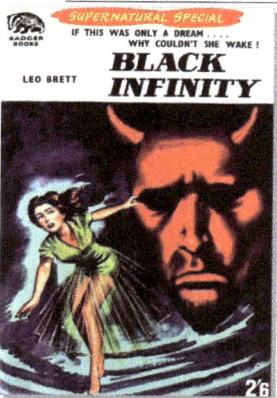

Series No/ Title	Supernatural Series #044
Date	1961 Imprint **Badger** Collected
Artist	Henry Fox
Notes	May.
Content	Black Infinity-Leo Brett(R. L. Fanthorpe)

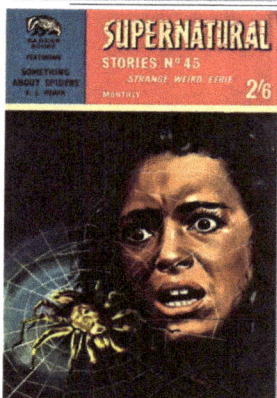

Series No/ Title	Supernatural Series #045
Date	1961 Imprint **Badger** Collected
Artist	D.Rainey
Notes	June.
Content	Something About Spiders-A. J. Merak(John Glasby), Mythos-Max Chartair(John Glasby), Not Without Sorcery-Randall Conway(John Glasby), When Darkness Falls-Michael Hamilton(John Glasby), Refugee-Peter Laynham(John Glasby)

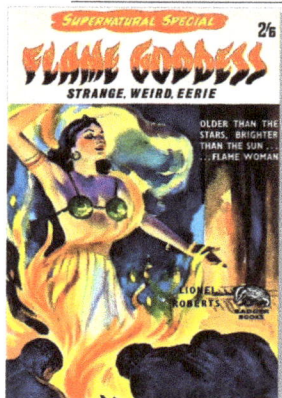

Series No/ Title	Supernatural Series #046
Date	1961 Imprint **Badger** Collected
Artist	
Notes	June.
Content	Flame Goddess-Lionel Roberts(R. L. Fanthorpe)

Supernatural/Out of this World Series

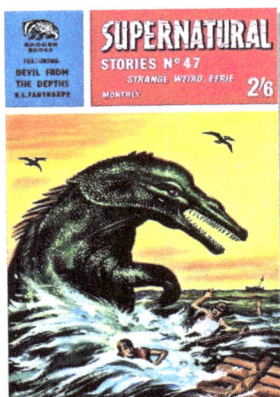

Series No/ Title	Supernatural Series #047
Date	1961
Imprint	Badger
Collected	
Artist	D.Rainey
Notes	August.
Content	Rusalka and the Vodyanol-Leo Brett(R. L. Fanthorpe), The Devil from the Depths-(R. L. Fanthorpe), Forbidden City-Bron Fane(R. L. Fanthorpe), Forest of Evil-Trebor Thorpe(R. L. Fanthorpe), Graven in the Rock-Pel Torro(R. L. Fanthorpe)

Series No/ Title	Supernatural Series #048
Date	1961
Imprint	Badger
Collected	
Artist	D.Rainey
Notes	August.
Content	The Phantom Ones-Pel Torro(R. L. Fanthorpe)

Series No/ Title	Supernatural Series #049
Date	1961
Imprint	Badger
Collected	
Artist	Henry Fox
Notes	October.
Content	The Centurion's Vengeance-(R. L. Fanthorpe), The Half Legs-Noel Bertram(Noel Boston), Contact with Satan-Leo Brett(R. L. Fanthorpe), The Secret of the Pyramid-Bron Fane(R. L. Fanthorpe), The House of Dreams-Trebor Thorpe(R. L. Fanthorpe), The Twisted Track-Pel Torro(R. L. Fanthorpe)

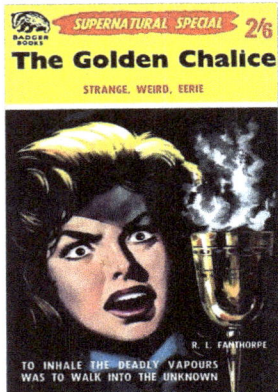

Series No/ Title	Supernatural Series #050
Date	1961
Imprint	Badger
Collected	
Artist	Henry Fox
Notes	November.
Content	The Golden Chalice-(R. L. Fanthorpe)

Supernatural/Out of this World Series

Series No/ Title	Supernatural Series #051		
Date	1961	Imprint	Badger	Collected
Artist	D.Rainey		
Notes	November.		
Content	The Grip of Fear-(R. L. Fanthorpe), The Brass Tombstone-Noel Bartram(Noel Boston), Mustapha-Leo Brett(R. L. Fanthorpe), Something at the Door-Bron Fane(R. L. Fanthorpe), The Eight Immortals-Trebor Thorpe(R. L. Fanthorpe), The Secret of Dr. Stark-Pel Torro(R. L. Fanthorpe)		

Series No/ Title	Supernatural Series #052		
Date	1962	Imprint	Badger	Collected
Artist	Henry Fox		
Notes	January.		
Content	Return of Zeus-John E. Muller(R. L. Fanthorpe)		

Series No/ Title	Supernatural Series #053		
Date	1962	Imprint	Badger	Collected
Artist	Henry Fox		
Notes	January.		
Content	Chariot of Apollo-(R. L. Fanthorpe), The North Cloister-Noel Bertram(Noel Boston), Fly, Witch, Fly-Leo Brett(R. L. Fanthorpe), Forbidden Island-Bron Fane(R. L. Fanthorpe), The Room With the Broken Floor-Pel Torro(R. L. Fanthorpe)		

Series No/ Title	Supernatural Series #054		
Date	1962	Imprint	Badger	Collected
Artist	Henry Fox		
Notes	March.		
Content	Nightmare-Leo Brett(R. L. Fanthorpe)		

Supernatural/Out of this World Series

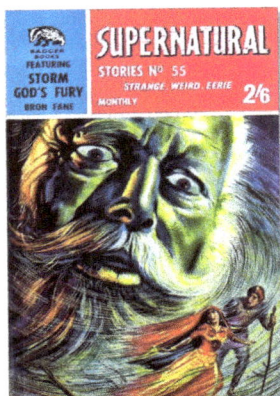

Series No/ Title Supernatural Series #055

Date 1962   Imprint Badger   Collected

Artist Henry Fox

Notes March.

Content Moonlight Island-Leo Brett(R. L. Fanthorpe), The Mountain Thing-(R. L. Fanthorpe), Storm God's Fury-Bron Fane(R. L. Fanthorpe), Return of Lilith-Trebor Thorpe(R. L. Fanthorpe), Vampire Castle-Pel Torro(R. L. Fanthorpe)

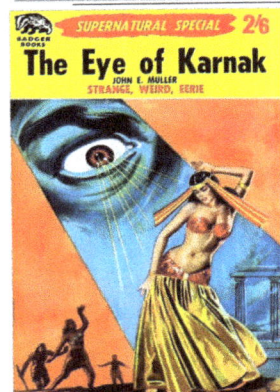

Series No/ Title Supernatural Series #056

Date 1962   Imprint Badger   Collected

Artist Henry Fox

Notes April.

Content The Eye of Karnack-John E. Muller(R. L. Fanthorpe)

Series No/ Title Supernatural Series #057

Date 1962   Imprint Badger   Collected

Artist Henry Fox

Notes April.

Content Hell Has Wings-(R. L. Fanthorpe), The Barrier-Noel Bertram(Noel Boston), The Phantom Schooner-Leo Brett(R. L. Fanthorpe), Vengeance of the Poltergeist-Bron Fane(R. L. Fanthorpe), The Eldritch Chair-Trebor Thorpe(R. L. Fanthorpe), The Frozen Claw-Pel Torro(R. L. Fanthorpe)

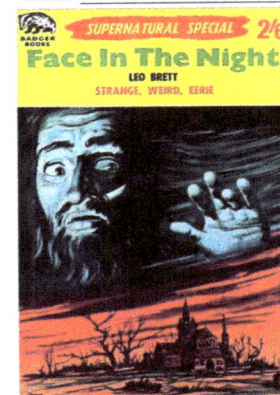

Series No/ Title Supernatural Series #058

Date 1962   Imprint Badger   Collected

Artist Henry Fox

Notes June.

Content Face In the Night-Leo Brett(R. L. Fanthorpe)

Supernatural/Out of this World Series

Series No/ Title Supernatural Series #059

Date 1962   **Imprint** Badger   Collected

Artist Henry Fox

Notes June.

Content Graveyard of the Damned-(R. L. Fanthorpe), Temple of Quetzalcoatl-Leo Brett(R. L. Fanthorpe), The Persian Cavern-Bron Fane(R. L. Fanthorpe), The Whisperer-Deutero Spartacus(R. L. Fanthorpe), The Dream of Camelot-Trebor Thorpe(R. L. Fanthorpe), The Voice-Pel Torro(R. L. Fanthorpe)

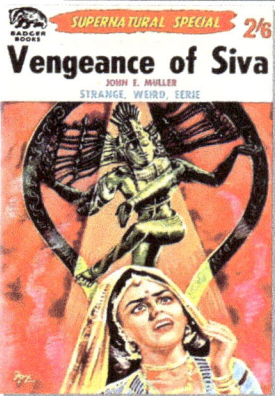

Series No/ Title Supernatural Series #060

Date 1962   **Imprint** Badger   Collected

Artist Henry Fox

Notes July.

Content Vengeance of Siva-John E. Muller(R. L. Fanthorpe)

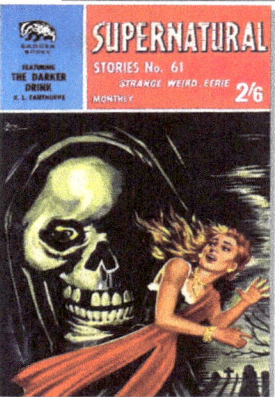

Series No/ Title Supernatural Series #061

Date 1962   **Imprint** Badger   Collected

Artist Henry Fox

Notes July. 'Chasm of Time' is listed as 'Charm of Time' in the TOC.

Content The Darker Drink-(R. L. Fanthorpe), Scraping the Barrel-Noel Bertram(Noel Boston), The Bevelled Casket-Leo Brett(R. L. Fanthorpe), Chasm of Time-Bron Fane(R. L. Fanthorpe), The Snarling Shadow-Trebor Thorpe(R. L. Fanthorpe), The Unfinished Chapter-Pel Torro(R. L. Fanthorpe)

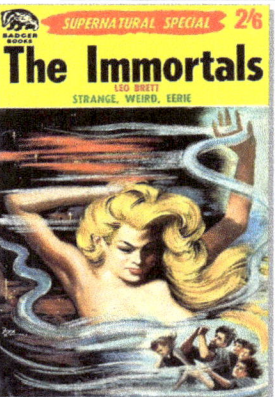

Series No/ Title Supernatural Series #062

Date 1962   **Imprint** Badger   Collected

Artist Henry Fox

Notes September.

Content The Immortals-Leo Brett(R. L. Fanthorpe)

Supernatural/Out of this World Series

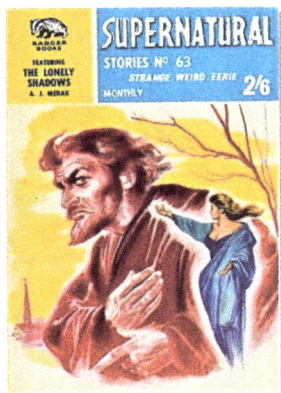

Series No/ Title	Supernatural Series #063
Date	1962
Imprint	Badger
Collected	
Artist	Henry Fox
Notes	September.
Content	The Lonely Shadows-A. J. Merak(John Glasby), The Beckoning Shade-Max Chartair(John Glasby), Dark Conquest-Randall Conway(John Glasby), And Midnight Falls-Michael Hamilton(John Glasby), To Suffer a Witch-Peter Laynham(John Glasby)

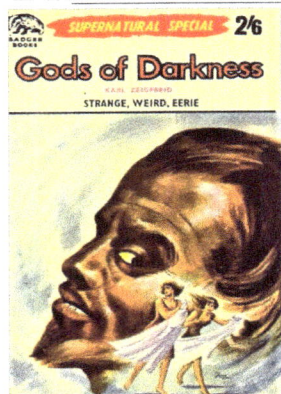

Series No/ Title	Supernatural Series #064
Date	1962
Imprint	Badger
Collected	
Artist	Henry Fox
Notes	October.
Content	Gods of Darkness-Karl Ziegfried(R. L. Fanthorpe)

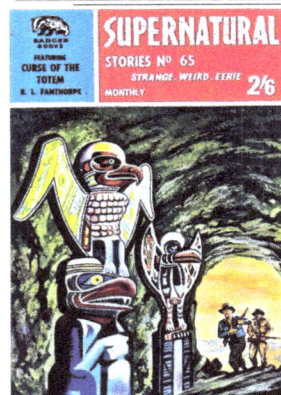

Series No/ Title	Supernatural Series #065
Date	1962
Imprint	Badger
Collected	
Artist	D.Rainey
Notes	October.
Content	Curse of the Totem-(R. L. Fanthorpe), Vengeance of Thor-Leo Brett(R. L. Fanthorpe), The Voice in the Wall-Bron Fane(R. L. Fanthorpe), Secret of the Shamen-Trebor Thorpe(R. L. Fanthorpe), Wokolo-Pel Torro(R. L. Fanthorpe)

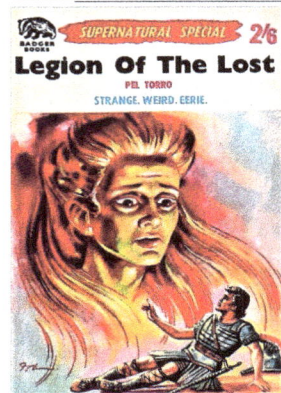

Series No/ Title	Supernatural Series #066
Date	1962
Imprint	Badger
Collected	
Artist	Henry Fox
Notes	November.
Content	Legion of the Lost-Pel Torro(R. L. Fanthorpe)

Supernatural/Out of this World Series

Series No/ Title	Supernatural Series #067
Date	1962
Imprint	Badger
Collected	
Artist	D.Rainey
Notes	November.
Content	The Frozen Tomb-Leo Brett(R. L. Fanthorpe), Sleeping Place-(R. L. Fanthorpe), Cry in the Night-Bron Fane(R. L. Fanthorpe), The Coveters-Deutero Spartacus(R. L. Fanthorpe), Strange Country-Trebor Thorpe(R. L. Fanthorpe), The Thing from Boulter's Cavern-Pel Torro(R. L. Fanthorpe)

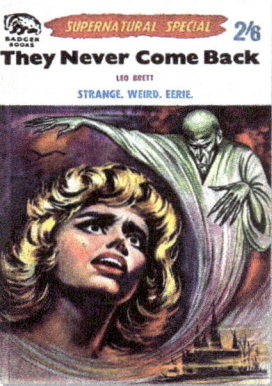

Series No/ Title	Supernatural Series #068
Date	1963
Imprint	Badger
Collected	
Artist	Henry Fox
Notes	January.
Content	They Never Came Back-Leo Brett(R. L. Fanthorpe)

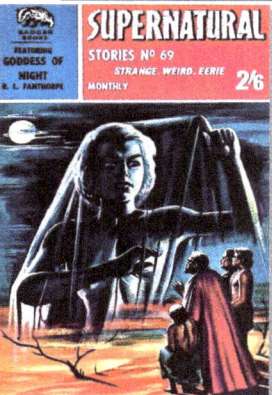

Series No/ Title	Supernatural Series #069
Date	1963
Imprint	Badger
Collected	
Artist	Henry Fox
Notes	January.
Content	The Silent Fleet-Leo Brett(R. L. Fanthorpe), Lilith - Goddess of Night-(R. L. Fanthorpe), The Nine Green Men-Bron Fane(R. L. Fanthorpe), The Swing of the Pendulum-Trebor Thorpe(R. L. Fanthorpe), Ventriloquist-Pel Torro(R. L. Fanthorpe)

Series No/ Title	Supernatural Series #070
Date	1963
Imprint	Badger
Collected	
Artist	Henry Fox
Notes	February.
Content	The Strange Ones-Pel Torro(R. L. Fanthorpe)

Supernatural/Out of this World Series

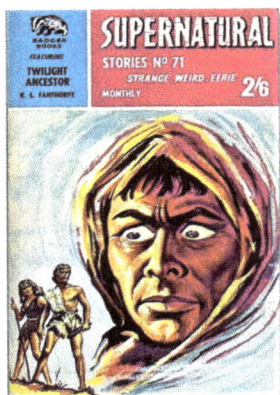

Series No/ Title	Supernatural Series #071		
Date	1963	Imprint	Badger	Collected
Artist	Henry Fox		
Notes	February.		
Content	Twilight Ancestor-(R. L. Fanthorpe), The Gliding Wraith-Leo Brett(R. L. Fanthorpe), The Man Who Never Smiled-Bron Fane(R. L. Fanthorpe), An Eye for an Eye-Trebor Thorpe(R. L. Fanthorpe), Fangs in the Night-Pel Torro(R. L. Fanthorpe)		

Series No/ Title	Supernatural Series #072		
Date	1963	Imprint	Badger	Collected
Artist	Henry Fox		
Notes	April.		
Content	The Forbidden-Leo Brett(R. L. Fanthorpe)		

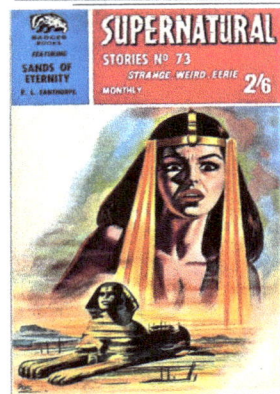

Series No/ Title	Supernatural Series #073		
Date	1963	Imprint	Badger	Collected
Artist	Henry Fox		
Notes	April.		
Content	Sands of Eternity-(R. L. Fanthorpe), House of Despair-Leo Brett(R. L. Fanthorpe), Return Ticket-Bron Fane(R. L. Fanthorpe), The Comedians-Deutero Spartacus(R. L. Fanthorpe), Spirit of Darkness-Trebor Thorpe(R. L. Fanthorpe), The Friendly Stranger-Pel Torro(R. L. Fanthorpe)		

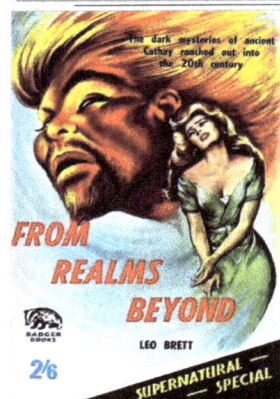

Series No/ Title	Supernatural Series #074		
Date	1963	Imprint	Badger	Collected
Artist	Henry Fox		
Notes	May.		
Content	From Realms Beyond-Leo Brett(R. L. Fanthorpe)		

Supernatural/Out of this World Series

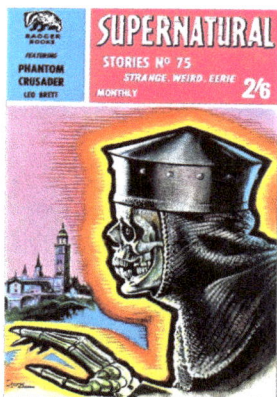

Series No/ Title   **Supernatural Series #075**

Date **1963**   Imprint **Badger**   Collected

Artist   **Henry Fox**

Notes   **May.**

Content   **The Phantom Crusader-Leo Brett(R. L. Fanthorpe), The Room That Never Was-Bron Fane(R. L. Fanthorpe), The Stockman-Deutero Spartacus(R. L. Fanthorpe), The Stone Tablet-Neil Thanet(R. L. Fanthorpe), Stranger in the Skull-Trebor Thorpe(R. L. Fanthorpe), Footprints in the Sand-Pel Torro(R. L. Fanthorpe), The Tunnel-Olaf Trent(R. L. Fanthorpe)**

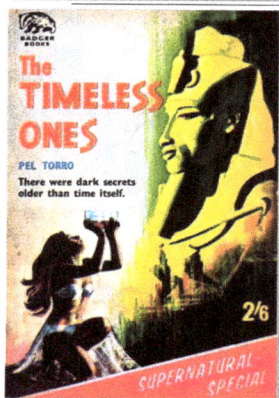

Series No/ Title   **Supernatural Series #076**

Date **1963**   Imprint **Badger**   Collected

Artist   **Henry Fox**

Notes   **June.**

Content   **The Timeless Ones-Pel Torro(R. L. Fanthorpe)**

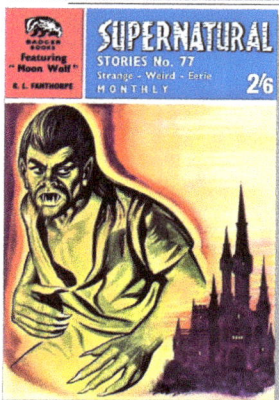

Series No/ Title   **Supernatural Series #077**

Date **1963**   Imprint **Badger**   Collected

Artist   **Henry Fox**

Notes   **June.**

Content   **Moon Wolf-(R. L. Fanthorpe), The Zombie-Erle Barton(R. L. Fanthorpe), The Grip of Time Unending-Leo Brett(Harry Mansfield), Blurred Horizon-Phil Noble(R. L. Fanthorpe), The Walker-Bron Fane(R. L. Fanthorpe), The Tragedians-Deutero Spartacus(R. L. Fanthorpe), Old Man of the Snow-Neil Thanet(R. L. Fanthorpe)**

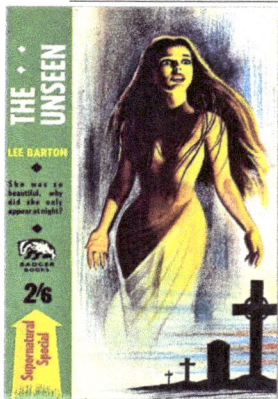

Series No/ Title   **Supernatural Series #078**

Date **1963**   Imprint **Badger**   Collected

Artist   **Henry Fox**

Notes   **July.**

Content   **The Unseen-Lee Barton(R. L. Fanthorpe)**

Supernatural/Out of this World Series

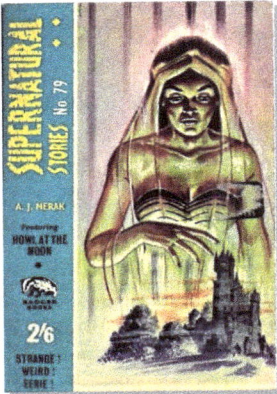

Series No/ Title	Supernatural Series #079		
Date	1963	Imprint **Badger**	Collected
Artist	Henry Fox		
Notes	July.		
Content	Howl at the Moon-A. J. Merak(John Glasby), Nightmare on Ice-Max Chartair(John Glasby), A Place of Shadows-Randall Conway(John Glasby), Solitude-Michael Hamilton(John Glasby), In the Midst of Night-Peter Laynham(John Glasby)		

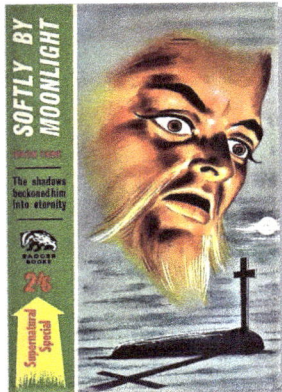

Series No/ Title	Supernatural Series #080		
Date	1963	Imprint **Badger**	Collected
Artist	Henry Fox		
Notes	September.		
Content	Softly By Moonlight-Bron Fane(R. L. Fanthorpe)		

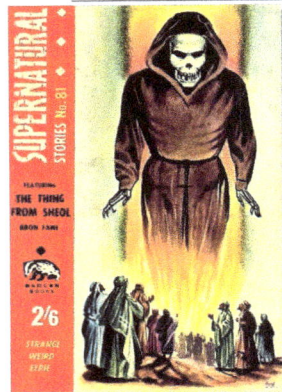

Series No/ Title	Supernatural Series #081		
Date	1963	Imprint **Badger**	Collected
Artist	Henry Fox		
Notes	September.		
Content	The Thing from Sheol-Bron Fane(R. L. Fanthorpe), Invisible Presence-(R. L. Fanthorpe), Forgotten Country-Peter O'Flinn(R. L. Fanthorpe), Midnight Ghoul-Robin Tate(R. L. Fanthorpe), Return of the Hag-Neil Thanet(R. L. Fanthorpe)		

Series No/ Title	Supernatural Series #082		
Date	1963	Imprint **Badger**	Collected
Artist	Henry Fox		
Notes	November.		
Content	The Face of Fear-Pel Torro(R. L. Fanthorpe)		

Supernatural/Out of this World Series

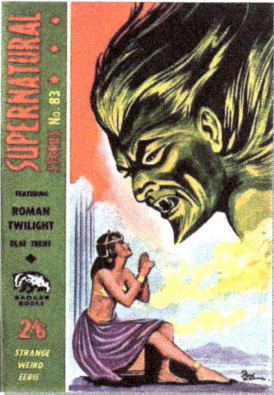

Series No/ Title Supernatural Series #083

Date	1963	Imprint	Badger	Collected	

Artist Henry Fox

Notes November.

Content Roman Twilight-Olaf Trent(R. L. Fanthorpe), The Clubmen-Leo Brett(Harry Mansfield), Psychic Circle-(R. L. Fanthorpe), The Reluctant Corpse-Rene Rolant(R. L. Fanthorpe), The Man Who Knew-Bron Fane(R. L. Fanthorpe), Land of the Green Shadows-Peter O'Flinn(R. L. Fanthorpe), Traveller's Rest-Trebor Thorpe(Ernest Kemp)

Series No/ Title Supernatural Series #084

Date	1964	Imprint	Badger	Collected	

Artist Henry Fox

Notes January.

Content Unknown Destiny-Bron Fane(R. L. Fanthorpe)

Series No/ Title Supernatural Series #085

Date	1964	Imprint	Badger	Collected	

Artist Henry Fox

Notes January.

Content Avenging Goddess-(R. L. Fanthorpe), Dark Staircase-Lee Barton(R. L. Fanthorpe), Endor's Daughter-Thornton Bell(R. L. Fanthorpe), The Abbot's Ring-Robin Tate(Harry Mansfield), The Sword and the Statue-Trebor Thorpe(R. L. Fanthorpe), Valley of the Kings-Olaf Trent(R. L. Fanthorpe)

Series No/ Title Supernatural Series #086

Date	1964	Imprint	Badger	Collected	

Artist Henry Fox

Notes March.

Content Beyond the Veil-Neil Thanet(R. L. Fanthorpe)

Supernatural/Out of this World Series

Series No/ Title	Supernatural Series #087
Date	1964	Imprint	Badger	Collected
Artist	Henry Fox
Notes	March.
Content	Death Has Two Faces-(R. L. Fanthorpe), Vengeance From the Past-Lee Barton(R. L. Fanthorpe), Bell Book and Candle-Thornton Bell(R. L. Fanthorpe), The Chinese Lustre Vase-Phil Noble(Harry Mansfield), The Warlock-Bron Fane(R. L. Fanthorpe), Lord of the Black Valley-Oben Lerteth(R. L. Fanthorpe), The Eldritch Guide-Robin Tate(R. L. Fanthorpe)

Series No/ Title	Supernatural Series #088
Date	1964	Imprint	Badger	Collected
Artist	Henry Fox
Notes	May.
Content	The Man Who Came Back-Neil Thanet(R. L. Fanthorpe)

Series No/ Title	Supernatural Series #089
Date	1964	Imprint	Badger	Collected
Artist	Henry Fox
Notes	May.
Content	The Shrouded Abbot-(R. L. Fanthorpe), The Phantom Galleon-Lee Barton(R. L. Fanthorpe), I'll Never Leave You-Phil Noble(Harry Mansfield), Return of the Banshee-Peter O'Flinn(R. L. Fanthorpe), Vampire's Moon-Rene Rolant(R. L. Fanthorpe), Curse of the Incas-Robin Tate(R. L. Fanthorpe)

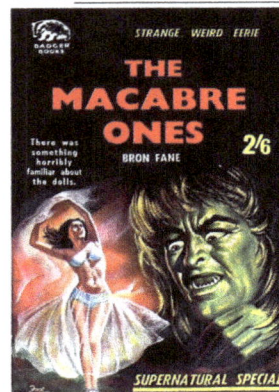

Series No/ Title	Supernatural Series #090
Date	1964	Imprint	Badger	Collected
Artist	Henry Fox
Notes	July.
Content	The Macabre Ones-Bron Fane(R. L. Fanthorpe)

Supernatural/Out of this World Series

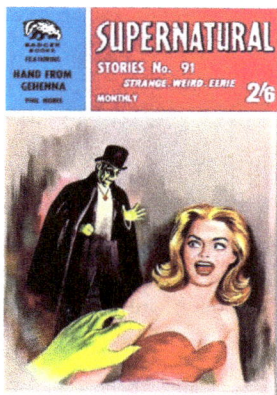

Series No/ Title	Supernatural Series #091
Date	1964 — Imprint Badger — Collected
Artist	Henry Fox
Notes	July.
Content	Hand From Gehanna-Phil Nobel(R. L. Fanthorpe), The Bow and the Bugle-Othello Baron(R. L. Fanthorpe), The Lady Loves Cats-Thornton Bell(Harry Mansfield), The Manhattan Warlock-Elton T. Neef(R. L. Fanthorpe), Suddenly...at Twilight-(R. L. Fanthorpe), The Troll-Bron Fane(R. L. Fanthorpe), The Devil's Brood-Robin Tate(R. L. Fanthorpe)

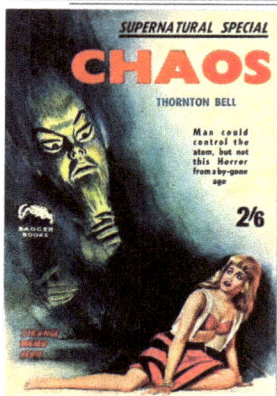

Series No/ Title	Supernatural Series #092
Date	1964 — Imprint Badger — Collected
Artist	Henry Fox
Notes	September. Given he seemed to be the only artist working on this series at the time, it is highly likely to have been Henry Fox.
Content	Chaos-Thornton Bell(R. L. Fanthorpe)

Series No/ Title	Supernatural Series #093
Date	1964 — Imprint Badger — Collected
Artist	Henry Fox
Notes	September.
Content	The Walking Shadow-Bron Fane(R. L. Fanthorpe), The Laird-Neil Balfort(R. L. Fanthorpe), Time Out of Mind-Lee Barton(R. L. Fanthorpe), The Ghoul and the Goddess-(R. L. Fanthorpe), In a Glass Darkly-Robin Tate(Harry Mansfield), Dungeon Castle-Trebor Thorpe(R. L. Fanthorpe), The Lake Thing-Pel Torro(R. L. Fanthorpe)

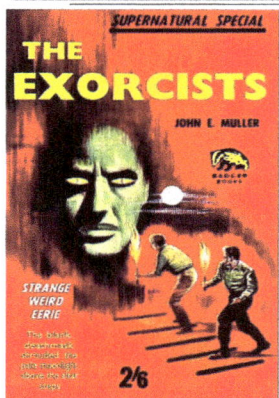

Series No/ Title	Supernatural Series #094
Date	1965 — Imprint Badger — Collected
Artist	Henry Fox
Notes	February.
Content	The Exorcists-John E. Muller(R. L. Fanthorpe)

Supernatural/Out of this World Series

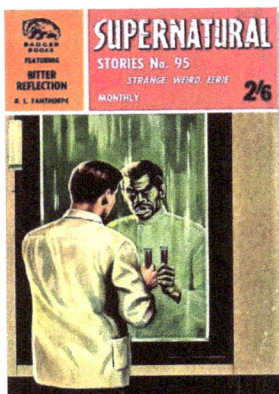

Series No/ Title	Supernatural Series #095		
Date	1965	Imprint	Badger
Artist	Henry Fox		Collected
Notes	February.		
Content	Bitter Reflection-(R. L. Fanthorpe), The Return of Albertus-Lee Barton(R. L. Fanthorpe), Grimoir-Thornton Bell(R. L. Fanthorpe), The Golem-Leo Brett(Harry Mansfield), Spring Fever-Robin Tate(Harry Mansfield), Dragon's Blood Mountain-Trebor Thorpe(R. L. Fanthorpe)		

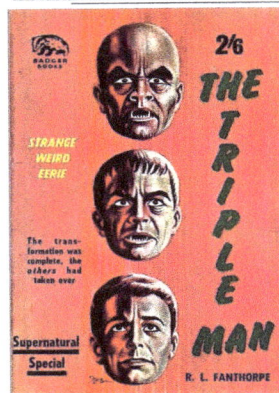

Series No/ Title	Supernatural Series #096		
Date	1965	Imprint	Badger
Artist	Henry Fox		Collected
Notes	April.		
Content	The Triple Man-(R. L. Fanthorpe)		

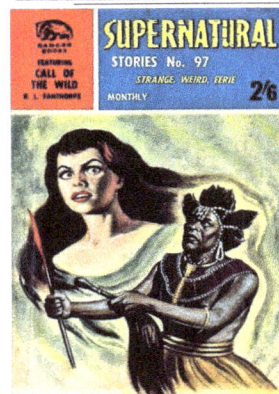

Series No/ Title	Supernatural Series #097		
Date	1965	Imprint	Badger
Artist	Henry Fox		Collected
Notes	June.		
Content	Call of the Wild-(R. L. Fanthorpe), The Accursed-Bron Fane(R. L. Fanthorpe), The Border Raider-Oben Lerteth(R. L. Fanthorpe), Isles of the Blessed-Peter O'Flynn(R. L. Fanthorpe), The Zoologist-Pel Torro(Harry Mansfield)		

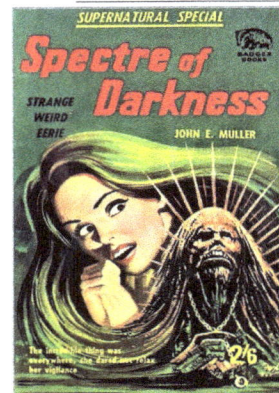

Series No/ Title	Supernatural Series #098		
Date	1965	Imprint	Badger
Artist	Henry Fox		Collected
Notes	August.		
Content	Spectre of the Darkness-John E. Muller(R. L. Fanthorpe)		

Supernatural/Out of this World Series

Series No/ Title	Supernatural Series #099
Date	1965	Imprint	Badger	Collected
Artist	Henry Fox
Notes	October.
Content	Vision of the Damned-(R. L. Fanthorpe), The Paint Box-Elton T. Neef(R. L. Fanthorpe), The Prodigy-Bron Fane(R. L. Fanthorpe), Reading Room-Oben Lerteth(R. L. Fanthorpe), Shadow of Fear-Rene Rolant(Harry Mansfield), The Attic-Deutero Spartacus(R. L. Fanthorpe)

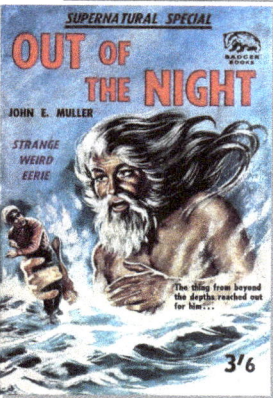

Series No/ Title	Supernatural Series #100
Date	1965	Imprint	Badger	Collected
Artist	Henry Fox
Notes	December.
Content	Out of the Night-John E. Muller(R. L. Fanthorpe)

Series No/ Title	Supernatural Series #101
Date	1965	Imprint	Badger	Collected
Artist	Henry Fox
Notes	December.
Content	The Sealed Sarcophagus-(R. L. Fanthorpe), The Unconfined-Othello Baron(R. L. Fanthorpe), Trouble in Mind-Neil Balfort(R. L. Fanthorpe), Girdle of Fear-Bron Fane(R. L. Fanthorpe), The Wanderer-Peter O'Flynn(R. L. Fanthorpe), God's Sin Eater-Robin Tate(Harry Mansfield)

Series No/ Title	Supernatural Series #102
Date	1966	Imprint	Badger	Collected
Artist	Henry Fox
Notes	April.
Content	The Unconfined-(R. L. Fanthorpe)

Supernatural/Out of this World Series

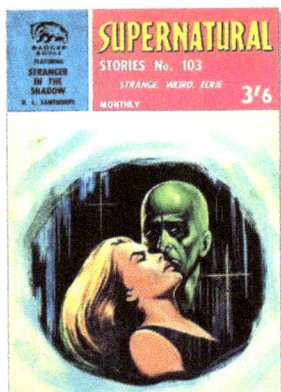

Series No/ Title	Supernatural Series #103		
Date	1966	Imprint **Badger**	Collected
Artist	Henry Fox		
Notes	April.		
Content	Stranger In the Shadow-Elton T. Neef(R. L. Fanthorpe), Corporal Death-Lee Barton(R. L. Fanthorpe), Repeat Programme-Bron Fane(R. L. Fanthorpe), Au Pair-Rene Rolant(R. L. Fanthorpe), The House That Wouldn't Die-Robin Tate(R. L. Fanthorpe), The Reluctant Corpse-(R. L. Fanthorpe)		

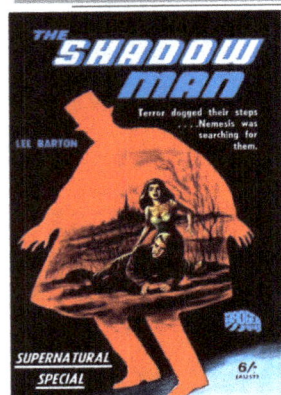

Series No/ Title	Supernatural Series #104		
Date	1966	Imprint **Badger**	Collected
Artist	Henry Fox		
Notes	July.		
Content	The Shadow Man-Lee Barton(R. L. Fanthorpe)		

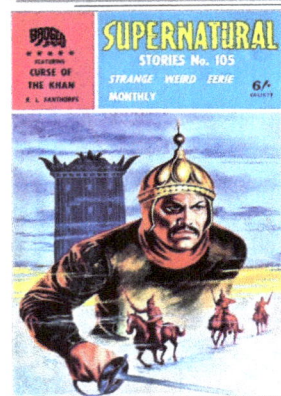

Series No/ Title	Supernatural Series #105		
Date	1966	Imprint **Badger**	Collected
Artist	Henry Fox		
Notes	October.		
Content	Curse of the Khan-(R. L. Fanthorpe), Uncle Julian's Typewriter-Elton T. Neefe(R. L. Fanthorpe), The Resurrected Enemy-Bron Fane(R. L. Fanthorpe), Lord of the Crags-Oben Lerteth(R. L. Fanthorpe), Chimney Piece-Peter O'Flinn(R. L. Fanthorpe)		

Series No/ Title	Supernatural Series #106		
Date	1967	Imprint **Badger**	Collected
Artist	Henry Fox		
Notes	May.		
Content	Dark Legion-John Crawford(John Glasby)		

Supernatural/Out of this World Series

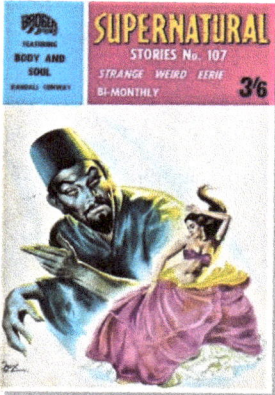

Series No/ Title   Supernatural Series #107

Date   1967   **Imprint**   Badger   **Collected**

Artist   Henry Fox

Notes   May.

Content   Body And Soul-Randall Conway(John Glasby), That Deep Black Yonder-A. J. Merak(John Glasby), Dust-Max Chartair(John Glasby), The Keeper of Dark Point-Michael Hamilton(John Glasby), The Visitors-J. J. Hansby(John Glasby), Where Dead Men Dream-Peter Laynham(John Glasby)

Not Issued

Series No/ Title   Supernatural Series #108

Date   1967   **Imprint**   **Collected**

Artist

Notes   It appears this number was not used/produced.

Content   Not Produced-()

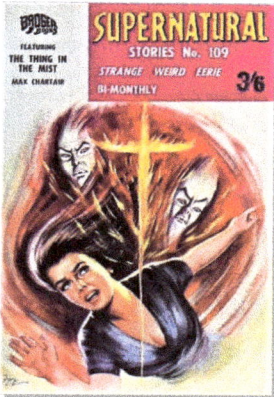

Series No/ Title   Supernatural Series #109

Date   1967   **Imprint**   Badger   **Collected**

Artist   Henry Fox

Notes   July.

Content   The Thing In the Mist-Max Chartair(John Glasby), Older Than Death-A. J. Merak(John Glasby), The Black Mirror-Randall Conway(John Glasby), The Haunting of Charles Quintain-Michael Hamilton(John Glasby), The Night-Comer-J. J. Hansby(John Glasby), The Dark Time-Peter Laynham(John Glasby)

Miscellaneous Series

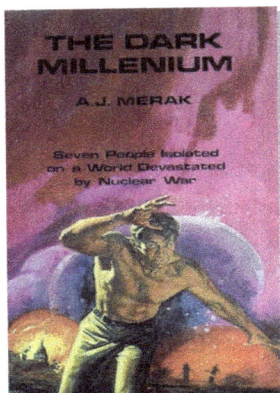

Series No/ Title Science Fiction #102

Date 1978 **Imprint** John Spencer **Collected**

Artist

Notes ISBN 854360212 . Reprint. Possibly the start of a new Science Fiction Series.

Content The Dark Millenium-A. J. Merak(John Glasby)

Series No/ Title The Macabre Ones

Date 1973 **Imprint** John Spencer **Collected**

Artist Henry Fox

Notes ISBN 0854360182 . Hardback. Seems to have been intended as a new Weird Fantasy Series. It mentions other titles in preparation but likely to have been the only one produced.

Content The Macabre Ones-Bron Fane(R. L. Fanthorpe)

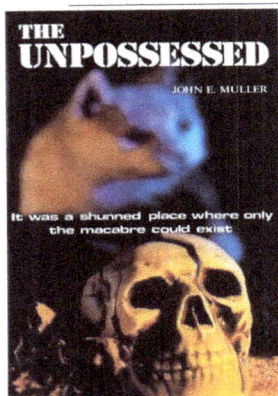

Series No/ Title Weird Fantasy #101

Date 1978 **Imprint** John Spencer **Collected**

Artist Photograph

Notes ISBN 854360204 . Reprint of SN42. Possibly the start of a new Weird Fantasy Series.

Content The Unpossessed-John E. Muller(John Glasby)

Unverified

no image available

Series No/ Title Spectre Stories #6

Date 1966   **Imprint** [   ]   **Collected** [   ]

Artist [   ]

Notes Although this is listed in various places I am not convinced it was ever released due to Spencer's comic run coming to an end around this time.

Content

---

no image available

Series No/ Title Strange Stories #6

Date 1966   **Imprint** [   ]   **Collected** [   ]

Artist [   ]

Notes Although this is listed in various places I am not convinced it was ever released due to Spencer's comic run coming to an end around this time.

Content

---

no image available

Series No/ Title The Man Who Came Back

Date 1974   **Imprint** John Spencer   **Collected** [   ]

Artist [   ]

Notes Reprint, along with Beyond the Veil, mentioned in the Hardback version of "The Macabre Ones" but likely never produced.

Content The Man Who Came Back-Neil Thanet(R. L. Fanthorpe)

John Spencer and Co. Illustrated Bibliography Vol. 1

Non-Fiction

Science Series

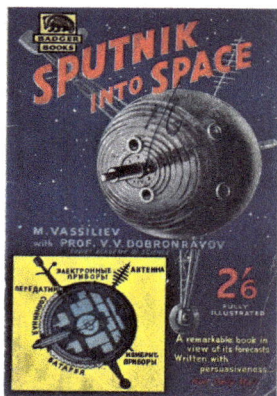

Series No/ Title Science Series #1

Date 1959 **Imprint** Badger **Collected**

Artist

Notes Reprint of a 1958 Russian book. Translated in Sovereign Press edition 1958

Content Sputnik Into Space-(M. Vassiliev/ V. V. Dobronravov)

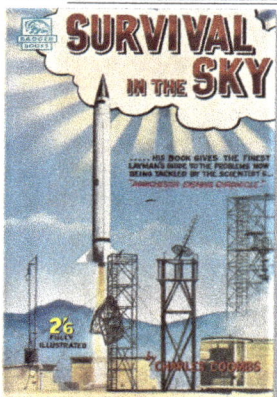

Series No/ Title Science Series #2

Date 1959 **Imprint** Badger **Collected**

Artist

Notes Reprint of a 1957 Robert Hale HB book.

Content Survival in the Sky-(Charlie Coombs)

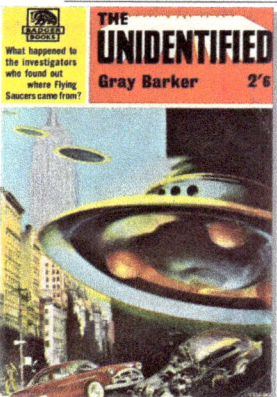

Series No/ Title Science Series #3

Date 1960 **Imprint** Badger **Collected**

Artist Curt Caesar

Notes Reprint of a 1956 University Press book. Barker used to edit the 'The Saucerian Bulletin' in the 1950s

Content The Unidentified-(Gray Barker)

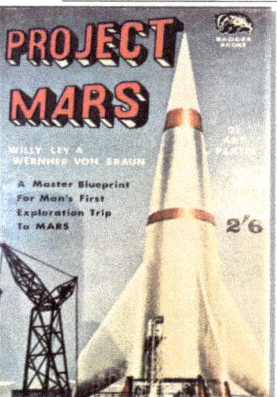

Series No/ Title Science Series #4

Date 1962 **Imprint** Badger **Collected**

Artist Chesley Bonestell

Notes Reprint of a 1956 Sidgwick & Jackson book.

Content Project Mars-(Willy Ley /Wernher Von Braun)

Type	Story Name	Date	Series No. /Title	Section
Fiction	12 To the Moon	1961	Science Fiction Series #059	02-Science Fiction
Fiction	3 Faces of Time	1960	Science Fiction Series #029	02-Science Fiction
Fiction	4 Dimensional Beam	1966	Macabre Stories #6	01-Comic
Fiction	A 1000 Years On	1961	Science Fiction Series #050	02-Science Fiction
Fiction	A little Devil Dancing	1954	Out of this World #2	03-Supernatural/Fantasy
Fiction	A little Devil Dancing	1960	Supernatural Series #036	03-Supernatural/Fantasy
Fiction	A Matter of Concealment	1953	Tales of Tomorrow #09	02-Science Fiction
Fiction	A Pattern of Evil	1959	Supernatural Series #028	03-Supernatural/Fantasy
Fiction	A Place of Madness	1954	Out of this World #1	03-Supernatural/Fantasy
Fiction	A Place of Madness	1960	Supernatural Series #034	03-Supernatural/Fantasy
Fiction	A Place of Meeting	1955	Supernatural Series #008	03-Supernatural/Fantasy
Fiction	A Place of Shadows	1963	Supernatural Series #079	03-Supernatural/Fantasy
Fiction	A Slip in Time	1966	Fantasy stories #3	01-Comic
Fiction	Adaptability	1952	Worlds of Fantasy #06	02-Science Fiction
Fiction	Adventure on the High Seas	1966	Strange Stories #1	01-Comic
Fiction	After the Atom	1953	After The Atom	02-Science Fiction
Fiction	Aftermath	1951	Tales of Tomorrow #02	02-Science Fiction
Fiction	Agent of Earth	1952	Worlds of Fantasy #05	02-Science Fiction
Fiction	Alien	1961	Science Fiction Series #061	02-Science Fiction
Fiction	Alien Threat	1954	Tales of Tomorrow #10	02-Science Fiction
Fiction	Alien From the Stars	1959	Science Fiction Series #015	02-Science Fiction
Fiction	All in the Mind	1966	Macabre Stories #6	01-Comic
Fiction	Allomorph	1953	Wonders of the Spaceways #08	02-Science Fiction
Fiction	An Eye for an Eye	1963	Supernatural Series #071	03-Supernatural/Fantasy
Fiction	And Midnight Falls	1962	Supernatural Series #063	03-Supernatural/Fantasy
Fiction	And Very Few Get Out	1954	Supernatural Series #002	03-Supernatural/Fantasy
Fiction	Android	1962	Science Fiction Series #079	02-Science Fiction
Fiction	Angel of the Bottomless Pit	1954	Out of this World #1	03-Supernatural/Fantasy
Fiction	Angel of the Bottomless Pit	1960	Supernatural Series #034	03-Supernatural/Fantasy
Fiction	Anno Mundi	1952	Wonders of the Spaceways #04	02-Science Fiction
Fiction	Assault From Infinity	1953	Assault From Infinity	02-Science Fiction
Fiction	Assignment in Venus	1952	Wonders of the Spaceways #04	02-Science Fiction
Fiction	Asteroid Man	1960	Science Fiction Series #035	02-Science Fiction
Fiction	Atomic Nemesis	1962	Science Fiction Series #080	02-Science Fiction
Fiction	Au Pair	1966	Supernatural Series #103	03-Supernatural/Fantasy
Fiction	Avenging Goddess	1964	Supernatural Series #085	03-Supernatural/Fantasy
Fiction	Back From the Dead	1966	Strange Stories #1	01-Comic
Fiction	Backtrack	1953	Worlds of Fantasy #11	02-Science Fiction
Fiction	Bardell's Wild Talent	1960	Supernatural Series #037	03-Supernatural/Fantasy
Fiction	Barrier 346	1965	Science Fiction Series #113	02-Science Fiction
Fiction	Barrier Unknown	1960	Science Fiction Series #030	02-Science Fiction

Type	Story Name	Date	Series No. /Title	Section
Fiction	Battle of the Giants!	1967	Mark Tyme #1	01-Comic
Fiction	Beast Men of Mars	1951	Futuristic Science Stories #04	02-Science Fiction
Fiction	Before the Beginning	1961	Supernatural Series #041	03-Supernatural/Fantasy
Fiction	Before the Beginning	1966	Macabre Stories #5	01-Comic
Fiction	Bell Book and Candle	1964	Supernatural Series #087	03-Supernatural/Fantasy
Fiction	Beyond the Galaxy	1953	Beyond The Galaxy	02-Science Fiction
Fiction	Beyond the Rim	1954	Worlds of Fantasy #14	02-Science Fiction
Fiction	Beyond the Veil	1964	Supernatural Series #086	03-Supernatural/Fantasy
Fiction	Beyond the Void	1965	Science Fiction Series #112	02-Science Fiction
Fiction	Beyond Time	1962	Science Fiction Series #071	02-Science Fiction
Fiction	Bifurcation	1953	Tales of Tomorrow #07	02-Science Fiction
Fiction	Bitter Reflection	1965	Supernatural Series #095	03-Supernatural/Fantasy
Fiction	Bitter Reflection	1966	Macabre Stories #3	01-Comic
Fiction	Black Abyss	1960	Science Fiction Series #032	02-Science Fiction
Fiction	Black Abyss	1961	Supernatural Series #043	03-Supernatural/Fantasy
Fiction	Black Abyss	1966	Spectre Stories #5	01-Comic
Fiction	Black Infinity	1961	Supernatural Series #044	03-Supernatural/Fantasy
Fiction	Black Marsh Mill	1961	Supernatural Series #038	03-Supernatural/Fantasy
Fiction	Black Pirate	1951	Tales of Tomorrow #02	02-Science Fiction
Fiction	Black River Mill	1958	Supernatural Series #015	03-Supernatural/Fantasy
Fiction	Blurred Horizon	1963	Supernatural Series #077	03-Supernatural/Fantasy
Fiction	Body And Soul	1967	Supernatural Series #107	03-Supernatural/Fantasy
Fiction	Bump in the Night	1960	Supernatural Series #037	03-Supernatural/Fantasy
Fiction	Buried in Space	1952	Wonders of the Spaceways #05	02-Science Fiction
Fiction	Call of the Werewolf	1958	Supernatural Series #017	03-Supernatural/Fantasy
Fiction	Call of the Wild	1965	Supernatural Series #097	03-Supernatural/Fantasy
Fiction	Call of the Wind	1966	Fantasy stories #2	01-Comic
Fiction	Candles of Death	1966	Fantasy stories #1	01-Comic
Fiction	Cano Sapiens	1952	Futuristic Science Stories #07	02-Science Fiction
Fiction	Captives of Vesta	1954	Wonders of the Spaceways #10	02-Science Fiction
Fiction	Chaos	1964	Supernatural Series #092	03-Supernatural/Fantasy
Fiction	Chaos In Arcturus	1953	Chaos In Arcturus	02-Science Fiction
Fiction	Chariot Into Time	1953	Chariot Into Time	02-Science Fiction
Fiction	Chariot of Apollo	1962	Supernatural Series #053	03-Supernatural/Fantasy
Fiction	Charlatan	1959	Supernatural Series #025	03-Supernatural/Fantasy
Fiction	Chasm of Time	1962	Supernatural Series #061	03-Supernatural/Fantasy
Fiction	Chimney Piece	1966	Supernatural Series #105	03-Supernatural/Fantasy
Fiction	Chronolel	1954	Wonders of the Spaceways #09	02-Science Fiction
Fiction	Colonist	1952	Worlds of Fantasy #06	02-Science Fiction
Fiction	Computer insane	1954	Tales of Tomorrow #11	02-Science Fiction
Fiction	Conquerors of the Moon	1950	Worlds of Fantasy #01	02-Science Fiction
Fiction	Conquest	1954	Worlds of Fantasy #14	02-Science Fiction

Type	Story Name	Date	Series No. /Title	Section
Fiction	Contact with Satan	1961	Supernatural Series #049	03-Supernatural/Fantasy
Fiction	Contract With Satan	1966	Fantasy stories #2	01-Comic
Fiction	Convoy to the Unknown	1951	Wonders of the Spaceways #01	02-Science Fiction
Fiction	Corporal Death	1966	Supernatural Series #103	03-Supernatural/Fantasy
Fiction	Cosmic Conception	1953	Futuristic Science Stories #10	02-Science Fiction
Fiction	Coven of Thirteen	1954	Out of this World #2	03-Supernatural/Fantasy
Fiction	Coven of Thirteen	1960	Supernatural Series #036	03-Supernatural/Fantasy
Fiction	Crimson Planet	1961	Science Fiction Series #060	02-Science Fiction
Fiction	Crimson Terror	1953	Futuristic Science Stories #10	02-Science Fiction
Fiction	Critical Age	1953	Futuristic Science Stories #12	02-Science Fiction
Fiction	Cry in the Night	1962	Supernatural Series #067	03-Supernatural/Fantasy
Fiction	Curse of the Incas	1964	Supernatural Series #089	03-Supernatural/Fantasy
Fiction	Curse of the Khan	1966	Supernatural Series #105	03-Supernatural/Fantasy
Fiction	Curse of the Totem	1962	Supernatural Series #065	03-Supernatural/Fantasy
Fiction	Curtain Up	1960	Supernatural Series #033	03-Supernatural/Fantasy
Fiction	Cyclops In the Sky	1960	Science Fiction Series #026	02-Science Fiction
Fiction	Danger Out of Space	1953	Tales of Tomorrow #09	02-Science Fiction
Fiction	Dangerous Moon	1950	Tales of Tomorrow #01	02-Science Fiction
Fiction	Dark Centauri	1954	Dark Centauri	02-Science Fiction
Fiction	Dark Conflict	1959	Supernatural Series #029	03-Supernatural/Fantasy
Fiction	Dark Conquest	1962	Supernatural Series #063	03-Supernatural/Fantasy
Fiction	Dark Continuum	1964	Science Fiction Series #104	02-Science Fiction
Fiction	Dark Kith and Kin	1958	Supernatural Series #018	03-Supernatural/Fantasy
Fiction	Dark Legion	1967	Supernatural Series #106	03-Supernatural/Fantasy
Fiction	Dark of the Dawn	1959	Supernatural Series #028	03-Supernatural/Fantasy
Fiction	Dark Staircase	1964	Supernatural Series #085	03-Supernatural/Fantasy
Fiction	Dark Staircase	1966	Macabre Stories #3	01-Comic
Fiction	Dawn of the Half-Gods	1953	Dawn Of The Half-Gods	02-Science Fiction
Fiction	Dawn of the Mutants	1959	Science Fiction Series #018	02-Science Fiction
Fiction	Day of the Beasts	1961	Science Fiction Series #051	02-Science Fiction
Fiction	Day of the Beasts	1966	Macabre Stories #2	01-Comic
Fiction	Dead or Alive?	1966	Spectre Stories #1	01-Comic
Fiction	Death From the Swamps	1952	Worlds of Fantasy #06	02-Science Fiction
Fiction	Death From the Swamps	1954	Futuristic Science Stories #14	02-Science Fiction
Fiction	Death Has Two Faces	1964	Supernatural Series #087	03-Supernatural/Fantasy
Fiction	Death Ships	1950	Futuristic Science Stories #02	02-Science Fiction
Fiction	Death-Note!	1966	Spectre Stories #5	01-Comic
Fiction	Deep Danger	1967	The Purple Hood #2	01-Comic
Fiction	Demon Dimension	1953	Futuristic Science Stories #12	02-Science Fiction
Fiction	Demons of Daavol	1952	Wonders of the Spaceways #05	02-Science Fiction
Fiction	Desert Fury!	1967	The Purple Hood #1	01-Comic
Fiction	Destination - Infinity	1954	Wonders of the Spaceways #10	02-Science Fiction

Type	Story Name	Date	Series No. /Title	Section
Fiction	Destination - Infinity	1959	Science Fiction Series #020	02-Science Fiction
Fiction	Destination Moon	1959	Science Fiction Series #014	02-Science Fiction
Fiction	Destroy the World!	1967	The Purple Hood #2	01-Comic
Fiction	Discovery	1952	Futuristic Science Stories #07	02-Science Fiction
Fiction	Doomed World	1951	Worlds of Fantasy #04	02-Science Fiction
Fiction	Doomed World	1960	Science Fiction Series #025	02-Science Fiction
Fiction	Doorway to Darkness	1959	Supernatural Series #026	03-Supernatural/Fantasy
Fiction	Dragon's Blood Mountain	1965	Supernatural Series #095	03-Supernatural/Fantasy
Fiction	Dragon's Blood Mountain	1966	Fantasy stories #4	01-Comic
Fiction	Dungeon Castle	1964	Supernatural Series #093	03-Supernatural/Fantasy
Fiction	Dungeon of Time	1953	Tales of Tomorrow #08	02-Science Fiction
Fiction	Dust	1967	Supernatural Series #107	03-Supernatural/Fantasy
Fiction	Ebb Tide	1959	Supernatural Series #026	03-Supernatural/Fantasy
Fiction	Edge of Darkness	1954	Worlds of Fantasy #14	02-Science Fiction
Fiction	Edge of Eternity	1962	Science Fiction Series #065	02-Science Fiction
Fiction	Emergency	1953	Worlds of Fantasy #10	02-Science Fiction
Fiction	Endor's Daughter	1964	Supernatural Series #085	03-Supernatural/Fantasy
Fiction	Escape or Die	1967	The Purple Hood #2	01-Comic
Fiction	Escape To Infinity	1963	Science Fiction Series #082	02-Science Fiction
Fiction	Excalibur	1960	Supernatural Series #030	03-Supernatural/Fantasy
Fiction	Exiles in Time	1950	Tales of Tomorrow #01	02-Science Fiction
Fiction	Exit Humanity	1960	Science Fiction Series #040	02-Science Fiction
Fiction	Expedition Eternity	1951	Tales of Tomorrow #03	02-Science Fiction
Fiction	Face In the Dark	1961	Supernatural Series #043	03-Supernatural/Fantasy
Fiction	Face in the Dark!	1966	Spectre Stories #5	01-Comic
Fiction	Face In the Night	1962	Supernatural Series #058	03-Supernatural/Fantasy
Fiction	Face of Evil	1960	Supernatural Series #036	03-Supernatural/Fantasy
Fiction	Faceless Planet	1961	Science Fiction Series #047	02-Science Fiction
Fiction	Fang	1957	Supernatural Series #012	03-Supernatural/Fantasy
Fiction	Fangs in the Night	1963	Supernatural Series #071	03-Supernatural/Fantasy
Fiction	Fear World	1953	Tales of Tomorrow #06	02-Science Fiction
Fiction	Fiends	1959	Science Fiction Series #022	02-Science Fiction
Fiction	Fight For Life	1967	Mark Tyme #2	01-Comic
Fiction	Final Answer	1958	Futuristic Science Stories Vol 2 #16	02-Science Fiction
Fiction	Fingers Of Darkness	1961	Supernatural Series #041	03-Supernatural/Fantasy
Fiction	Fire-Ray Invaders	1951	Tales of Tomorrow #02	02-Science Fiction
Fiction	First Effort	1952	Worlds of Fantasy #07	02-Science Fiction
Fiction	Five Faces of Fear	1960	Supernatural Series #032	03-Supernatural/Fantasy
Fiction	Flame Goddess	1961	Supernatural Series #046	03-Supernatural/Fantasy
Fiction	Flamemass	1961	Science Fiction Series #049	02-Science Fiction
Fiction	Fly, Witch, Fly	1962	Supernatural Series #053	03-Supernatural/Fantasy
Fiction	Footprints in the Sand	1963	Supernatural Series #075	03-Supernatural/Fantasy

Type	Story Name	Date	Series No. /Title	Section
Fiction	Forbidden City	1961	Supernatural Series #047	03-Supernatural/Fantasy
Fiction	Forbidden Island	1962	Supernatural Series #053	03-Supernatural/Fantasy
Fiction	Forbidden Planet	1961	Science Fiction Series #063	02-Science Fiction
Fiction	Force 97X	1965	Science Fiction Series #110	02-Science Fiction
Fiction	Forest of Evil	1961	Supernatural Series #047	03-Supernatural/Fantasy
Fiction	Forgotten Country	1963	Supernatural Series #081	03-Supernatural/Fantasy
Fiction	Forgotten Country	1966	Fantasy stories #1	01-Comic
Fiction	Forgotten World	1951	Tales of Tomorrow #03	02-Science Fiction
Fiction	Formula 29X	1963	Science Fiction Series #087	02-Science Fiction
Fiction	Frog	1954	Supernatural Series #002	03-Supernatural/Fantasy
Fiction	From Realms Beyond	1960	Supernatural Series #037	03-Supernatural/Fantasy
Fiction	From Realms Beyond	1963	Supernatural Series #074	03-Supernatural/Fantasy
Fiction	Frozen Planet	1960	Science Fiction Series #042	02-Science Fiction
Fiction	Galactic Interlude	1953	Tales of Tomorrow #06	02-Science Fiction
Fiction	Galactic Twin	1954	Worlds of Fantasy #14	02-Science Fiction
Fiction	Galaxy 666	1963	Science Fiction Series #086	02-Science Fiction
Fiction	Genesis	1954	Worlds of Fantasy #13	02-Science Fiction
Fiction	Gestalt	1959	Supernatural Series #027	03-Supernatural/Fantasy
Fiction	Ghost Moon	1952	Worlds of Fantasy #07	02-Science Fiction
Fiction	Ghost Rider	1966	Spectre Stories #3	01-Comic
Fiction	Ghost Ship	1957	Supernatural Series #013	03-Supernatural/Fantasy
Fiction	Girdle of Fear	1965	Supernatural Series #101	03-Supernatural/Fantasy
Fiction	Girl From Tomorrow	1965	Science Fiction Series #114	02-Science Fiction
Fiction	Globe of Dread	1953	Tales of Tomorrow #09	02-Science Fiction
Fiction	Gods of Darkness	1962	Supernatural Series #064	03-Supernatural/Fantasy
Fiction	Gods of Helle	1950	Worlds of Fantasy #01	02-Science Fiction
Fiction	God's Sin Eater	1965	Supernatural Series #101	03-Supernatural/Fantasy
Fiction	Graven in the Rock	1961	Supernatural Series #047	03-Supernatural/Fantasy
Fiction	Graveyard of the Damned	1962	Supernatural Series #059	03-Supernatural/Fantasy
Fiction	Graveyard of the Damned	1966	Fantasy stories #4	01-Comic
Fiction	Grimoir	1965	Supernatural Series #095	03-Supernatural/Fantasy
Fiction	Grip of Fear	1966	Macabre Stories #6	01-Comic
Fiction	Guardians of the Tomb	1958	Supernatural Series #016	03-Supernatural/Fantasy
Fiction	Guest of Honour	1966	Macabre Stories #2	01-Comic
Fiction	Hand From Gehanna	1964	Supernatural Series #091	03-Supernatural/Fantasy
Fiction	Hand of Doom	1960	Science Fiction Series #044	02-Science Fiction
Fiction	Haunt of the Vampire	1954	Supernatural Series #003	03-Supernatural/Fantasy
Fiction	Hell Has Wings	1962	Supernatural Series #057	03-Supernatural/Fantasy
Fiction	Hell Planet	1951	Tales of Tomorrow #03	02-Science Fiction
Fiction	Helping Hand	1952	Wonders of the Spaceways #05	02-Science Fiction
Fiction	Heritage	1952	Futuristic Science Stories #06	02-Science Fiction
Fiction	Hexere!	1966	Strange Stories #3	01-Comic

Checklist 1 - Story Titles (Alphabetical)

Type	Story Name	Date	Series No. /Title	Section
Fiction	Hexerei	1959	Supernatural Series #022	03-Supernatural/Fantasy
Fiction	Honour Bright	1953	Futuristic Science Stories #12	02-Science Fiction
Fiction	House of Despair	1963	Supernatural Series #073	03-Supernatural/Fantasy
Fiction	House of Despair	1966	Spectre Stories #4	01-Comic
Fiction	House of Unreason	1954	Supernatural Series #004	03-Supernatural/Fantasy
Fiction	Howl at the Moon	1963	Supernatural Series #079	03-Supernatural/Fantasy
Fiction	Hunter's Moon	1954	Supernatural Series #002	03-Supernatural/Fantasy
Fiction	Hydrosphere	1960	Science Fiction Series #036	02-Science Fiction
Fiction	Hyper Space	1959	Science Fiction Series #017	02-Science Fiction
Fiction	Ice Tomb	1966	Spectre Stories #5	01-Comic
Fiction	Idol of the Igorot	1966	Fantasy stories #5	01-Comic
Fiction	I'll Never Leave You	1964	Supernatural Series #089	03-Supernatural/Fantasy
Fiction	In a Glass Darkly	1964	Supernatural Series #093	03-Supernatural/Fantasy
Fiction	In a Glass Darkly	1966	Fantasy stories #3	01-Comic
Fiction	In The Beginning	1962	Science Fiction Series #076	02-Science Fiction
Fiction	In the Midst of Night	1963	Supernatural Series #079	03-Supernatural/Fantasy
Fiction	Infinity Machine	1962	Science Fiction Series #072	02-Science Fiction
Fiction	Integral Menace	1954	Wonders of the Spaceways #09	02-Science Fiction
Fiction	Interplanetary Zoo	1953	Tales of Tomorrow #07	02-Science Fiction
Fiction	Intrigue on Io	1952	Tales of Tomorrow #05	02-Science Fiction
Fiction	Invaders From the Stars	1950	Tales of Tomorrow #01	02-Science Fiction
Fiction	Invisible Presence	1963	Supernatural Series #081	03-Supernatural/Fantasy
Fiction	Invisible Witness	1958	Supernatural Series #019	03-Supernatural/Fantasy
Fiction	Island of Fear	1967	Mark Tyme #1	01-Comic
Fiction	Isles of the Blessed	1965	Supernatural Series #097	03-Supernatural/Fantasy
Fiction	It Came by Appointment	1957	Supernatural Series #011	03-Supernatural/Fantasy
Fiction	I've Been Here Before	1957	Supernatural Series #012	03-Supernatural/Fantasy
Fiction	Jaws of Steel	1966	Strange Stories #5	01-Comic
Fiction	Journey into Tomorrow	1953	Futuristic Science Stories #09	02-Science Fiction
Fiction	Journey to the Dawn	1952	Worlds of Fantasy #08	02-Science Fiction
Fiction	Jovian Flypaper	1952	Wonders of the Spaceways #04	02-Science Fiction
Fiction	Juggernaut	1960	Science Fiction Series #041	02-Science Fiction
Fiction	Jungle of Death	1959	Supernatural Series #027	03-Supernatural/Fantasy
Fiction	Lambda Point	1953	Wonders of the Spaceways #07	02-Science Fiction
Fiction	Land of the Green Shadows	1963	Supernatural Series #083	03-Supernatural/Fantasy
Fiction	Land of the Living Dead	1961	Supernatural Series #039	03-Supernatural/Fantasy
Fiction	Land of the Living Dead	1966	Spectre Stories #4	01-Comic
Fiction	Last Bus to Llangery	1958	Supernatural Series #016	03-Supernatural/Fantasy
Fiction	Last Command	1953	Worlds of Fantasy #10	02-Science Fiction
Fiction	Last Man on Earth	1961	Science Fiction Series #046	02-Science Fiction
Fiction	Last Survivor	1954	Worlds of Fantasy #12	02-Science Fiction
Fiction	Last Throw From Ganymede	1952	Futuristic Science Stories #08	02-Science Fiction

Type	Story Name	Date	Series No. /Title	Section
Fiction	Laughing Gas	1953	Tales of Tomorrow #07	02-Science Fiction
Fiction	Legend of the Lost World	1966	Strange Stories #4	01-Comic
Fiction	Legion of the Lost	1962	Supernatural Series #066	03-Supernatural/Fantasy
Fiction	Light of Mars	1959	Science Fiction Series #012	02-Science Fiction
Fiction	Lightning World	1960	Science Fiction Series #038	02-Science Fiction
Fiction	Lilith - Goddess of Night	1963	Supernatural Series #069	03-Supernatural/Fantasy
Fiction	Lord of the Black Valley	1964	Supernatural Series #087	03-Supernatural/Fantasy
Fiction	Lord of the Crag	1966	Macabre Stories #6	01-Comic
Fiction	Lord of the Crags	1966	Supernatural Series #105	03-Supernatural/Fantasy
Fiction	Lord of the Necromancers	1957	Supernatural Series #011	03-Supernatural/Fantasy
Fiction	Lorelei	1955	Supernatural Series #006	03-Supernatural/Fantasy
Fiction	Lost in Space	1953	Futuristic Science Stories #13	02-Science Fiction
Fiction	Lost Land of Lemuria	1961	Supernatural Series #041	03-Supernatural/Fantasy
Fiction	Lunar Flight	1958	Science Fiction Series #007	02-Science Fiction
Fiction	Lunar Revolt	1950	Worlds of Fantasy #02	02-Science Fiction
Fiction	Lurani	1955	Supernatural Series #005	03-Supernatural/Fantasy
Fiction	Lust for conquest	1951	Wonders of the Spaceways #01	02-Science Fiction
Fiction	Lycanthrope	1954	Supernatural Series #001	03-Supernatural/Fantasy
Fiction	Machine-Men of Avaion	1952	Wonders of the Spaceways #04	02-Science Fiction
Fiction	Mad Heritage	1953	Futuristic Science Stories #11	02-Science Fiction
Fiction	Marauders of the Void	1954	Wonders of the Spaceways #10	02-Science Fiction
Fiction	March of The Robots	1961	Science Fiction Series #053	02-Science Fiction
Fiction	Mark of The Beast	1964	Science Fiction Series #105	02-Science Fiction
Fiction	Marooned on Venus	1953	Worlds of Fantasy #11	02-Science Fiction
Fiction	Martian Apemen	1950	Futuristic Science Stories #03	02-Science Fiction
Fiction	Martian Bonanza	1954	Worlds of Fantasy #12	02-Science Fiction
Fiction	Martian Outcast	1952	Wonders of the Spaceways #03	02-Science Fiction
Fiction	Martian Terror	1950	Worlds of Fantasy #01	02-Science Fiction
Fiction	Martian Terror	1952	Worlds of Fantasy #08	02-Science Fiction
Fiction	Mask of Asmodeus	1955	Supernatural Series #007	03-Supernatural/Fantasy
Fiction	Menace From Mercury	1954	Menace From Mercury	02-Science Fiction
Fiction	Menace from the Atom	1950	Futuristic Science Stories #03	02-Science Fiction
Fiction	Menace of the Deep	1966	Fantasy stories #6	01-Comic
Fiction	Mermaid Reef	1959	Supernatural Series #023	03-Supernatural/Fantasy
Fiction	Mermaid Reef	1966	Strange Stories #2	01-Comic
Fiction	Micro Infinity	1962	Science Fiction Series #070	02-Science Fiction
Fiction	Midnight Ghoul	1963	Supernatural Series #081	03-Supernatural/Fantasy
Fiction	Midnight Ghoul	1966	Fantasy stories #1	01-Comic
Fiction	Mightier Weapon	1952	Worlds of Fantasy #06	02-Science Fiction
Fiction	Mind Force	1961	Science Fiction Series #054	02-Science Fiction
Fiction	Minerals From Mars	1952	Futuristic Science Stories #08	02-Science Fiction
Fiction	Mischa	1954	Wonders of the Spaceways #09	02-Science Fiction

Type	Story Name	Date	Series No. /Title	Section
Fiction	Mission to the Red Moon	1952	Futuristic Science Stories #08	02-Science Fiction
Fiction	Mission Venus	1953	Wonders of the Spaceways #07	02-Science Fiction
Fiction	Mistakes Do Happen	1952	Wonders of the Spaceways #05	02-Science Fiction
Fiction	Moon King	1953	Wonders of the Spaceways #08	02-Science Fiction
Fiction	Moon Wolf	1963	Supernatural Series #077	03-Supernatural/Fantasy
Fiction	Moon Wolf!	1966	Macabre Stories #4	01-Comic
Fiction	Moonbeast	1955	Supernatural Series #007	03-Supernatural/Fantasy
Fiction	Moondust	1952	Futuristic Science Stories #08	02-Science Fiction
Fiction	Moonlight Island	1962	Supernatural Series #055	03-Supernatural/Fantasy
Fiction	Moonlight Island	1966	Spectre Stories #5	01-Comic
Fiction	Moons of fear	1951	Worlds of Fantasy #03	02-Science Fiction
Fiction	More Than Mortal	1954	Menace From Mercury	02-Science Fiction
Fiction	Mr Pilkington's Ghost	1957	Supernatural Series #010	03-Supernatural/Fantasy
Fiction	Museum Piece	1954	Futuristic Science Stories #15	02-Science Fiction
Fiction	Mustapha	1961	Supernatural Series #051	03-Supernatural/Fantasy
Fiction	My Name Is Satan	1955	Supernatural Series #005	03-Supernatural/Fantasy
Fiction	Mythos	1961	Supernatural Series #045	03-Supernatural/Fantasy
Fiction	Negative Minus	1963	Science Fiction Series #088	02-Science Fiction
Fiction	Negative Ones	1965	Science Fiction Series #109	02-Science Fiction
Fiction	Nemesis	1964	Science Fiction Series #100	02-Science Fiction
Fiction	Neuron World	1965	Science Fiction Series #108	02-Science Fiction
Fiction	Never Look Behind You	1960	Supernatural Series #031	03-Supernatural/Fantasy
Fiction	Night Cry	1966	Macabre Stories #2	01-Comic
Fiction	Night of The Big Fire	1962	Science Fiction Series #075	02-Science Fiction
Fiction	Night of the Black Horror	1962	Science Fiction Series #064	02-Science Fiction
Fiction	Night of the Ghoul	1958	Supernatural Series #019	03-Supernatural/Fantasy
Fiction	Night of the Ghoul	1966	Spectre Stories #2	01-Comic
Fiction	Night Walkers	1966	Fantasy stories #6	01-Comic
Fiction	Nightmare	1957	Supernatural Series #010	03-Supernatural/Fantasy
Fiction	Nightmare	1962	Supernatural Series #054	03-Supernatural/Fantasy
Fiction	Nightmare on Ice	1963	Supernatural Series #079	03-Supernatural/Fantasy
Fiction	Nightmare on Ice	1966	Strange Stories #3	01-Comic
Fiction	Nightmare Planet	1950	Futuristic Science Stories #01	02-Science Fiction
Fiction	No Dawn and No Horizon	1959	Science Fiction Series #016	02-Science Fiction
Fiction	No Moon Tonight	1953	Tales of Tomorrow #09	02-Science Fiction
Fiction	No Tomorrow	1954	Futuristic Science Stories #14	02-Science Fiction
Fiction	No Way Back	1964	Science Fiction Series #107	02-Science Fiction
Fiction	Not Produced	1958	Science Fiction Series #002	02-Science Fiction
Fiction	Not Produced	1958	Science Fiction Series #008	02-Science Fiction
Fiction	Not Produced	1967	Supernatural Series #108	03-Supernatural/Fantasy
Fiction	Not Without Sorcery	1961	Supernatural Series #045	03-Supernatural/Fantasy
Fiction	Objective Pluto	1953	Tales of Tomorrow #08	02-Science Fiction

Type	Story Name	Date	Series No. /Title	Section
Fiction	Objective Venus	1958	Science Fiction Series #004	02-Science Fiction
Fiction	Old Man of the Snow	1963	Supernatural Series #077	03-Supernatural/Fantasy
Fiction	Older Than Death	1967	Supernatural Series #109	03-Supernatural/Fantasy
Fiction	One Million Years Ago	1950	Futuristic Science Stories #02	02-Science Fiction
Fiction	Operation Satellite	1958	Science Fiction Series #005	02-Science Fiction
Fiction	Orbit One	1962	Science Fiction Series #069	02-Science Fiction
Fiction	Out of the Blue	1952	Worlds of Fantasy #07	02-Science Fiction
Fiction	Out of the Darkness	1960	Supernatural Series #035	03-Supernatural/Fantasy
Fiction	Out of the Night	1965	Supernatural Series #100	03-Supernatural/Fantasy
Fiction	Out of the Past	1952	Futuristic Science Stories #06	02-Science Fiction
Fiction	Out of The Shadows	1959	Supernatural Series #022	03-Supernatural/Fantasy
Fiction	Out of the Vault	1958	Supernatural Series #015	03-Supernatural/Fantasy
Fiction	Out of the Vault	1966	Spectre Stories #4	01-Comic
Fiction	Outpost on Orbit 097	1953	Futuristic Science Stories #10	02-Science Fiction
Fiction	Paradise Planet	1954	Worlds of Fantasy #13	02-Science Fiction
Fiction	Perilous Expedition	1951	Worlds of Fantasy #04	02-Science Fiction
Fiction	Perilous Galaxy	1962	Science Fiction Series #066	02-Science Fiction
Fiction	Perseus	1952	Futuristic Science Stories #07	02-Science Fiction
Fiction	Phantom Crusader	1966	Strange Stories #4	01-Comic
Fiction	Phenomena X	1966	Science Fiction Series #116	02-Science Fiction
Fiction	Pioneers For Saturn	1953	Futuristic Science Stories #09	02-Science Fiction
Fiction	Plan for Conquest	1950	Worlds of Fantasy #02	02-Science Fiction
Fiction	Plan for Conquest	1963	Science Fiction Series #090	02-Science Fiction
Fiction	Planet of Desire	1954	Tales of Tomorrow #11	02-Science Fiction
Fiction	Planet of Fear	1967	Mark Tyme #2	01-Comic
Fiction	Planetoid of Peril	1953	Futuristic Science Stories #11	02-Science Fiction
Fiction	Plasma Men Bring Death	1950	Futuristic Science Stories #02	02-Science Fiction
Fiction	Point in Time	1952	Wonders of the Spaceways #05	02-Science Fiction
Fiction	Point of No Return	1953	Tales of Tomorrow #06	02-Science Fiction
Fiction	Point of No Return	1959	Science Fiction Series #013	02-Science Fiction
Fiction	Power Mad	1966	Macabre Stories #1	01-Comic
Fiction	Power of the Phantom Genie	1966	Spectre Stories #4	01-Comic
Fiction	Power Politics	1953	Futuristic Science Stories #09	02-Science Fiction
Fiction	Power Sphere	1963	Science Fiction Series #095	02-Science Fiction
Fiction	Princess in a Bubble	1953	Worlds of Fantasy #10	02-Science Fiction
Fiction	Prison Planet	1950	Futuristic Science Stories #03	02-Science Fiction
Fiction	Prisoners of Mars	1953	Wonders of the Spaceways #06	02-Science Fiction
Fiction	Project Survival	1953	Tales of Tomorrow #08	02-Science Fiction
Fiction	Projection Infinity	1964	Science Fiction Series #103	02-Science Fiction
Fiction	Psychic Circle	1963	Supernatural Series #083	03-Supernatural/Fantasy
Fiction	Pursuit	1959	Supernatural Series #025	03-Supernatural/Fantasy
Fiction	Pyramid Problem	1958	Futuristic Science Stories Vol 2 #16	02-Science Fiction

Type	Story Name	Date	Series No. /Title	Section
Fiction	Quest for Atlantis	1959	Supernatural Series #024	03-Supernatural/Fantasy
Fiction	Quietus	1952	Worlds of Fantasy #07	02-Science Fiction
Fiction	Radar Alert	1963	Science Fiction Series #083	02-Science Fiction
Fiction	Rake's Progress	1951	Wonders of the Spaceways #01	02-Science Fiction
Fiction	Raw Material	1953	Futuristic Science Stories #11	02-Science Fiction
Fiction	Reaction	1951	Tales of Tomorrow #03	02-Science Fiction
Fiction	Reactor Xk9	1963	Science Fiction Series #096	02-Science Fiction
Fiction	Reading Room	1965	Supernatural Series #099	03-Supernatural/Fantasy
Fiction	Realm of Danger	1953	Worlds of Fantasy #09	02-Science Fiction
Fiction	Rebels of Venus	1952	Futuristic Science Stories #07	02-Science Fiction
Fiction	Re-Creation	1951	Futuristic Science Stories #05	02-Science Fiction
Fiction	Refugee	1961	Supernatural Series #045	03-Supernatural/Fantasy
Fiction	Renegades of the Void	1954	Wonders of the Spaceways #10	02-Science Fiction
Fiction	Repeat Programme	1966	Supernatural Series #103	03-Supernatural/Fantasy
Fiction	Repercussions	1953	Tales of Tomorrow #08	02-Science Fiction
Fiction	Resting Place	1966	Macabre Stories #2	01-Comic
Fiction	Resurgam	1957	Supernatural Series #012	03-Supernatural/Fantasy
Fiction	Return from Space	1958	Science Fiction Series #009	02-Science Fiction
Fiction	Return of Lilith	1962	Supernatural Series #055	03-Supernatural/Fantasy
Fiction	Return of the Banshee	1964	Supernatural Series #089	03-Supernatural/Fantasy
Fiction	Return of the Hag	1963	Supernatural Series #081	03-Supernatural/Fantasy
Fiction	Return of Zeus	1962	Supernatural Series #052	03-Supernatural/Fantasy
Fiction	Return Ticket	1963	Supernatural Series #073	03-Supernatural/Fantasy
Fiction	Revolt!	1951	Worlds of Fantasy #03	02-Science Fiction
Fiction	Riddle of the Robots	1954	Worlds of Fantasy #12	02-Science Fiction
Fiction	Right Through My Hair	1960	Supernatural Series #030	03-Supernatural/Fantasy
Fiction	Robot Rebels	1954	Worlds of Fantasy #12	02-Science Fiction
Fiction	Robot Threat	1953	Wonders of the Spaceways #06	02-Science Fiction
Fiction	Rodent Mutation	1961	Science Fiction Series #055	02-Science Fiction
Fiction	Rogue Ship	1953	Worlds of Fantasy #09	02-Science Fiction
Fiction	Roman Twilight	1963	Supernatural Series #083	03-Supernatural/Fantasy
Fiction	Rusalka and the Vodyanol	1961	Supernatural Series #047	03-Supernatural/Fantasy
Fiction	Safari on Venus	1953	Tales of Tomorrow #06	02-Science Fiction
Fiction	Sands of Eternity	1963	Supernatural Series #073	03-Supernatural/Fantasy
Fiction	Sands of Eternity	1966	Macabre Stories #5	01-Comic
Fiction	Sargasso of Space	1952	Tales of Tomorrow #04	02-Science Fiction
Fiction	Satellite	1960	Science Fiction Series #027	02-Science Fiction
Fiction	Satellite in Space	1954	Wonders of the Spaceways #09	02-Science Fiction
Fiction	Satellite Peril	1953	Tales of Tomorrow #08	02-Science Fiction
Fiction	Saucers From Space	1954	Futuristic Science Stories #14	02-Science Fiction
Fiction	Scarlet Invaders	1950	Worlds of Fantasy #01	02-Science Fiction
Fiction	Scourge of Space	1952	Wonders of the Spaceways #03	02-Science Fiction

Checklist 1 - Story Titles (Alphabetical)

Type	Story Name	Date	Series No. /Title	Section
Fiction	Scraping the Barrel	1962	Supernatural Series #061	03-Supernatural/Fantasy
Fiction	Search the Dark Stars	1961	Science Fiction Series #048	02-Science Fiction
Fiction	Secret of the Pyramid	1966	Fantasy stories #2	01-Comic
Fiction	Secret of the Shamen	1962	Supernatural Series #065	03-Supernatural/Fantasy
Fiction	Secret of the Snows	1957	Supernatural Series #013	03-Supernatural/Fantasy
Fiction	Shadow of Fear	1965	Supernatural Series #099	03-Supernatural/Fantasy
Fiction	Shadow of the Atom	1958	Futuristic Science Stories Vol 2 #16	02-Science Fiction
Fiction	Shadow Over Endor	1955	Supernatural Series #007	03-Supernatural/Fantasy
Fiction	Sillisian Menace	1953	Wonders of the Spaceways #07	02-Science Fiction
Fiction	Sinister Stranger	1958	Supernatural Series #020	03-Supernatural/Fantasy
Fiction	Sirius Rampant	1952	Futuristic Science Stories #06	02-Science Fiction
Fiction	Sky Herd	1957	Supernatural Series #013	03-Supernatural/Fantasy
Fiction	Slave God of the Norsu	1966	Strange Stories #4	01-Comic
Fiction	Slave Ships	1952	Tales of Tomorrow #04	02-Science Fiction
Fiction	Slaves of Space	1953	Futuristic Science Stories #09	02-Science Fiction
Fiction	Sleeping Place	1962	Supernatural Series #067	03-Supernatural/Fantasy
Fiction	Snake Vengeance	1957	Supernatural Series #009	03-Supernatural/Fantasy
Fiction	Softly By Moonlight	1963	Supernatural Series #080	03-Supernatural/Fantasy
Fiction	Soldiers of Space	1951	Tales of Tomorrow #02	02-Science Fiction
Fiction	Solitude	1963	Supernatural Series #079	03-Supernatural/Fantasy
Fiction	Something About Gargoyles	1958	Supernatural Series #018	03-Supernatural/Fantasy
Fiction	Something About Spiders	1961	Supernatural Series #045	03-Supernatural/Fantasy
Fiction	Something at the Door	1961	Supernatural Series #051	03-Supernatural/Fantasy
Fiction	Something at the Door	1966	Fantasy stories #6	01-Comic
Fiction	Something from the Sea	1954	Supernatural Series #003	03-Supernatural/Fantasy
Fiction	Something Old	1960	Supernatural Series #031	03-Supernatural/Fantasy
Fiction	Somewhere in the Moonlight	1955	Supernatural Series #005	03-Supernatural/Fantasy
Fiction	Somewhere Out There	1963	Science Fiction Series #092	02-Science Fiction
Fiction	Somewhere the Devil Hides	1959	Supernatural Series #022	03-Supernatural/Fantasy
Fiction	Song of the Banshee	1958	Supernatural Series #014	03-Supernatural/Fantasy
Fiction	Space Adventurer	1952	Worlds of Fantasy #08	02-Science Fiction
Fiction	Space Fury	1962	Science Fiction Series #077	02-Science Fiction
Fiction	Space Menace	1954	Worlds of Fantasy #13	02-Science Fiction
Fiction	Space No Barrier	1964	Science Fiction Series #106	02-Science Fiction
Fiction	Space Patrol	1951	Futuristic Science Stories #05	02-Science Fiction
Fiction	Space Pirates	1950	Worlds of Fantasy #02	02-Science Fiction
Fiction	Space Trader	1951	Futuristic Science Stories #04	02-Science Fiction
Fiction	Space Trap	1964	Science Fiction Series #098	02-Science Fiction
Fiction	Space Void	1960	Science Fiction Series #034	02-Science Fiction
Fiction	Space Warning	1953	Wonders of the Spaceways #06	02-Science Fiction
Fiction	Space-Borne	1959	Science Fiction Series #020	02-Science Fiction
Fiction	Spacemen's Luck	1953	Futuristic Science Stories #12	02-Science Fiction

Type	Story Name	Date	Series No. /Title	Section
Fiction	Spawn of Space	1953	Wonders of the Spaceways #07	02-Science Fiction
Fiction	Spawn of the Void	1951	Futuristic Science Stories #04	02-Science Fiction
Fiction	Special Mission	1963	Science Fiction Series #097	02-Science Fiction
Fiction	Spectre of the Darkness	1965	Supernatural Series #098	03-Supernatural/Fantasy
Fiction	Spirit of Darkness	1963	Supernatural Series #073	03-Supernatural/Fantasy
Fiction	Spring Fever	1965	Supernatural Series #095	03-Supernatural/Fantasy
Fiction	Stanhope's Moon	1950	Futuristic Science Stories #01	02-Science Fiction
Fiction	Star's End	1953	Wonders of the Spaceways #08	02-Science Fiction
Fiction	Station Neptune	1951	Futuristic Science Stories #05	02-Science Fiction
Fiction	Stone Age Menace!	1967	Mark Tyme #1	01-Comic
Fiction	Stone Face	1966	Fantasy stories #5	01-Comic
Fiction	Storm God's Fury	1962	Supernatural Series #055	03-Supernatural/Fantasy
Fiction	Stowaway	1954	Tales of Tomorrow #10	02-Science Fiction
Fiction	Strange Company	1960	Supernatural Series #031	03-Supernatural/Fantasy
Fiction	Strange Country	1962	Supernatural Series #067	03-Supernatural/Fantasy
Fiction	Strange Country	1966	Macabre Stories #2	01-Comic
Fiction	Strange Door	1966	Macabre Stories #6	01-Comic
Fiction	Strange Land	1966	Spectre Stories #3	01-Comic
Fiction	Stranger In the Shadow	1966	Supernatural Series #103	03-Supernatural/Fantasy
Fiction	Stranger in the Skull	1963	Supernatural Series #075	03-Supernatural/Fantasy
Fiction	Stratoship X9	1951	Worlds of Fantasy #03	02-Science Fiction
Fiction	Struggle For Calisto	1952	Wonders of the Spaceways #02	02-Science Fiction
Fiction	Such Worlds Are Dangerous	1954	Futuristic Science Stories #15	02-Science Fiction
Fiction	Suddenly...at Twilight	1964	Supernatural Series #091	03-Supernatural/Fantasy
Fiction	Suddenly…at Twilight	1966	Macabre Stories #4	01-Comic
Fiction	Suicide Mission	1952	Tales of Tomorrow #04	02-Science Fiction
Fiction	Suns in Duo	1953	Suns In Duo	02-Science Fiction
Fiction	Survival Project	1966	Science Fiction Series #117	02-Science Fiction
Fiction	Suspension	1964	Science Fiction Series #102	02-Science Fiction
Fiction	Swamp Thing	1961	Supernatural Series #043	03-Supernatural/Fantasy
Fiction	Synthesis of Knowledge	1952	Wonders of the Spaceways #03	02-Science Fiction
Fiction	Tables Turned	1953	Worlds of Fantasy #10	02-Science Fiction
Fiction	Take the Last Train	1959	Supernatural Series #022	03-Supernatural/Fantasy
Fiction	Temple of Quetzalcoatl	1962	Supernatural Series #059	03-Supernatural/Fantasy
Fiction	Terror From the Skies	1951	Futuristic Science Stories #04	02-Science Fiction
Fiction	That Deep Black Yonder	1967	Supernatural Series #107	03-Supernatural/Fantasy
Fiction	The 7th Dimension	1953	The 7th Dimension	02-Science Fiction
Fiction	The Abbot's Ring	1964	Supernatural Series #085	03-Supernatural/Fantasy
Fiction	The Abbot's Ring	1966	Strange Stories #3	01-Comic
Fiction	The Accursed	1965	Supernatural Series #097	03-Supernatural/Fantasy
Fiction	The Alien	1951	Futuristic Science Stories #05	02-Science Fiction
Fiction	The Alien Ones	1963	Science Fiction Series #094	02-Science Fiction

Type	Story Name	Date	Series No. /Title	Section
Fiction	The Ancient Alchemist	1957	Supernatural Series #009	03-Supernatural/Fantasy
Fiction	The Aphesian Riddle	1954	Futuristic Science Stories #15	02-Science Fiction
Fiction	The Aquatic Piracy	1952	Worlds of Fantasy #05	02-Science Fiction
Fiction	The Artist's Model	1957	Supernatural Series #009	03-Supernatural/Fantasy
Fiction	The Attic	1965	Supernatural Series #099	03-Supernatural/Fantasy
Fiction	The Audit Chamber	1960	Supernatural Series #033	03-Supernatural/Fantasy
Fiction	The Avenging Goddess	1966	Fantasy stories #3	01-Comic
Fiction	The Barrier	1962	Supernatural Series #057	03-Supernatural/Fantasy
Fiction	The Beckoning Shade	1962	Supernatural Series #063	03-Supernatural/Fantasy
Fiction	The Bellarmine Jars	1961	Supernatural Series #041	03-Supernatural/Fantasy
Fiction	The Bevelled Casket	1962	Supernatural Series #061	03-Supernatural/Fantasy
Fiction	The Big Slowdown	1954	Tales of Tomorrow #10	02-Science Fiction
Fiction	The Black Hound	1957	Supernatural Series #013	03-Supernatural/Fantasy
Fiction	The Black Mirror	1967	Supernatural Series #109	03-Supernatural/Fantasy
Fiction	The Black Sphere	1952	The Black Sphere	02-Science Fiction
Fiction	The Border Raider	1965	Supernatural Series #097	03-Supernatural/Fantasy
Fiction	The Bow and the Bugle	1964	Supernatural Series #091	03-Supernatural/Fantasy
Fiction	The Bow and the Bugle	1966	Macabre Stories #5	01-Comic
Fiction	The Brain Stealers	1960	Science Fiction Series #033	02-Science Fiction
Fiction	The Brass Tombstone	1961	Supernatural Series #051	03-Supernatural/Fantasy
Fiction	The Byarkil Eaters	1954	Worlds of Fantasy #13	02-Science Fiction
Fiction	The Carnival Horror	1961	Supernatural Series #038	03-Supernatural/Fantasy
Fiction	The Centurion's Vengeance	1961	Supernatural Series #049	03-Supernatural/Fantasy
Fiction	The Chair	1954	Supernatural Series #004	03-Supernatural/Fantasy
Fiction	The Chalice of Circe	1958	Supernatural Series #018	03-Supernatural/Fantasy
Fiction	The Challenge	1966	Spectre Stories #1	01-Comic
Fiction	The Chinese Lustre Vase	1964	Supernatural Series #087	03-Supernatural/Fantasy
Fiction	The City	1953	Tales of Tomorrow #07	02-Science Fiction
Fiction	The Clipper Ships of Space	1953	Futuristic Science Stories #11	02-Science Fiction
Fiction	The Cloak of Darkness	1954	Supernatural Series #001	03-Supernatural/Fantasy
Fiction	The Cloak of Darkness	1957	Supernatural Series #010	03-Supernatural/Fantasy
Fiction	The Clock That Struck Thirteen	1959	Supernatural Series #023	03-Supernatural/Fantasy
Fiction	The Clubmen	1963	Supernatural Series #083	03-Supernatural/Fantasy
Fiction	The Coffin	1966	Macabre Stories #1	01-Comic
Fiction	The Comedians	1963	Supernatural Series #073	03-Supernatural/Fantasy
Fiction	The Coveters	1962	Supernatural Series #067	03-Supernatural/Fantasy
Fiction	The Crawling Fiend	1960	Supernatural Series #030	03-Supernatural/Fantasy
Fiction	The Creature	1958	Supernatural Series #014	03-Supernatural/Fantasy
Fiction	The Creature in the Depths	1959	Supernatural Series #028	03-Supernatural/Fantasy
Fiction	The Creatures from Below	1958	Supernatural Series #016	03-Supernatural/Fantasy
Fiction	The Creatures That Came After	1966	Macabre Stories #4	01-Comic
Fiction	The Crimson Evil	1959	Supernatural Series #026	03-Supernatural/Fantasy

Type	Story Name	Date	Series No. /Title	Section
Fiction	The Crusade That Was Different	1966	Fantasy stories #3	01-Comic
Fiction	The Crystal Fear	1955	Supernatural Series #007	03-Supernatural/Fantasy
Fiction	The Crystal Skull	1954	Supernatural Series #003	03-Supernatural/Fantasy
Fiction	The Crystalline World	1952	Tales of Tomorrow #05	02-Science Fiction
Fiction	The Dancing Wraiths	1958	Supernatural Series #017	03-Supernatural/Fantasy
Fiction	The Dark Millenium	1959	Science Fiction Series #019	02-Science Fiction
Fiction	The Dark Millenium	1978	Science Fiction #102	Misc Series -1
Fiction	The Dark Ones	1955	Supernatural Series #005	03-Supernatural/Fantasy
Fiction	The Dark Possessed	1959	Supernatural Series #026	03-Supernatural/Fantasy
Fiction	The Dark Time	1967	Supernatural Series #109	03-Supernatural/Fantasy
Fiction	The Darker Drink	1962	Supernatural Series #061	03-Supernatural/Fantasy
Fiction	The Day the World Died	1962	Science Fiction Series #073	02-Science Fiction
Fiction	The Death Note	1958	Supernatural Series #020	03-Supernatural/Fantasy
Fiction	The Death Planet	1951	Worlds of Fantasy #04	02-Science Fiction
Fiction	The Deathless Wings	1961	Supernatural Series #039	03-Supernatural/Fantasy
Fiction	The Destroyers	1958	Science Fiction Series #011	02-Science Fiction
Fiction	The Devil at My Elbow	1954	Out of this World #1	03-Supernatural/Fantasy
Fiction	The Devil at My Elbow	1960	Supernatural Series #034	03-Supernatural/Fantasy
Fiction	The Devil from the Depths	1961	Supernatural Series #047	03-Supernatural/Fantasy
Fiction	The Devil's Brood	1964	Supernatural Series #091	03-Supernatural/Fantasy
Fiction	The Devil's Canvas	1954	Supernatural Series #001	03-Supernatural/Fantasy
Fiction	The Devil's Dictionary	1957	Supernatural Series #009	03-Supernatural/Fantasy
Fiction	The Devil's Weed	1953	Futuristic Science Stories #13	02-Science Fiction
Fiction	The Dolmen	1957	Supernatural Series #009	03-Supernatural/Fantasy
Fiction	The Dream of Camelot	1962	Supernatural Series #059	03-Supernatural/Fantasy
Fiction	The Dreamer	1966	Macabre Stories #1	01-Comic
Fiction	The Drud	1959	Supernatural Series #024	03-Supernatural/Fantasy
Fiction	The Drud	1966	Strange Stories #2	01-Comic
Fiction	The Earthen Vessel	1958	Supernatural Series #015	03-Supernatural/Fantasy
Fiction	The Effigy	1958	Supernatural Series #016	03-Supernatural/Fantasy
Fiction	The Eight Immortals	1961	Supernatural Series #051	03-Supernatural/Fantasy
Fiction	The Elder Race	1951	Worlds of Fantasy #03	02-Science Fiction
Fiction	The Eldritch Chair	1962	Supernatural Series #057	03-Supernatural/Fantasy
Fiction	The Eldritch Guide	1964	Supernatural Series #087	03-Supernatural/Fantasy
Fiction	The Encompassed Globe	1951	Tales of Tomorrow #03	02-Science Fiction
Fiction	The Entropists	1958	Futuristic Science Stories Vol 2 #16	02-Science Fiction
Fiction	The Evil One!	1966	Macabre Stories #6	01-Comic
Fiction	The Exorcists	1965	Supernatural Series #094	03-Supernatural/Fantasy
Fiction	The Expanding Bacillus	1953	Worlds of Fantasy #10	02-Science Fiction
Fiction	The Eye of Karnack	1962	Supernatural Series #056	03-Supernatural/Fantasy
Fiction	The Face at the Window	1961	Supernatural Series #043	03-Supernatural/Fantasy
Fiction	The Face of Fear	1963	Supernatural Series #082	03-Supernatural/Fantasy

Type	Story Name	Date	Series No. /Title	Section
Fiction	The Face of Stone	1961	Supernatural Series #038	03-Supernatural/Fantasy
Fiction	The Face of X	1960	Science Fiction Series #039	02-Science Fiction
Fiction	The Family	1966	Spectre Stories #3	01-Comic
Fiction	The Final Threat	1954	Wonders of the Spaceways #10	02-Science Fiction
Fiction	The Fire Goddess	1950	Futuristic Science Stories #02	02-Science Fiction
Fiction	The Flaming Sword	1966	Macabre Stories #5	01-Comic
Fiction	The Flight of The Valkyries	1958	Supernatural Series #014	03-Supernatural/Fantasy
Fiction	The Forbidden	1963	Supernatural Series #072	03-Supernatural/Fantasy
Fiction	The Forgotten days	1950	Tales of Tomorrow #01	02-Science Fiction
Fiction	The Fox on the Prowl	1967	The Purple Hood #1	01-Comic
Fiction	The Friendly Stranger	1963	Supernatural Series #073	03-Supernatural/Fantasy
Fiction	The Frozen Claw	1962	Supernatural Series #057	03-Supernatural/Fantasy
Fiction	The Frozen Tomb	1962	Supernatural Series #067	03-Supernatural/Fantasy
Fiction	The Fugitive	1954	Tales of Tomorrow #10	02-Science Fiction
Fiction	The Ghost	1966	Macabre Stories #1	01-Comic
Fiction	The Ghost Rider	1959	Supernatural Series #027	03-Supernatural/Fantasy
Fiction	The Ghoul and the Goddess	1964	Supernatural Series #093	03-Supernatural/Fantasy
Fiction	The Gliding Wraith	1963	Supernatural Series #071	03-Supernatural/Fantasy
Fiction	The Gods of Fear	1954	Supernatural Series #001	03-Supernatural/Fantasy
Fiction	The Golden Chalice	1961	Supernatural Series #050	03-Supernatural/Fantasy
Fiction	The Golden Hibiscus	1953	Wonders of the Spaceways #06	02-Science Fiction
Fiction	The Golden Scarab	1955	Supernatural Series #008	03-Supernatural/Fantasy
Fiction	The Golden Warrior	1958	Supernatural Series #019	03-Supernatural/Fantasy
Fiction	The Golden Warrior	1966	Macabre Stories #3	01-Comic
Fiction	The Golem	1965	Supernatural Series #095	03-Supernatural/Fantasy
Fiction	The Green Cloud	1951	Wonders of the Spaceways #01	02-Science Fiction
Fiction	The Green Cloud	1959	Supernatural Series #024	03-Supernatural/Fantasy
Fiction	The Green Hell of Venus	1954	Futuristic Science Stories #15	02-Science Fiction
Fiction	The Green Ray	1950	Futuristic Science Stories #01	02-Science Fiction
Fiction	The Green Sarcophagus	1961	Supernatural Series #041	03-Supernatural/Fantasy
Fiction	The Green Sarcophagus	1966	Fantasy stories #5	01-Comic
Fiction	The Grimoire	1966	Fantasy stories #4	01-Comic
Fiction	The Grip of Fear	1961	Supernatural Series #051	03-Supernatural/Fantasy
Fiction	The Grip of Time Unending	1963	Supernatural Series #077	03-Supernatural/Fantasy
Fiction	The Guide and the God	1959	Supernatural Series #025	03-Supernatural/Fantasy
Fiction	The Hag	1966	Fantasy stories #5	01-Comic
Fiction	The Half Legs	1961	Supernatural Series #049	03-Supernatural/Fantasy
Fiction	The Hand of Gehenna	1966	Macabre Stories #4	01-Comic
Fiction	The Haunted Pool	1959	Supernatural Series #021	03-Supernatural/Fantasy
Fiction	The Haunter	1957	Supernatural Series #011	03-Supernatural/Fantasy
Fiction	The Haunting of Charles Quintain	1967	Supernatural Series #109	03-Supernatural/Fantasy
Fiction	The House of Dreams	1961	Supernatural Series #049	03-Supernatural/Fantasy

Type	Story Name	Date	Series No. /Title	Section
Fiction	The House That Wouldn't Die	1966	Supernatural Series #103	03-Supernatural/Fantasy
Fiction	The Hungry Gods	1955	Supernatural Series #007	03-Supernatural/Fantasy
Fiction	The Hungry House	1955	Supernatural Series #006	03-Supernatural/Fantasy
Fiction	The Hungry Ones	1958	Supernatural Series #018	03-Supernatural/Fantasy
Fiction	The Hypnotist	1959	Supernatural Series #024	03-Supernatural/Fantasy
Fiction	The Hypnotist	1966	Strange Stories #2	01-Comic
Fiction	The Immortals	1962	Supernatural Series #062	03-Supernatural/Fantasy
Fiction	The Impending Heritage	1952	Worlds of Fantasy #05	02-Science Fiction
Fiction	The Incredible Scourge	1952	Tales of Tomorrow #05	02-Science Fiction
Fiction	The Incredulist	1954	Supernatural Series #002	03-Supernatural/Fantasy
Fiction	The Indigenous Revolt	1953	Futuristic Science Stories #13	02-Science Fiction
Fiction	The Intruders	1963	Science Fiction Series #089	02-Science Fiction
Fiction	The In-World	1960	Science Fiction Series #037	02-Science Fiction
Fiction	The Iron Oven	1958	Supernatural Series #016	03-Supernatural/Fantasy
Fiction	The Irreparable Sunset	1951	Futuristic Science Stories #05	02-Science Fiction
Fiction	The Isle of the Blessed	1966	Fantasy stories #2	01-Comic
Fiction	The Isolationists	1952	Wonders of the Spaceways #02	02-Science Fiction
Fiction	The Joker!	1966	Strange Stories #5	01-Comic
Fiction	The Juggernaut Who Walked	1966	Macabre Stories #1	01-Comic
Fiction	The Keeper of Dark Point	1967	Supernatural Series #107	03-Supernatural/Fantasy
Fiction	The Kraken	1958	Supernatural Series #019	03-Supernatural/Fantasy
Fiction	The Kraken	1966	Macabre Stories #3	01-Comic
Fiction	The Lady Labyrinth	1959	Supernatural Series #028	03-Supernatural/Fantasy
Fiction	The Lady Loves Cats	1964	Supernatural Series #091	03-Supernatural/Fantasy
Fiction	The Laird	1964	Supernatural Series #093	03-Supernatural/Fantasy
Fiction	The Lake Thing	1964	Supernatural Series #093	03-Supernatural/Fantasy
Fiction	The Lamia	1959	Supernatural Series #021	03-Supernatural/Fantasy
Fiction	The Last Astronaut	1963	Science Fiction Series #093	02-Science Fiction
Fiction	The Last Chance	1954	Tales of Tomorrow #11	02-Science Fiction
Fiction	The Last Ten Men on Earth	1950	Tales of Tomorrow #01	02-Science Fiction
Fiction	The Last Valkyrie	1961	Supernatural Series #040	03-Supernatural/Fantasy
Fiction	The Laughter of Space	1954	Wonders of the Spaceways #09	02-Science Fiction
Fiction	The Legacy	1952	Futuristic Science Stories #06	02-Science Fiction
Fiction	The Lethal Mist	1954	Tales of Tomorrow #11	02-Science Fiction
Fiction	The Lighter	1952	Wonders of the Spaceways #03	02-Science Fiction
Fiction	The Loch Ness Terror	1961	Supernatural Series #038	03-Supernatural/Fantasy
Fiction	The Loch Ness Terror	1966	Macabre Stories #4	01-Comic
Fiction	The Lonely Shadows	1962	Supernatural Series #063	03-Supernatural/Fantasy
Fiction	The Lonely Things	1957	Supernatural Series #011	03-Supernatural/Fantasy
Fiction	The Long Trek	1953	Futuristic Science Stories #13	02-Science Fiction
Fiction	The Macabre Ones	1964	Supernatural Series #090	03-Supernatural/Fantasy
Fiction	The Macabre Ones	1973	The Macabre Ones	Misc Series -1

Type	Story Name	Date	Series No. /Title	Section
Fiction	The Magician Sleeps	1961	Supernatural Series #039	03-Supernatural/Fantasy
Fiction	The Man From Beyond	1965	Science Fiction Series #111	02-Science Fiction
Fiction	The Man From The Bomb	1959	Science Fiction Series #021	02-Science Fiction
Fiction	The Man Who Ate Fire	1966	Spectre Stories #2	01-Comic
Fiction	The Man Who Came Back	1964	Supernatural Series #088	03-Supernatural/Fantasy
Fiction	The Man Who Came Back	1974	The Man Who Came Back	Unverified - 1
Fiction	The Man Who Conquered Time	1962	Science Fiction Series #068	02-Science Fiction
Fiction	The Man Who Conquered Time	1966	Strange Stories #3	01-Comic
Fiction	The Man Who Could not Die	1960	Supernatural Series #033	03-Supernatural/Fantasy
Fiction	The Man Who Knew	1963	Supernatural Series #083	03-Supernatural/Fantasy
Fiction	The Man Who Lost Thursday	1955	Supernatural Series #008	03-Supernatural/Fantasy
Fiction	The Man Who Never Smiled	1963	Supernatural Series #071	03-Supernatural/Fantasy
Fiction	The Man Who Was Nothing	1959	Supernatural Series #027	03-Supernatural/Fantasy
Fiction	The Man Within	1959	Supernatural Series #025	03-Supernatural/Fantasy
Fiction	The Manhattan Warlock	1964	Supernatural Series #091	03-Supernatural/Fantasy
Fiction	The Manhattan Warlock	1966	Spectre Stories #3	01-Comic
Fiction	The Manipulators	1952	Futuristic Science Stories #08	02-Science Fiction
Fiction	The Mechans of Muah	1950	Futuristic Science Stories #03	02-Science Fiction
Fiction	The Menace of the Discoids	1952	Wonders of the Spaceways #03	02-Science Fiction
Fiction	The Merman of Destruction Bay	1966	Fantasy stories #1	01-Comic
Fiction	The Microscopic Ones	1960	Science Fiction Series #043	02-Science Fiction
Fiction	The Midnight Museum	1960	Supernatural Series #033	03-Supernatural/Fantasy
Fiction	The Midnight Museum	1966	Macabre Stories #3	01-Comic
Fiction	The Midnight Walkers	1957	Supernatural Series #010	03-Supernatural/Fantasy
Fiction	The Minacious Termites	1952	Wonders of the Spaceways #02	02-Science Fiction
Fiction	The Mind Makers	1961	Science Fiction Series #058	02-Science Fiction
Fiction	The Moment in Time	1953	Tales of Tomorrow #09	02-Science Fiction
Fiction	The Monument	1952	Wonders of the Spaceways #02	02-Science Fiction
Fiction	The Mountain Thing	1962	Supernatural Series #055	03-Supernatural/Fantasy
Fiction	The Mountain Thing!	1966	Strange Stories #5	01-Comic
Fiction	The Night Creatures	1957	Supernatural Series #011	03-Supernatural/Fantasy
Fiction	The Night-Comer	1967	Supernatural Series #109	03-Supernatural/Fantasy
Fiction	The Nightmare Road	1954	Out of this World #1	03-Supernatural/Fantasy
Fiction	The Nightmare Road	1960	Supernatural Series #034	03-Supernatural/Fantasy
Fiction	The Nine Green Men	1963	Supernatural Series #069	03-Supernatural/Fantasy
Fiction	The Nine Green Men	1966	Fantasy stories #4	01-Comic
Fiction	The North Cloister	1962	Supernatural Series #053	03-Supernatural/Fantasy
Fiction	The Old House	1958	Supernatural Series #014	03-Supernatural/Fantasy
Fiction	The Old Man of the Sea	1966	Spectre Stories #1	01-Comic
Fiction	The Other Driver	1958	Supernatural Series #020	03-Supernatural/Fantasy
Fiction	The Other Line	1959	Supernatural Series #023	03-Supernatural/Fantasy
Fiction	The Other Séance	1954	Supernatural Series #003	03-Supernatural/Fantasy

Type	Story Name	Date	Series No. /Title	Section
Fiction	The Other Side of Night	1960	Science Fiction Series #024	02-Science Fiction
Fiction	The Outlaw of Space	1950	Worlds of Fantasy #02	02-Science Fiction
Fiction	The Paint Box	1965	Supernatural Series #099	03-Supernatural/Fantasy
Fiction	The Parrot	1966	Macabre Stories #1	01-Comic
Fiction	The Peril from the Moon	1951	Wonders of the Spaceways #01	02-Science Fiction
Fiction	The Persian Cavern	1962	Supernatural Series #059	03-Supernatural/Fantasy
Fiction	The Phantom Crusader	1963	Supernatural Series #075	03-Supernatural/Fantasy
Fiction	The Phantom Galleon	1964	Supernatural Series #089	03-Supernatural/Fantasy
Fiction	The Phantom Hand	1958	Supernatural Series #017	03-Supernatural/Fantasy
Fiction	The Phantom of the Goodwins	1958	Supernatural Series #019	03-Supernatural/Fantasy
Fiction	The Phantom Ones	1961	Supernatural Series #048	03-Supernatural/Fantasy
Fiction	The Phantom Schooner	1962	Supernatural Series #057	03-Supernatural/Fantasy
Fiction	The Phantom Wakes	1960	Supernatural Series #031	03-Supernatural/Fantasy
Fiction	The Pipes of Pan	1959	Supernatural Series #028	03-Supernatural/Fantasy
Fiction	The Pirate Who Was Indestructible	1966	Macabre Stories #3	01-Comic
Fiction	The Pirates of the Black Moon	1952	Futuristic Science Stories #07	02-Science Fiction
Fiction	The Planet Seekers	1964	Science Fiction Series #099	02-Science Fiction
Fiction	The Planeteer	1950	Worlds of Fantasy #02	02-Science Fiction
Fiction	The Poltergeist	1959	Supernatural Series #024	03-Supernatural/Fantasy
Fiction	The Power	1966	Spectre Stories #2	01-Comic
Fiction	The Power From Out There	1966	Fantasy stories #4	01-Comic
Fiction	The Problem Ship	1951	Futuristic Science Stories #04	02-Science Fiction
Fiction	The Prodigy	1965	Supernatural Series #099	03-Supernatural/Fantasy
Fiction	The Purple Flower	1951	Wonders of the Spaceways #01	02-Science Fiction
Fiction	The Purple Sun	1953	Wonders of the Spaceways #08	02-Science Fiction
Fiction	The Quest of the Seeker	1958	Science Fiction Series #010	02-Science Fiction
Fiction	The Reincarnate	1955	Supernatural Series #008	03-Supernatural/Fantasy
Fiction	The Reluctant Corpse	1963	Supernatural Series #083	03-Supernatural/Fantasy
Fiction	The Reluctant Corpse	1966	Strange Stories #4	01-Comic
Fiction	The Reluctant Corpse	1966	Supernatural Series #103	03-Supernatural/Fantasy
Fiction	The Resurrected Enemy	1966	Supernatural Series #105	03-Supernatural/Fantasy
Fiction	The Return	1959	Supernatural Series #025	03-Supernatural/Fantasy
Fiction	The Return	1964	Science Fiction Series #101	02-Science Fiction
Fiction	The Return	1966	Strange Stories #5	01-Comic
Fiction	The Return of Albertus	1965	Supernatural Series #095	03-Supernatural/Fantasy
Fiction	The Road to Anywhere	1954	Tales of Tomorrow #11	02-Science Fiction
Fiction	The Robots	1966	Strange Stories #1	01-Comic
Fiction	The Rocket Caper!	1967	The Purple Hood #1	01-Comic
Fiction	The Room That Never Was	1963	Supernatural Series #075	03-Supernatural/Fantasy
Fiction	The Room With the Broken Floor	1962	Supernatural Series #053	03-Supernatural/Fantasy
Fiction	The Saga of the Mighty Midget	1966	Strange Stories #1	01-Comic
Fiction	The Saviour	1954	Tales of Tomorrow #10	02-Science Fiction

Type	Story Name	Date	Series No. /Title	Section
Fiction	The Screaming Skull	1958	Supernatural Series #017	03-Supernatural/Fantasy
Fiction	The Sea Thing	1960	Supernatural Series #034	03-Supernatural/Fantasy
Fiction	The Sealed Sarcophagus	1965	Supernatural Series #101	03-Supernatural/Fantasy
Fiction	The Séance	1958	Supernatural Series #014	03-Supernatural/Fantasy
Fiction	The Secret of Dr. Stark	1961	Supernatural Series #051	03-Supernatural/Fantasy
Fiction	The Secret of Dr. Stark	1966	Strange Stories #5	01-Comic
Fiction	The Secret of the Lake	1960	Supernatural Series #037	03-Supernatural/Fantasy
Fiction	The Secret of the Pyramid	1961	Supernatural Series #049	03-Supernatural/Fantasy
Fiction	The Secret Room	1958	Supernatural Series #017	03-Supernatural/Fantasy
Fiction	The Serpent Ring	1959	Supernatural Series #022	03-Supernatural/Fantasy
Fiction	The Serpent Ring	1966	Strange Stories #3	01-Comic
Fiction	The Seventh Image	1954	Out of this World #1	03-Supernatural/Fantasy
Fiction	The Seventh Image	1960	Supernatural Series #034	03-Supernatural/Fantasy
Fiction	The Shadow Man	1966	Supernatural Series #104	03-Supernatural/Fantasy
Fiction	The Shadow of Terror	1959	Supernatural Series #026	03-Supernatural/Fantasy
Fiction	The Shrouded Abbot	1964	Supernatural Series #089	03-Supernatural/Fantasy
Fiction	The Shrouded Abbot	1966	Strange Stories #2	01-Comic
Fiction	The Silent Fleet	1963	Supernatural Series #069	03-Supernatural/Fantasy
Fiction	The Silent Stranger	1959	Supernatural Series #021	03-Supernatural/Fantasy
Fiction	The Sinister Circle	1960	Supernatural Series #033	03-Supernatural/Fantasy
Fiction	The Sleeper	1966	Macabre Stories #2	01-Comic
Fiction	The Snarling Shadow	1962	Supernatural Series #061	03-Supernatural/Fantasy
Fiction	The Sorcerer's Cave	1957	Supernatural Series #012	03-Supernatural/Fantasy
Fiction	The Sorcerers of Bast	1960	Supernatural Series #031	03-Supernatural/Fantasy
Fiction	The Space Trap	1966	Spectre Stories #3	01-Comic
Fiction	The Space Warp	1966	Strange Stories #1	01-Comic
Fiction	The Spawn of Satan	1958	Supernatural Series #020	03-Supernatural/Fantasy
Fiction	The Spectre of the Tower	1957	Supernatural Series #013	03-Supernatural/Fantasy
Fiction	The Stairway	1954	Out of this World #2	03-Supernatural/Fantasy
Fiction	The Stairway	1960	Supernatural Series #036	03-Supernatural/Fantasy
Fiction	The Star Ship	1951	Tales of Tomorrow #02	02-Science Fiction
Fiction	The Stockman	1963	Supernatural Series #075	03-Supernatural/Fantasy
Fiction	The Stone Crusader	1959	Supernatural Series #021	03-Supernatural/Fantasy
Fiction	The Stone Tablet	1963	Supernatural Series #075	03-Supernatural/Fantasy
Fiction	The Stone Tablets	1966	Fantasy stories #6	01-Comic
Fiction	The Storm Movers	1953	Worlds of Fantasy #11	02-Science Fiction
Fiction	The Strange One	1966	Fantasy stories #1	01-Comic
Fiction	The Strange Ones	1963	Supernatural Series #070	03-Supernatural/Fantasy
Fiction	The Supernaturalist	1955	Supernatural Series #006	03-Supernatural/Fantasy
Fiction	The Swan Mea	1959	Supernatural Series #023	03-Supernatural/Fantasy
Fiction	The Swing of the Pendulum	1963	Supernatural Series #069	03-Supernatural/Fantasy
Fiction	The Sword and the Statue	1964	Supernatural Series #085	03-Supernatural/Fantasy

Type	Story Name	Date	Series No. /Title	Section
Fiction	The Synthetic Ones	1961	Science Fiction Series #052	02-Science Fiction
Fiction	The Tartars	1966	Macabre Stories #1	01-Comic
Fiction	The Thing	1966	Fantasy stories #1	01-Comic
Fiction	The Thing from Beyond the Void	1966	Fantasy stories #2	01-Comic
Fiction	The Thing from Boulter's Cavern	1962	Supernatural Series #067	03-Supernatural/Fantasy
Fiction	The Thing from Sheol	1963	Supernatural Series #081	03-Supernatural/Fantasy
Fiction	The Thing from Sheol	1966	Fantasy stories #5	01-Comic
Fiction	The Thing In the Mist	1967	Supernatural Series #109	03-Supernatural/Fantasy
Fiction	The Things That are Mars	1958	Futuristic Science Stories Vol 2 #16	02-Science Fiction
Fiction	The Thought Machine	1953	Tales of Tomorrow #06	02-Science Fiction
Fiction	The Three Green Sisters	1957	Supernatural Series #010	03-Supernatural/Fantasy
Fiction	The Time Kings	1958	Science Fiction Series #006	02-Science Fiction
Fiction	The Timeless Ones	1963	Supernatural Series #076	03-Supernatural/Fantasy
Fiction	The Tiny World…	1966	Spectre Stories #1	01-Comic
Fiction	The Tragedians	1963	Supernatural Series #077	03-Supernatural/Fantasy
Fiction	The Triple Man	1965	Supernatural Series #096	03-Supernatural/Fantasy
Fiction	The Troll	1964	Supernatural Series #091	03-Supernatural/Fantasy
Fiction	The Tunnel	1963	Supernatural Series #075	03-Supernatural/Fantasy
Fiction	The Tunnel of Fear	1958	Supernatural Series #018	03-Supernatural/Fantasy
Fiction	The Twisted Track	1961	Supernatural Series #049	03-Supernatural/Fantasy
Fiction	The Twisted Track	1966	Fantasy stories #5	01-Comic
Fiction	The Ugly Ones	1955	Supernatural Series #008	03-Supernatural/Fantasy
Fiction	The Ultimate	1958	Science Fiction Series #003	02-Science Fiction
Fiction	The Uncanny Affair at Greycove	1957	Supernatural Series #012	03-Supernatural/Fantasy
Fiction	The Unconfined	1965	Supernatural Series #101	03-Supernatural/Fantasy
Fiction	The Unconfined	1966	Supernatural Series #102	03-Supernatural/Fantasy
Fiction	The Unfinished Chapter	1962	Supernatural Series #061	03-Supernatural/Fantasy
Fiction	The Uninvited	1961	Science Fiction Series #057	02-Science Fiction
Fiction	The Unpossessed	1961	Supernatural Series #042	03-Supernatural/Fantasy
Fiction	The Unpossessed	1978	Weird Fantasy #101	Misc Series -1
Fiction	The Unrealistic Theatre	1959	Supernatural Series #023	03-Supernatural/Fantasy
Fiction	The Unseen	1954	Out of this World #2	03-Supernatural/Fantasy
Fiction	The Unseen	1960	Supernatural Series #036	03-Supernatural/Fantasy
Fiction	The Unseen	1963	Supernatural Series #078	03-Supernatural/Fantasy
Fiction	The Uranium Seekers	1953	The Uranium Seekers	02-Science Fiction
Fiction	The Valley of the Vampire	1958	Supernatural Series #020	03-Supernatural/Fantasy
Fiction	The Vampire	1966	Strange Stories #4	01-Comic
Fiction	The Venus Venture	1961	Science Fiction Series #062	02-Science Fiction
Fiction	The Visitors	1950	Worlds of Fantasy #02	02-Science Fiction
Fiction	The Visitors	1967	Supernatural Series #107	03-Supernatural/Fantasy
Fiction	The Voice	1962	Supernatural Series #059	03-Supernatural/Fantasy
Fiction	The Voice in the Wall	1962	Supernatural Series #065	03-Supernatural/Fantasy

Type	Story Name	Date	Series No. /Title	Section
Fiction	The Waiting World	1958	Science Fiction Series #001	02-Science Fiction
Fiction	The Walker	1963	Supernatural Series #077	03-Supernatural/Fantasy
Fiction	The Walking Dead	1966	Spectre Stories #2	01-Comic
Fiction	The Walking Shadow	1964	Supernatural Series #093	03-Supernatural/Fantasy
Fiction	The Wanderer	1965	Supernatural Series #101	03-Supernatural/Fantasy
Fiction	The Warlock	1964	Supernatural Series #087	03-Supernatural/Fantasy
Fiction	The Warlock	1966	Strange Stories #3	01-Comic
Fiction	The Watching World	1966	Science Fiction Series #118	02-Science Fiction
Fiction	The Web of Cerian	1966	Spectre Stories #1	01-Comic
Fiction	The Weird Lovers	1954	Supernatural Series #004	03-Supernatural/Fantasy
Fiction	The Werewolf	1966	Spectre Stories #3	01-Comic
Fiction	The Whisper of the Wind	1955	Supernatural Series #005	03-Supernatural/Fantasy
Fiction	The Whisperer	1962	Supernatural Series #059	03-Supernatural/Fantasy
Fiction	The Witch of Peronia	1957	Supernatural Series #009	03-Supernatural/Fantasy
Fiction	The Witch?	1966	Fantasy stories #2	01-Comic
Fiction	The World Beyond	1953	Worlds of Fantasy #11	02-Science Fiction
Fiction	The World Makers	1958	Science Fiction Series #003	02-Science Fiction
Fiction	The World of the Sun	1966	Spectre Stories #1	01-Comic
Fiction	The World That Never Was	1963	Science Fiction Series #085	02-Science Fiction
Fiction	The Worm of Venus	1950	Futuristic Science Stories #01	02-Science Fiction
Fiction	The Zegrembi Bracelet	1954	Supernatural Series #004	03-Supernatural/Fantasy
Fiction	The Zombie	1963	Supernatural Series #077	03-Supernatural/Fantasy
Fiction	The Zoologist	1965	Supernatural Series #097	03-Supernatural/Fantasy
Fiction	The Zuku Plant	1966	Strange Stories #1	01-Comic
Fiction	There is No Future	1954	Worlds of Fantasy #12	02-Science Fiction
Fiction	There's No Tomorrow	1952	Worlds of Fantasy #07	02-Science Fiction
Fiction	They Flew by Night	1961	Supernatural Series #043	03-Supernatural/Fantasy
Fiction	They Flew by Night	1966	Strange Stories #5	01-Comic
Fiction	They Fly by Night	1954	Supernatural Series #004	03-Supernatural/Fantasy
Fiction	They Never Came Back	1963	Supernatural Series #068	03-Supernatural/Fantasy
Fiction	Things of the Dark	1954	Supernatural Series #002	03-Supernatural/Fantasy
Fiction	This Second Earth	1957	Science (Fiction) Series #1	02-Science Fiction
Fiction	Threat from Mars	1952	Worlds of Fantasy #06	02-Science Fiction
Fiction	Threat from Space	1952	Tales of Tomorrow #04	02-Science Fiction
Fiction	Through The Barrier	1963	Science Fiction Series #091	02-Science Fiction
Fiction	Time Echo	1959	Science Fiction Series #023	02-Science Fiction
Fiction	Time Out of Mind	1964	Supernatural Series #093	03-Supernatural/Fantasy
Fiction	Time Out of Mind	1966	Spectre Stories #2	01-Comic
Fiction	Time Pit	1953	Futuristic Science Stories #10	02-Science Fiction
Fiction	Time To Die	1954	Out of this World #2	03-Supernatural/Fantasy
Fiction	Time To Die	1960	Supernatural Series #036	03-Supernatural/Fantasy
Fiction	Time Triangle	1953	Futuristic Science Stories #13	02-Science Fiction

Type	Story Name	Date	Series No. /Title	Section
Fiction	Time Trouble	1954	Worlds of Fantasy #13	02-Science Fiction
Fiction	Time Warp	1954	Worlds of Fantasy #13	02-Science Fiction
Fiction	To Suffer a Witch	1962	Supernatural Series #063	03-Supernatural/Fantasy
Fiction	To Tame a Tyrant	1967	Mark Tyme #2	01-Comic
Fiction	Tomorrow is Also a Day	1953	Worlds of Fantasy #10	02-Science Fiction
Fiction	Traitors of the Void	1954	Futuristic Science Stories #14	02-Science Fiction
Fiction	Traveller's Rest	1963	Supernatural Series #083	03-Supernatural/Fantasy
Fiction	Treachery From Venus	1951	Worlds of Fantasy #03	02-Science Fiction
Fiction	Treasure in Space	1950	Futuristic Science Stories #03	02-Science Fiction
Fiction	Trouble in Mind	1965	Supernatural Series #101	03-Supernatural/Fantasy
Fiction	Tunnel of Fear	1966	Fantasy stories #4	01-Comic
Fiction	Twilight Ancestor	1963	Supernatural Series #071	03-Supernatural/Fantasy
Fiction	Twilight Ancestor	1966	Strange Stories #2	01-Comic
Fiction	Twilight Zone	1954	Twilight Zone	02-Science Fiction
Fiction	Twilight Zone	1959	Science Fiction Series #013	02-Science Fiction
Fiction	U.F.O 517	1965	Science Fiction Series #115	02-Science Fiction
Fiction	Ultimate Man	1961	Science Fiction Series #056	02-Science Fiction
Fiction	Uncle Julian's Typewriter	1966	Supernatural Series #105	03-Supernatural/Fantasy
Fiction	Unknown Destiny	1964	Supernatural Series #084	03-Supernatural/Fantasy
Fiction	Unknown Realm	1959	Supernatural Series #021	03-Supernatural/Fantasy
Fiction	Unrecorded Incident	1953	Wonders of the Spaceways #08	02-Science Fiction
Fiction	Uranium 235	1962	Science Fiction Series #067	02-Science Fiction
Fiction	Valley of the Kings	1964	Supernatural Series #085	03-Supernatural/Fantasy
Fiction	Valley of the Kings	1966	Spectre Stories #4	01-Comic
Fiction	Valley of the Shadow	1966	Spectre Stories #5	01-Comic
Fiction	Vampire Castle	1962	Supernatural Series #055	03-Supernatural/Fantasy
Fiction	Vampire's Moon	1964	Supernatural Series #089	03-Supernatural/Fantasy
Fiction	Vandal of the Void	1950	Worlds of Fantasy #01	02-Science Fiction
Fiction	Vault of Terror	1960	Supernatural Series #030	03-Supernatural/Fantasy
Fiction	Veiled Planet	1953	Futuristic Science Stories #11	02-Science Fiction
Fiction	Vengeance From the Past	1964	Supernatural Series #087	03-Supernatural/Fantasy
Fiction	Vengeance of Set	1954	Supernatural Series #001	03-Supernatural/Fantasy
Fiction	Vengeance of Siva	1962	Supernatural Series #060	03-Supernatural/Fantasy
Fiction	Vengeance of the Poltergeist	1962	Supernatural Series #057	03-Supernatural/Fantasy
Fiction	Vengeance of Thor	1962	Supernatural Series #065	03-Supernatural/Fantasy
Fiction	Vengeance of Thor	1966	Spectre Stories #2	01-Comic
Fiction	Vengeance of Trelko	1952	Worlds of Fantasy #05	02-Science Fiction
Fiction	Ventriloquist	1963	Supernatural Series #069	03-Supernatural/Fantasy
Fiction	Vision of the Damned	1965	Supernatural Series #099	03-Supernatural/Fantasy
Fiction	Visiting Celebrity	1954	Futuristic Science Stories #14	02-Science Fiction
Fiction	Voice in the Wall	1966	Fantasy stories #3	01-Comic
Fiction	Voice of the Drum	1955	Supernatural Series #006	03-Supernatural/Fantasy

Type	Story Name	Date	Series No. /Title	Section
Fiction	Voice of the Drum	1966	Strange Stories #2	01-Comic
Fiction	Void Warp	1953	Wonders of the Spaceways #07	02-Science Fiction
Fiction	Voodoo Hell Drums	1961	Supernatural Series #039	03-Supernatural/Fantasy
Fiction	Voodoo Hell Drums	1966	Spectre Stories #4	01-Comic
Fiction	Voodoo Vengeance	1958	Supernatural Series #015	03-Supernatural/Fantasy
Fiction	Voodoo Vengeance	1966	Macabre Stories #5	01-Comic
Fiction	Vultures of the Void	1950	Futuristic Science Stories #02	02-Science Fiction
Fiction	Walk Through Tomorrow	1962	Science Fiction Series #078	02-Science Fiction
Fiction	War Potential	1952	Tales of Tomorrow #05	02-Science Fiction
Fiction	Watchers of the Forest	1958	Supernatural Series #015	03-Supernatural/Fantasy
Fiction	Weird Castle	1966	Fantasy stories #6	01-Comic
Fiction	Weird Plant	1952	Worlds of Fantasy #08	02-Science Fiction
Fiction	We're Human Too	1953	Worlds of Fantasy #09	02-Science Fiction
Fiction	Werewolf at Large	1960	Supernatural Series #037	03-Supernatural/Fantasy
Fiction	Werewolf at Large	1966	Fantasy stories #3	01-Comic
Fiction	When Darkness Falls	1961	Supernatural Series #045	03-Supernatural/Fantasy
Fiction	When The Gods Came	1960	Science Fiction Series #031	02-Science Fiction
Fiction	Whence? Wither?	1960	Supernatural Series #030	03-Supernatural/Fantasy
Fiction	Where Dead Men Dream	1967	Supernatural Series #107	03-Supernatural/Fantasy
Fiction	Whirlwind of Death	1961	Supernatural Series #038	03-Supernatural/Fantasy
Fiction	Whirlwind of Death	1966	Strange Stories #4	01-Comic
Fiction	White Wolf	1959	Supernatural Series #027	03-Supernatural/Fantasy
Fiction	Who?	1960	Science Fiction Series #028	02-Science Fiction
Fiction	Will O' the Wisp	1954	Supernatural Series #003	03-Supernatural/Fantasy
Fiction	Witches Brew	1966	Fantasy stories #6	01-Comic
Fiction	Witch-Water	1957	Supernatural Series #010	03-Supernatural/Fantasy
Fiction	Without a Shadow of a Doubt	1955	Supernatural Series #006	03-Supernatural/Fantasy
Fiction	Wokolo	1962	Supernatural Series #065	03-Supernatural/Fantasy
Fiction	Wolf Man's Vengeance	1961	Supernatural Series #039	03-Supernatural/Fantasy
Fiction	Wolfman's Vengeance	1966	Macabre Stories #5	01-Comic
Fiction	World of Dread	1954	Futuristic Science Stories #14	02-Science Fiction
Fiction	World of Fear	1953	Futuristic Science Stories #12	02-Science Fiction
Fiction	World of the Ancients	1951	Worlds of Fantasy #04	02-Science Fiction
Fiction	World of the Gods	1960	Science Fiction Series #045	02-Science Fiction
Fiction	World of Tomorrow	1954	Futuristic Science Stories #15	02-Science Fiction
Fiction	World of Tomorrow	1963	Science Fiction Series #084	02-Science Fiction
Fiction	Worlds of Fear	1950	Futuristic Science Stories #01	02-Science Fiction
Fiction	Worlds Without End	1952	Futuristic Science Stories #06	02-Science Fiction
Fiction	Wreckers of Space	1952	Worlds of Fantasy #06	02-Science Fiction
Fiction	X-Machine	1962	Science Fiction Series #074	02-Science Fiction
Fiction	Zero Minus	1962	Science Fiction Series #081	02-Science Fiction
Fiction	Zerzuran Plague	1953	Worlds of Fantasy #11	02-Science Fiction

Checklist 1 - Story Titles (Alphabetical)

Type	Story Name	Date	Series No. /Title	Section
Fiction	Zombie	1966	Macabre Stories #4	01-Comic

Checklist 1 - Story Titles (Alphabetical)

Type	Story Name	Date	Series No. /Title	Section
Non-Fiction	Project Mars	1962	Science Series #4	02-Science Fiction
Non-Fiction	Sputnik Into Space	1959	Science Series #1	02-Science Fiction
Non-Fiction	Survival in the Sky	1959	Science Series #2	02-Science Fiction
Non-Fiction	The Unidentified	1960	Science Series #3	02-Science Fiction

Psuedo/(Author)	Story Name	Date	Serie No./ Title	Section
()	Not Produced	1958	Science Fiction Series #002	02-Science Fiction
()	Not Produced	1958	Science Fiction Series #008	02-Science Fiction
()	Not Produced	1967	Supernatural Series #108	03-Supernatural/Fantasy
(A. A. Glynn)	Demon Dimension	1953	Futuristic Science Stories #12	02-Science Fiction
(A. A. Glynn)	Fear World	1953	Tales of Tomorrow #06	02-Science Fiction
(A. A. Glynn)	Mission to the Red Moon	1952	Futuristic Science Stories #08	02-Science Fiction
(A. A. Glynn)	Objective Pluto	1953	Tales of Tomorrow #08	02-Science Fiction
(A. A. Glynn)	Perseus	1952	Futuristic Science Stories #07	02-Science Fiction
(A. A. Glynn)	Plan for Conquest	1963	Science Fiction Series #090	02-Science Fiction
(A. A. Glynn)	Planetoid of Peril	1953	Futuristic Science Stories #11	02-Science Fiction
(A. A. Glynn)	Realm of Danger	1953	Worlds of Fantasy #09	02-Science Fiction
(A. A. Glynn)	Sargasso of Space	1952	Tales of Tomorrow #04	02-Science Fiction
(A. A. Glynn)	Tables Turned	1953	Worlds of Fantasy #10	02-Science Fiction
(A. A. Glynn)	Unrecorded Incident	1953	Wonders of the Spaceways #08	02-Science Fiction
(A. A. Glynn)	The Weird Lovers	1954	Supernatural Series #004	03-Supernatural/Fantasy
(Alfred E. Hind)	Out of the Blue	1952	Worlds of Fantasy #07	02-Science Fiction
(Alfred E. Hind)	Rogue Ship	1953	Worlds of Fantasy #09	02-Science Fiction
(Algis Budrys)	Who?	1960	Science Fiction Series #028	02-Science Fiction
(C. D. Ellis)	World of the Ancients	1951	Worlds of Fantasy #04	02-Science Fiction
(Comic Strip)	4 Dimensional Beam	1966	Macabre Stories #6	01-Comic
(Comic Strip)	A Slip in Time	1966	Fantasy stories #3	01-Comic
(Comic Strip)	Adventure on the High Seas	1966	Strange Stories #1	01-Comic
(Comic Strip)	All in the Mind	1966	Macabre Stories #6	01-Comic
(Comic Strip)	Back From the Dead	1966	Strange Stories #1	01-Comic
(Comic Strip)	Battle of the Giants!	1967	Mark Tyme #1	01-Comic
(Comic Strip)	Before the Beginning	1966	Macabre Stories #5	01-Comic
(Comic Strip)	Bitter Reflection	1966	Macabre Stories #3	01-Comic
(Comic Strip)	Black Abyss	1966	Spectre Stories #5	01-Comic
(Comic Strip)	Call of the Wind	1966	Fantasy stories #2	01-Comic
(Comic Strip)	Candles of Death	1966	Fantasy stories #1	01-Comic
(Comic Strip)	Contract With Satan	1966	Fantasy stories #2	01-Comic
(Comic Strip)	Dark Staircase	1966	Macabre Stories #3	01-Comic
(Comic Strip)	Day of the Beasts	1966	Macabre Stories #2	01-Comic
(Comic Strip)	Dead or Alive?	1966	Spectre Stories #1	01-Comic
(Comic Strip)	Death-Note!	1966	Spectre Stories #5	01-Comic
(Comic Strip)	Deep Danger	1967	The Purple Hood #2	01-Comic

Psuedo/(Author)	Story Name	Date	Serie No./ Title	Section
(Comic Strip)	Desert Fury!	1967	The Purple Hood #1	01-Comic
(Comic Strip)	Destroy the World!	1967	The Purple Hood #2	01-Comic
(Comic Strip)	Dragon's Blood Mountain	1966	Fantasy stories #4	01-Comic
(Comic Strip)	Escape or Die	1967	The Purple Hood #2	01-Comic
(Comic Strip)	Face in the Dark!	1966	Spectre Stories #5	01-Comic
(Comic Strip)	Fight For Life	1967	Mark Tyme #2	01-Comic
(Comic Strip)	Forgotten Country	1966	Fantasy stories #1	01-Comic
(Comic Strip)	Ghost Rider	1966	Spectre Stories #3	01-Comic
(Comic Strip)	Graveyard of the Damned	1966	Fantasy stories #4	01-Comic
(Comic Strip)	Grip of Fear	1966	Macabre Stories #6	01-Comic
(Comic Strip)	Guest of Honour	1966	Macabre Stories #2	01-Comic
(Comic Strip)	Hexere!	1966	Strange Stories #3	01-Comic
(Comic Strip)	House of Despair	1966	Spectre Stories #4	01-Comic
(Comic Strip)	Ice Tomb	1966	Spectre Stories #5	01-Comic
(Comic Strip)	Idol of the Igorot	1966	Fantasy stories #5	01-Comic
(Comic Strip)	In a Glass Darkly	1966	Fantasy stories #3	01-Comic
(Comic Strip)	Island of Fear	1967	Mark Tyme #1	01-Comic
(Comic Strip)	Jaws of Steel	1966	Strange Stories #5	01-Comic
(Comic Strip)	Land of the Living Dead	1966	Spectre Stories #4	01-Comic
(Comic Strip)	Legend of the Lost World	1966	Strange Stories #4	01-Comic
(Comic Strip)	Lord of the Crag	1966	Macabre Stories #6	01-Comic
(Comic Strip)	Menace of the Deep	1966	Fantasy stories #6	01-Comic
(Comic Strip)	Mermaid Reef	1966	Strange Stories #2	01-Comic
(Comic Strip)	Midnight Ghoul	1966	Fantasy stories #1	01-Comic
(Comic Strip)	Moon Wolf!	1966	Macabre Stories #4	01-Comic
(Comic Strip)	Moonlight Island	1966	Spectre Stories #5	01-Comic
(Comic Strip)	Night Cry	1966	Macabre Stories #2	01-Comic
(Comic Strip)	Night of the Ghoul	1966	Spectre Stories #2	01-Comic
(Comic Strip)	Night Walkers	1966	Fantasy stories #6	01-Comic
(Comic Strip)	Nightmare on Ice	1966	Strange Stories #3	01-Comic
(Comic Strip)	Out of the Vault	1966	Spectre Stories #4	01-Comic
(Comic Strip)	Phantom Crusader	1966	Strange Stories #4	01-Comic
(Comic Strip)	Planet of Fear	1967	Mark Tyme #2	01-Comic
(Comic Strip)	Power of the Phantom Genie	1966	Spectre Stories #4	01-Comic
(Comic Strip)	Resting Place	1966	Macabre Stories #2	01-Comic
(Comic Strip)	Sands of Eternity	1966	Macabre Stories #5	01-Comic
(Comic Strip)	Secret of the Pyramid	1966	Fantasy stories #2	01-Comic

Psuedo/(Author)	Story Name	Date	Serie No./ Title	Section
(Comic Strip)	Slave God of the Norsu	1966	Strange Stories #4	01-Comic
(Comic Strip)	Something at the Door	1966	Fantasy stories #6	01-Comic
(Comic Strip)	Stone Age Menace!	1967	Mark Tyme #1	01-Comic
(Comic Strip)	Stone Face	1966	Fantasy stories #5	01-Comic
(Comic Strip)	Strange Country	1966	Macabre Stories #2	01-Comic
(Comic Strip)	Strange Door	1966	Macabre Stories #6	01-Comic
(Comic Strip)	Strange Land	1966	Spectre Stories #3	01-Comic
(Comic Strip)	Suddenly…at Twilight	1966	Macabre Stories #4	01-Comic
(Comic Strip)	The Abbot's Ring	1966	Strange Stories #3	01-Comic
(Comic Strip)	The Avenging Goddess	1966	Fantasy stories #3	01-Comic
(Comic Strip)	The Bow and the Bugle	1966	Macabre Stories #5	01-Comic
(Comic Strip)	The Challenge	1966	Spectre Stories #1	01-Comic
(Comic Strip)	The Coffin	1966	Macabre Stories #1	01-Comic
(Comic Strip)	The Creatures That Came After	1966	Macabre Stories #4	01-Comic
(Comic Strip)	The Crusade That Was Different	1966	Fantasy stories #3	01-Comic
(Comic Strip)	The Dreamer	1966	Macabre Stories #1	01-Comic
(Comic Strip)	The Drud	1966	Strange Stories #2	01-Comic
(Comic Strip)	The Evil One!	1966	Macabre Stories #6	01-Comic
(Comic Strip)	The Family	1966	Spectre Stories #3	01-Comic
(Comic Strip)	The Flaming Sword	1966	Macabre Stories #5	01-Comic
(Comic Strip)	The Fox on the Prowl	1967	The Purple Hood #1	01-Comic
(Comic Strip)	The Ghost	1966	Macabre Stories #1	01-Comic
(Comic Strip)	The Golden Warrior	1966	Macabre Stories #3	01-Comic
(Comic Strip)	The Green Sarcophagus	1966	Fantasy stories #5	01-Comic
(Comic Strip)	The Grimoire	1966	Fantasy stories #4	01-Comic
(Comic Strip)	The Hag	1966	Fantasy stories #5	01-Comic
(Comic Strip)	The Hand of Gehenna	1966	Macabre Stories #4	01-Comic
(Comic Strip)	The Hypnotist	1966	Strange Stories #2	01-Comic
(Comic Strip)	The Isle of the Blessed	1966	Fantasy stories #2	01-Comic
(Comic Strip)	The Joker!	1966	Strange Stories #5	01-Comic
(Comic Strip)	The Juggernaut Who Walked	1966	Macabre Stories #1	01-Comic
(Comic Strip)	The Kraken	1966	Macabre Stories #3	01-Comic
(Comic Strip)	The Loch Ness Terror	1966	Macabre Stories #4	01-Comic
(Comic Strip)	The Man Who Ate Fire	1966	Spectre Stories #2	01-Comic
(Comic Strip)	The Man Who Conquered Time	1966	Strange Stories #3	01-Comic
(Comic Strip)	The Manhattan Warlock	1966	Spectre Stories #3	01-Comic
(Comic Strip)	The Merman of Destruction Bay	1966	Fantasy stories #1	01-Comic

Psuedo/(Author)	Story Name	Date	Serie No./ Title	Section
(Comic Strip)	The Midnight Museum	1966	Macabre Stories #3	01-Comic
(Comic Strip)	The Mountain Thing!	1966	Strange Stories #5	01-Comic
(Comic Strip)	The Nine Green Men	1966	Fantasy stories #4	01-Comic
(Comic Strip)	The Old Man of the Sea	1966	Spectre Stories #1	01-Comic
(Comic Strip)	The Parrot	1966	Macabre Stories #1	01-Comic
(Comic Strip)	The Pirate Who Was Indestructible	1966	Macabre Stories #3	01-Comic
(Comic Strip)	The Power	1966	Spectre Stories #2	01-Comic
(Comic Strip)	The Power From Out There	1966	Fantasy stories #4	01-Comic
(Comic Strip)	The Reluctant Corpse	1966	Strange Stories #4	01-Comic
(Comic Strip)	The Return	1966	Strange Stories #5	01-Comic
(Comic Strip)	The Robots	1966	Strange Stories #1	01-Comic
(Comic Strip)	The Rocket Caper!	1967	The Purple Hood #1	01-Comic
(Comic Strip)	The Saga of the Mighty Midget	1966	Strange Stories #1	01-Comic
(Comic Strip)	The Secret of Dr. Stark	1966	Strange Stories #5	01-Comic
(Comic Strip)	The Serpent Ring	1966	Strange Stories #3	01-Comic
(Comic Strip)	The Shrouded Abbot	1966	Strange Stories #2	01-Comic
(Comic Strip)	The Sleeper	1966	Macabre Stories #2	01-Comic
(Comic Strip)	The Space Trap	1966	Spectre Stories #3	01-Comic
(Comic Strip)	The Space Warp	1966	Strange Stories #1	01-Comic
(Comic Strip)	The Stone Tablets	1966	Fantasy stories #6	01-Comic
(Comic Strip)	The Strange One	1966	Fantasy stories #1	01-Comic
(Comic Strip)	The Tartars	1966	Macabre Stories #1	01-Comic
(Comic Strip)	The Thing	1966	Fantasy stories #1	01-Comic
(Comic Strip)	The Thing from Beyond the Void	1966	Fantasy stories #2	01-Comic
(Comic Strip)	The Thing from Sheol	1966	Fantasy stories #5	01-Comic
(Comic Strip)	The Tiny World...	1966	Spectre Stories #1	01-Comic
(Comic Strip)	The Twisted Track	1966	Fantasy stories #5	01-Comic
(Comic Strip)	The Vampire	1966	Strange Stories #4	01-Comic
(Comic Strip)	The Walking Dead	1966	Spectre Stories #2	01-Comic
(Comic Strip)	The Warlock	1966	Strange Stories #3	01-Comic
(Comic Strip)	The Web of Cerian	1966	Spectre Stories #1	01-Comic
(Comic Strip)	The Werewolf	1966	Spectre Stories #3	01-Comic
(Comic Strip)	The Witch?	1966	Fantasy stories #2	01-Comic
(Comic Strip)	The World of the Sun	1966	Spectre Stories #1	01-Comic
(Comic Strip)	The Zuku Plant	1966	Strange Stories #1	01-Comic
(Comic Strip)	They Flew by Night	1966	Strange Stories #5	01-Comic

Psuedo/(Author)	Story Name	Date	Serie No./ Title	Section
(Comic Strip)	Time Out of Mind	1966	Spectre Stories #2	01-Comic
(Comic Strip)	To Tame a Tyrant	1967	Mark Tyme #2	01-Comic
(Comic Strip)	Tunnel of Fear	1966	Fantasy stories #4	01-Comic
(Comic Strip)	Twilight Ancestor	1966	Strange Stories #2	01-Comic
(Comic Strip)	Valley of the Kings	1966	Spectre Stories #4	01-Comic
(Comic Strip)	Valley of the Shadow	1966	Spectre Stories #5	01-Comic
(Comic Strip)	Vengeance of Thor	1966	Spectre Stories #2	01-Comic
(Comic Strip)	Voice in the Wall	1966	Fantasy stories #3	01-Comic
(Comic Strip)	Voice of the Drum	1966	Strange Stories #2	01-Comic
(Comic Strip)	Voodoo Hell Drums	1966	Spectre Stories #4	01-Comic
(Comic Strip)	Voodoo Vengeance	1966	Macabre Stories #5	01-Comic
(Comic Strip)	Weird Castle	1966	Fantasy stories #6	01-Comic
(Comic Strip)	Werewolf at Large	1966	Fantasy stories #3	01-Comic
(Comic Strip)	Whirlwind of Death	1966	Strange Stories #4	01-Comic
(Comic Strip)	Witches Brew	1966	Fantasy stories #6	01-Comic
(Comic Strip)	Wolfman's Vengeance	1966	Macabre Stories #5	01-Comic
(Comic Strip)	Zombie	1966	Macabre Stories #4	01-Comic
(Frederick T. Foden)	Stanhope's Moon	1950	Futuristic Science Stories #01	02-Science Fiction
(Gerald Evans)	Re-Creation	1951	Futuristic Science Stories #05	02-Science Fiction
(Laurence Sandfield)	Emergency	1953	Worlds of Fantasy #10	02-Science Fiction
(Laurence Sandfield)	Mightier Weapon	1952	Worlds of Fantasy #06	02-Science Fiction
(Leonard G. Fish)	Hell Planet	1951	Tales of Tomorrow #03	02-Science Fiction
(Leonard G. Fish)	The Alien	1951	Futuristic Science Stories #05	02-Science Fiction
(Leslie V. Heald)	Out of the Past	1952	Futuristic Science Stories #06	02-Science Fiction
(Leslie V. Heald)	The Monument	1952	Wonders of the Spaceways #02	02-Science Fiction
(Norman Lazenby)	Gods of Helle	1950	Worlds of Fantasy #01	02-Science Fiction
(Norman Lazenby)	Moons of fear	1951	Worlds of Fantasy #03	02-Science Fiction
(Norman Lazenby)	Nightmare Planet	1950	Futuristic Science Stories #01	02-Science Fiction
(Norman Lazenby)	Plasma Men Bring Death	1950	Futuristic Science Stories #02	02-Science Fiction
(Norman Lazenby)	The Mechans of Muah	1950	Futuristic Science Stories #03	02-Science Fiction
(Paul Charkin)	Light of Mars	1959	Science Fiction Series #012	02-Science Fiction
(Paul Charkin)	The Other Side of Night	1960	Science Fiction Series #024	02-Science Fiction
(Peter J. Ridley)	Rake's Progress	1951	Wonders of the Spaceways #01	02-Science Fiction
(R. Chetwynd-Hayes)	The Man From The Bomb	1959	Science Fiction Series #021	02-Science Fiction
(R. L. Fanthorpe)	Alien From the Stars	1959	Science Fiction Series #015	02-Science Fiction
(R. L. Fanthorpe)	Asteroid Man	1960	Science Fiction Series #035	02-Science Fiction
(R. L. Fanthorpe)	Doomed World	1960	Science Fiction Series #025	02-Science Fiction

Psuedo/(Author)	Story Name	Date	Serie No./ Title	Section
(R. L. Fanthorpe)	Fiends	1959	Science Fiction Series #022	02-Science Fiction
(R. L. Fanthorpe)	Flamemass	1961	Science Fiction Series #049	02-Science Fiction
(R. L. Fanthorpe)	Hand of Doom	1960	Science Fiction Series #044	02-Science Fiction
(R. L. Fanthorpe)	Hyper Space	1959	Science Fiction Series #017	02-Science Fiction
(R. L. Fanthorpe)	Negative Minus	1963	Science Fiction Series #088	02-Science Fiction
(R. L. Fanthorpe)	Neuron World	1965	Science Fiction Series #108	02-Science Fiction
(R. L. Fanthorpe)	Satellite	1960	Science Fiction Series #027	02-Science Fiction
(R. L. Fanthorpe)	Space Fury	1962	Science Fiction Series #077	02-Science Fiction
(R. L. Fanthorpe)	Space-Borne	1959	Science Fiction Series #020	02-Science Fiction
(R. L. Fanthorpe)	The Clipper Ships of Space	1953	Futuristic Science Stories #11	02-Science Fiction
(R. L. Fanthorpe)	The Waiting World	1958	Science Fiction Series #001	02-Science Fiction
(R. L. Fanthorpe)	The Watching World	1966	Science Fiction Series #118	02-Science Fiction
(R. L. Fanthorpe)	And Very Few Get Out	1954	Supernatural Series #002	03-Supernatural/Fantasy
(R. L. Fanthorpe)	Avenging Goddess	1964	Supernatural Series #085	03-Supernatural/Fantasy
(R. L. Fanthorpe)	Bitter Reflection	1965	Supernatural Series #095	03-Supernatural/Fantasy
(R. L. Fanthorpe)	Call of the Werewolf	1958	Supernatural Series #017	03-Supernatural/Fantasy
(R. L. Fanthorpe)	Call of the Wild	1965	Supernatural Series #097	03-Supernatural/Fantasy
(R. L. Fanthorpe)	Chariot of Apollo	1962	Supernatural Series #053	03-Supernatural/Fantasy
(R. L. Fanthorpe)	Curse of the Khan	1966	Supernatural Series #105	03-Supernatural/Fantasy
(R. L. Fanthorpe)	Curse of the Totem	1962	Supernatural Series #065	03-Supernatural/Fantasy
(R. L. Fanthorpe)	Death Has Two Faces	1964	Supernatural Series #087	03-Supernatural/Fantasy
(R. L. Fanthorpe)	Face In the Dark	1961	Supernatural Series #043	03-Supernatural/Fantasy
(R. L. Fanthorpe)	Face of Evil	1960	Supernatural Series #036	03-Supernatural/Fantasy
(R. L. Fanthorpe)	Fingers Of Darkness	1961	Supernatural Series #041	03-Supernatural/Fantasy
(R. L. Fanthorpe)	Graveyard of the Damned	1962	Supernatural Series #059	03-Supernatural/Fantasy
(R. L. Fanthorpe)	Hell Has Wings	1962	Supernatural Series #057	03-Supernatural/Fantasy
(R. L. Fanthorpe)	Invisible Presence	1963	Supernatural Series #081	03-Supernatural/Fantasy
(R. L. Fanthorpe)	Invisible Witness	1958	Supernatural Series #019	03-Supernatural/Fantasy
(R. L. Fanthorpe)	Lilith - Goddess of Night	1963	Supernatural Series #069	03-Supernatural/Fantasy
(R. L. Fanthorpe)	Mermaid Reef	1959	Supernatural Series #023	03-Supernatural/Fantasy
(R. L. Fanthorpe)	Moon Wolf	1963	Supernatural Series #077	03-Supernatural/Fantasy
(R. L. Fanthorpe)	Out of the Darkness	1960	Supernatural Series #035	03-Supernatural/Fantasy
(R. L. Fanthorpe)	Psychic Circle	1963	Supernatural Series #083	03-Supernatural/Fantasy
(R. L. Fanthorpe)	Quest for Atlantis	1959	Supernatural Series #024	03-Supernatural/Fantasy
(R. L. Fanthorpe)	Resurgam	1957	Supernatural Series #012	03-Supernatural/Fantasy
(R. L. Fanthorpe)	Sands of Eternity	1963	Supernatural Series #073	03-Supernatural/Fantasy
(R. L. Fanthorpe)	Secret of the Snows	1957	Supernatural Series #013	03-Supernatural/Fantasy

Psuedo/(Author)	Story Name	Date	Serie No./ Title	Section
(R. L. Fanthorpe)	Sleeping Place	1962	Supernatural Series #067	03-Supernatural/Fantasy
(R. L. Fanthorpe)	Suddenly...at Twilight	1964	Supernatural Series #091	03-Supernatural/Fantasy
(R. L. Fanthorpe)	The Centurion's Vengeance	1961	Supernatural Series #049	03-Supernatural/Fantasy
(R. L. Fanthorpe)	The Creatures from Below	1958	Supernatural Series #016	03-Supernatural/Fantasy
(R. L. Fanthorpe)	The Darker Drink	1962	Supernatural Series #061	03-Supernatural/Fantasy
(R. L. Fanthorpe)	The Death Note	1958	Supernatural Series #020	03-Supernatural/Fantasy
(R. L. Fanthorpe)	The Devil from the Depths	1961	Supernatural Series #047	03-Supernatural/Fantasy
(R. L. Fanthorpe)	The Flight of The Valkyries	1958	Supernatural Series #014	03-Supernatural/Fantasy
(R. L. Fanthorpe)	The Ghost Rider	1959	Supernatural Series #027	03-Supernatural/Fantasy
(R. L. Fanthorpe)	The Ghoul and the Goddess	1964	Supernatural Series #093	03-Supernatural/Fantasy
(R. L. Fanthorpe)	The Golden Chalice	1961	Supernatural Series #050	03-Supernatural/Fantasy
(R. L. Fanthorpe)	The Grip of Fear	1961	Supernatural Series #051	03-Supernatural/Fantasy
(R. L. Fanthorpe)	The Guide and the God	1959	Supernatural Series #025	03-Supernatural/Fantasy
(R. L. Fanthorpe)	The Magician Sleeps	1961	Supernatural Series #039	03-Supernatural/Fantasy
(R. L. Fanthorpe)	The Man Who Could not Die	1960	Supernatural Series #033	03-Supernatural/Fantasy
(R. L. Fanthorpe)	The Mountain Thing	1962	Supernatural Series #055	03-Supernatural/Fantasy
(R. L. Fanthorpe)	The Reluctant Corpse	1966	Supernatural Series #103	03-Supernatural/Fantasy
(R. L. Fanthorpe)	The Sealed Sarcophagus	1965	Supernatural Series #101	03-Supernatural/Fantasy
(R. L. Fanthorpe)	The Shrouded Abbot	1964	Supernatural Series #089	03-Supernatural/Fantasy
(R. L. Fanthorpe)	The Stone Crusader	1959	Supernatural Series #021	03-Supernatural/Fantasy
(R. L. Fanthorpe)	The Triple Man	1965	Supernatural Series #096	03-Supernatural/Fantasy
(R. L. Fanthorpe)	The Unconfined	1966	Supernatural Series #102	03-Supernatural/Fantasy
(R. L. Fanthorpe)	Twilight Ancestor	1963	Supernatural Series #071	03-Supernatural/Fantasy
(R. L. Fanthorpe)	Vision of the Damned	1965	Supernatural Series #099	03-Supernatural/Fantasy
(R. L. Fanthorpe)	Watchers of the Forest	1958	Supernatural Series #015	03-Supernatural/Fantasy
(R. L. Fanthorpe)	Werewolf at Large	1960	Supernatural Series #037	03-Supernatural/Fantasy
(R. L. Fanthorpe)	Whence? Wither?	1960	Supernatural Series #030	03-Supernatural/Fantasy
(R. L. Fanthorpe)	Whirlwind of Death	1961	Supernatural Series #038	03-Supernatural/Fantasy
(Robert A. Wise)	12 To the Moon	1961	Science Fiction Series #059	02-Science Fiction
(Sam Merwin Jr.)	3 Faces of Time	1960	Science Fiction Series #029	02-Science Fiction
(Tom W. Wade)	Assignment in Venus	1952	Wonders of the Spaceways #04	02-Science Fiction
(Tom W. Wade)	Globe of Dread	1953	Tales of Tomorrow #09	02-Science Fiction
(Tom W. Wade)	Integral Menace	1954	Wonders of the Spaceways #09	02-Science Fiction
(Tom W. Wade)	Journey to the Dawn	1952	Worlds of Fantasy #08	02-Science Fiction
(Tom W. Wade)	Minerals From Mars	1952	Futuristic Science Stories #08	02-Science Fiction
(Tom W. Wade)	Mistakes Do Happen	1952	Wonders of the Spaceways #05	02-Science Fiction
(Tom W. Wade)	Pioneers For Saturn	1953	Futuristic Science Stories #09	02-Science Fiction

Psuedo/(Author)	Story Name	Date	Serie No./ Title	Section
(Tom W. Wade)	Sirius Rampant	1952	Futuristic Science Stories #06	02-Science Fiction
(Tom W. Wade)	The Impending Heritage	1952	Worlds of Fantasy #05	02-Science Fiction
(Tom W. Wade)	The Incredible Scourge	1952	Tales of Tomorrow #05	02-Science Fiction
(Tom W. Wade)	The Indigenous Revolt	1953	Futuristic Science Stories #13	02-Science Fiction
(Tom W. Wade)	The Irreparable Sunset	1951	Futuristic Science Stories #05	02-Science Fiction
(Tom W. Wade)	The Minacious Termites	1952	Wonders of the Spaceways #02	02-Science Fiction
(Tom W. Wade)	The Peril from the Moon	1951	Wonders of the Spaceways #01	02-Science Fiction
(Tom W. Wade)	There is No Future	1954	Worlds of Fantasy #12	02-Science Fiction
(Victor Norwood)	Night of the Black Horror	1962	Science Fiction Series #064	02-Science Fiction
(W. H. Fear)	Lunar Flight	1958	Science Fiction Series #007	02-Science Fiction
(W. H. Fear)	Operation Satellite	1958	Science Fiction Series #005	02-Science Fiction
(W. H. Fear)	Return from Space	1958	Science Fiction Series #009	02-Science Fiction
(W. H. Fear)	The Ultimate	1958	Science Fiction Series #003	02-Science Fiction
(W. Shaw)	Quietus	1952	Worlds of Fantasy #07	02-Science Fiction
(W. Shaw)	The Manipulators	1952	Futuristic Science Stories #08	02-Science Fiction
A. J. Merak(John Glasby)	Barrier Unknown	1960	Science Fiction Series #030	02-Science Fiction
A. J. Merak(John Glasby)	Beyond the Rim	1954	Worlds of Fantasy #14	02-Science Fiction
A. J. Merak(John Glasby)	Bifurcation	1953	Tales of Tomorrow #07	02-Science Fiction
A. J. Merak(John Glasby)	Hydrosphere	1960	Science Fiction Series #036	02-Science Fiction
A. J. Merak(John Glasby)	Mischa	1954	Wonders of the Spaceways #09	02-Science Fiction
A. J. Merak(John Glasby)	Moon King	1953	Wonders of the Spaceways #08	02-Science Fiction
A. J. Merak(John Glasby)	Moondust	1952	Futuristic Science Stories #08	02-Science Fiction
A. J. Merak(John Glasby)	No Dawn and No Horizon	1959	Science Fiction Series #016	02-Science Fiction
A. J. Merak(John Glasby)	Planet of Desire	1954	Tales of Tomorrow #11	02-Science Fiction
A. J. Merak(John Glasby)	Shadow of the Atom	1958	Futuristic Science Stories Vol 2 #16	02-Science Fiction
A. J. Merak(John Glasby)	Stowaway	1954	Tales of Tomorrow #10	02-Science Fiction
A. J. Merak(John Glasby)	Such Worlds Are Dangerous	1954	Futuristic Science Stories #15	02-Science Fiction
A. J. Merak(John Glasby)	The Byarkil Eaters	1954	Worlds of Fantasy #13	02-Science Fiction
A. J. Merak(John Glasby)	The Dark Millenium	1959	Science Fiction Series #019	02-Science Fiction
A. J. Merak(John Glasby)	The Golden Hibiscus	1953	Wonders of the Spaceways #06	02-Science Fiction
A. J. Merak(John Glasby)	The Storm Movers	1953	Worlds of Fantasy #11	02-Science Fiction
A. J. Merak(John Glasby)	Veiled Planet	1953	Futuristic Science Stories #11	02-Science Fiction
A. J. Merak(John Glasby)	A Pattern of Evil	1959	Supernatural Series #028	03-Supernatural/Fantasy
A. J. Merak(John Glasby)	A Place of Madness	1954	Out of this World #1	03-Supernatural/Fantasy
A. J. Merak(John Glasby)	A Place of Madness	1960	Supernatural Series #034	03-Supernatural/Fantasy
A. J. Merak(John Glasby)	Dark Conflict	1959	Supernatural Series #029	03-Supernatural/Fantasy
A. J. Merak(John Glasby)	Doorway to Darkness	1959	Supernatural Series #026	03-Supernatural/Fantasy

Psuedo/(Author)	Story Name	Date	Serie No./ Title	Section
A. J. Merak(John Glasby)	Howl at the Moon	1963	Supernatural Series #079	03-Supernatural/Fantasy
A. J. Merak(John Glasby)	Moonbeast	1955	Supernatural Series #007	03-Supernatural/Fantasy
A. J. Merak(John Glasby)	My Name Is Satan	1955	Supernatural Series #005	03-Supernatural/Fantasy
A. J. Merak(John Glasby)	Older Than Death	1967	Supernatural Series #109	03-Supernatural/Fantasy
A. J. Merak(John Glasby)	Something About Spiders	1961	Supernatural Series #045	03-Supernatural/Fantasy
A. J. Merak(John Glasby)	Take the Last Train	1959	Supernatural Series #022	03-Supernatural/Fantasy
A. J. Merak(John Glasby)	That Deep Black Yonder	1967	Supernatural Series #107	03-Supernatural/Fantasy
A. J. Merak(John Glasby)	The Chalice of Circe	1958	Supernatural Series #018	03-Supernatural/Fantasy
A. J. Merak(John Glasby)	The Crystal Skull	1954	Supernatural Series #003	03-Supernatural/Fantasy
A. J. Merak(John Glasby)	The Devil's Canvas	1954	Supernatural Series #001	03-Supernatural/Fantasy
A. J. Merak(John Glasby)	The Haunter	1957	Supernatural Series #011	03-Supernatural/Fantasy
A. J. Merak(John Glasby)	The Lonely Shadows	1962	Supernatural Series #063	03-Supernatural/Fantasy
A. J. Merak(John Glasby)	The Reincarnate	1955	Supernatural Series #008	03-Supernatural/Fantasy
A. J. Merak(John Glasby)	The Sorcerers of Bast	1960	Supernatural Series #031	03-Supernatural/Fantasy
A. J. Merak(John Glasby)	The Supernaturalist	1955	Supernatural Series #006	03-Supernatural/Fantasy
A. J. Merak(John Glasby)	The Three Green Sisters	1957	Supernatural Series #010	03-Supernatural/Fantasy
A. J. Merak(John Glasby)	The Unseen	1954	Out of this World #2	03-Supernatural/Fantasy
A. J. Merak(John Glasby)	The Unseen	1960	Supernatural Series #036	03-Supernatural/Fantasy
A. J. Merak(John Glasby)	Things of the Dark	1954	Supernatural Series #002	03-Supernatural/Fantasy
A. J. Merak(John Glasby)	The Dark Millenium	1978	Science Fiction #102	Misc Series -1
Andrew Sutton(E. C. Tubb)	Snake Vengeance	1957	Supernatural Series #009	03-Supernatural/Fantasy
Anthony Martin(A. A. Glynn)	Backtrack	1953	Worlds of Fantasy #11	02-Science Fiction
Anthony Martin(A. A. Glynn)	Dungeon of Time	1953	Tales of Tomorrow #08	02-Science Fiction
Art Smith(Art Smith)	The Big Slowdown	1954	Tales of Tomorrow #10	02-Science Fiction
B. Ward(Barney Ward)	The Pirates of the Black Moon	1952	Futuristic Science Stories #07	02-Science Fiction
B. Ward(Barney Ward)	Weird Plant	1952	Worlds of Fantasy #08	02-Science Fiction
Basil Sitty(Norman Lazenby)	The Last Ten Men on Earth	1950	Tales of Tomorrow #01	02-Science Fiction
Branson D. Carter(Tom W. Wade)	Anno Mundi	1952	Wonders of the Spaceways #04	02-Science Fiction
Bron Fane(R. L. Fanthorpe)	Conquest	1954	Worlds of Fantasy #14	02-Science Fiction
Bron Fane(R. L. Fanthorpe)	Juggernaut	1960	Science Fiction Series #041	02-Science Fiction
Bron Fane(R. L. Fanthorpe)	Last Man on Earth	1961	Science Fiction Series #046	02-Science Fiction
Bron Fane(R. L. Fanthorpe)	Nemesis	1964	Science Fiction Series #100	02-Science Fiction
Bron Fane(R. L. Fanthorpe)	Rodent Mutation	1961	Science Fiction Series #055	02-Science Fiction
Bron Fane(R. L. Fanthorpe)	Somewhere Out There	1963	Science Fiction Series #092	02-Science Fiction
Bron Fane(R. L. Fanthorpe)	Suspension	1964	Science Fiction Series #102	02-Science Fiction
Bron Fane(R. L. Fanthorpe)	The Intruders	1963	Science Fiction Series #089	02-Science Fiction

Psuedo/(Author)	Story Name	Date	Serie No./ Title	Section
Bron Fane(R. L. Fanthorpe)	U.F.O 517	1965	Science Fiction Series #115	02-Science Fiction
Bron Fane(R. L. Fanthorpe)	Black Abyss	1961	Supernatural Series #043	03-Supernatural/Fantasy
Bron Fane(R. L. Fanthorpe)	Chasm of Time	1962	Supernatural Series #061	03-Supernatural/Fantasy
Bron Fane(R. L. Fanthorpe)	Cry in the Night	1962	Supernatural Series #067	03-Supernatural/Fantasy
Bron Fane(R. L. Fanthorpe)	Curtain Up	1960	Supernatural Series #033	03-Supernatural/Fantasy
Bron Fane(R. L. Fanthorpe)	Forbidden City	1961	Supernatural Series #047	03-Supernatural/Fantasy
Bron Fane(R. L. Fanthorpe)	Forbidden Island	1962	Supernatural Series #053	03-Supernatural/Fantasy
Bron Fane(R. L. Fanthorpe)	Girdle of Fear	1965	Supernatural Series #101	03-Supernatural/Fantasy
Bron Fane(R. L. Fanthorpe)	Jungle of Death	1959	Supernatural Series #027	03-Supernatural/Fantasy
Bron Fane(R. L. Fanthorpe)	Night of the Ghoul	1958	Supernatural Series #019	03-Supernatural/Fantasy
Bron Fane(R. L. Fanthorpe)	Pursuit	1959	Supernatural Series #025	03-Supernatural/Fantasy
Bron Fane(R. L. Fanthorpe)	Repeat Programme	1966	Supernatural Series #103	03-Supernatural/Fantasy
Bron Fane(R. L. Fanthorpe)	Return Ticket	1963	Supernatural Series #073	03-Supernatural/Fantasy
Bron Fane(R. L. Fanthorpe)	Sky Herd	1957	Supernatural Series #013	03-Supernatural/Fantasy
Bron Fane(R. L. Fanthorpe)	Softly By Moonlight	1963	Supernatural Series #080	03-Supernatural/Fantasy
Bron Fane(R. L. Fanthorpe)	Something at the Door	1961	Supernatural Series #051	03-Supernatural/Fantasy
Bron Fane(R. L. Fanthorpe)	Storm God's Fury	1962	Supernatural Series #055	03-Supernatural/Fantasy
Bron Fane(R. L. Fanthorpe)	The Accursed	1965	Supernatural Series #097	03-Supernatural/Fantasy
Bron Fane(R. L. Fanthorpe)	The Crawling Fiend	1960	Supernatural Series #030	03-Supernatural/Fantasy
Bron Fane(R. L. Fanthorpe)	The Deathless Wings	1961	Supernatural Series #039	03-Supernatural/Fantasy
Bron Fane(R. L. Fanthorpe)	The Green Cloud	1959	Supernatural Series #024	03-Supernatural/Fantasy
Bron Fane(R. L. Fanthorpe)	The Green Sarcophagus	1961	Supernatural Series #041	03-Supernatural/Fantasy
Bron Fane(R. L. Fanthorpe)	The Loch Ness Terror	1961	Supernatural Series #038	03-Supernatural/Fantasy
Bron Fane(R. L. Fanthorpe)	The Macabre Ones	1964	Supernatural Series #090	03-Supernatural/Fantasy
Bron Fane(R. L. Fanthorpe)	The Man Who Knew	1963	Supernatural Series #083	03-Supernatural/Fantasy
Bron Fane(R. L. Fanthorpe)	The Man Who Never Smiled	1963	Supernatural Series #071	03-Supernatural/Fantasy
Bron Fane(R. L. Fanthorpe)	The Nine Green Men	1963	Supernatural Series #069	03-Supernatural/Fantasy
Bron Fane(R. L. Fanthorpe)	The Other Line	1959	Supernatural Series #023	03-Supernatural/Fantasy
Bron Fane(R. L. Fanthorpe)	The Persian Cavern	1962	Supernatural Series #059	03-Supernatural/Fantasy
Bron Fane(R. L. Fanthorpe)	The Prodigy	1965	Supernatural Series #099	03-Supernatural/Fantasy
Bron Fane(R. L. Fanthorpe)	The Resurrected Enemy	1966	Supernatural Series #105	03-Supernatural/Fantasy
Bron Fane(R. L. Fanthorpe)	The Room That Never Was	1963	Supernatural Series #075	03-Supernatural/Fantasy
Bron Fane(R. L. Fanthorpe)	The Séance	1958	Supernatural Series #014	03-Supernatural/Fantasy
Bron Fane(R. L. Fanthorpe)	The Secret of the Lake	1960	Supernatural Series #037	03-Supernatural/Fantasy
Bron Fane(R. L. Fanthorpe)	The Secret of the Pyramid	1961	Supernatural Series #049	03-Supernatural/Fantasy
Bron Fane(R. L. Fanthorpe)	The Secret Room	1958	Supernatural Series #017	03-Supernatural/Fantasy
Bron Fane(R. L. Fanthorpe)	The Silent Stranger	1959	Supernatural Series #021	03-Supernatural/Fantasy

Psuedo/(Author)	Story Name	Date	Serie No./ Title	Section
Bron Fane(R. L. Fanthorpe)	The Thing from Sheol	1963	Supernatural Series #081	03-Supernatural/Fantasy
Bron Fane(R. L. Fanthorpe)	The Troll	1964	Supernatural Series #091	03-Supernatural/Fantasy
Bron Fane(R. L. Fanthorpe)	The Valley of the Vampire	1958	Supernatural Series #020	03-Supernatural/Fantasy
Bron Fane(R. L. Fanthorpe)	The Voice in the Wall	1962	Supernatural Series #065	03-Supernatural/Fantasy
Bron Fane(R. L. Fanthorpe)	The Walker	1963	Supernatural Series #077	03-Supernatural/Fantasy
Bron Fane(R. L. Fanthorpe)	The Walking Shadow	1964	Supernatural Series #093	03-Supernatural/Fantasy
Bron Fane(R. L. Fanthorpe)	The Warlock	1964	Supernatural Series #087	03-Supernatural/Fantasy
Bron Fane(R. L. Fanthorpe)	Unknown Destiny	1964	Supernatural Series #084	03-Supernatural/Fantasy
Bron Fane(R. L. Fanthorpe)	Vengeance of the Poltergeist	1962	Supernatural Series #057	03-Supernatural/Fantasy
Bron Fane(R. L. Fanthorpe)	Voodoo Vengeance	1958	Supernatural Series #015	03-Supernatural/Fantasy
Bron Fane(R. L. Fanthorpe)	The Macabre Ones	1973	The Macabre Ones	Misc Series -1
Bruce Fenton(John F. Watt)	Marooned on Venus	1953	Worlds of Fantasy #11	02-Science Fiction
Bruce Fenton(John F. Watt)	Robot Rebels	1954	Worlds of Fantasy #12	02-Science Fiction
Bruce Fenton(John F. Watt)	Satellite Peril	1953	Tales of Tomorrow #08	02-Science Fiction
Bruce Fenton(John F. Watt)	Slaves of Space	1953	Futuristic Science Stories #09	02-Science Fiction
Bruce Fenton(John F. Watt)	Space Menace	1954	Worlds of Fantasy #13	02-Science Fiction
Bruce Fenton(John F. Watt)	The Fugitive	1954	Tales of Tomorrow #10	02-Science Fiction
Bruce Fenton(John F. Watt)	Threat from Space	1952	Tales of Tomorrow #04	02-Science Fiction
Charles Gray(E. C. Tubb)	Museum Piece	1954	Futuristic Science Stories #15	02-Science Fiction
Charles Grey(E. C. Tubb)	Helping Hand	1952	Wonders of the Spaceways #05	02-Science Fiction
Charles Grey(E. C. Tubb)	Honour Bright	1953	Futuristic Science Stories #12	02-Science Fiction
Charles Grey(E. C. Tubb)	Intrigue on Io	1952	Tales of Tomorrow #05	02-Science Fiction
Charles Grey(E. C. Tubb)	There's No Tomorrow	1952	Worlds of Fantasy #07	02-Science Fiction
Charles Grey(E. C. Tubb)	Visiting Celebrity	1954	Futuristic Science Stories #14	02-Science Fiction
Clifford Wallace(Sydney J. Bounds)	Vultures of the Void	1950	Futuristic Science Stories #02	02-Science Fiction
D. A. LeGraeme(Dale Graham)	Adaptability	1952	Worlds of Fantasy #06	02-Science Fiction
D. A. LeGraeme(Dale Graham)	Lambda Point	1953	Wonders of the Spaceways #07	02-Science Fiction
D. A. LeGraeme(Dale Graham)	Safari on Venus	1953	Tales of Tomorrow #06	02-Science Fiction
D. A. LeGraeme(Dale Graham)	The Lighter	1952	Wonders of the Spaceways #03	02-Science Fiction
D. A. LeGraeme(Dale Graham)	Time Warp	1954	Worlds of Fantasy #13	02-Science Fiction
D. F. Jameson(D. F. Jameson)	Jovian Flypaper	1952	Wonders of the Spaceways #04	02-Science Fiction
D. J. Mencet(John F. Watt)	Plan for Conquest	1950	Worlds of Fantasy #02	02-Science Fiction
D. J. Mencet(John F. Watt)	The Death Planet	1951	Worlds of Fantasy #04	02-Science Fiction
D. J. Mencet(John F. Watt)	The Fire Goddess	1950	Futuristic Science Stories #02	02-Science Fiction
D. R. Le Graeme(Dale Graham)	The Expanding Bacillus	1953	Worlds of Fantasy #10	02-Science Fiction
D. R. Mencet(John F. Watt)	Convoy to the Unknown	1951	Wonders of the Spaceways #01	02-Science Fiction

Checklist 2 - Story Title by Author

Psuedo/(Author)	Story Name	Date	Serie No./ Title	Section
D. R. Mencet(John F. Watt)	Lost in Space	1953	Futuristic Science Stories #13	02-Science Fiction
D. R. Mencet(John F. Watt)	Prisoners of Mars	1953	Wonders of the Spaceways #06	02-Science Fiction
D. R. Mencet(John F. Watt)	Scarlet Invaders	1950	Worlds of Fantasy #01	02-Science Fiction
D. R. Mencet(John F. Watt)	Scourge of Space	1952	Wonders of the Spaceways #03	02-Science Fiction
D. R. Mencet(John F. Watt)	Traitors of the Void	1954	Futuristic Science Stories #14	02-Science Fiction
D. R. Mencet(John F. Watt)	World of Fear	1953	Futuristic Science Stories #12	02-Science Fiction
David Campbell(Leonard G. Fish)	Expedition Eternity	1951	Tales of Tomorrow #03	02-Science Fiction
David Campbell(Leonard G. Fish)	The Problem Ship	1951	Futuristic Science Stories #04	02-Science Fiction
Dean Ryan()	Buried in Space	1952	Wonders of the Spaceways #05	02-Science Fiction
Dean Ryan()	Cosmic Conception	1953	Futuristic Science Stories #10	02-Science Fiction
Dean Ryan()	Tomorrow is Also a Day	1953	Worlds of Fantasy #10	02-Science Fiction
Deutero Spartacus(R. L. Fanthorpe)	The Attic	1965	Supernatural Series #099	03-Supernatural/Fantasy
Deutero Spartacus(R. L. Fanthorpe)	The Comedians	1963	Supernatural Series #073	03-Supernatural/Fantasy
Deutero Spartacus(R. L. Fanthorpe)	The Coveters	1962	Supernatural Series #067	03-Supernatural/Fantasy
Deutero Spartacus(R. L. Fanthorpe)	The Stockman	1963	Supernatural Series #075	03-Supernatural/Fantasy
Deutero Spartacus(R. L. Fanthorpe)	The Tragedians	1963	Supernatural Series #077	03-Supernatural/Fantasy
Deutero Spartacus(R. L. Fanthorpe)	The Whisperer	1962	Supernatural Series #059	03-Supernatural/Fantasy
Earl Van Loden(Ernest Lister Hale(Lisle) Willis)	Interplanetary Zoo	1953	Tales of Tomorrow #07	02-Science Fiction
Edward Stokes(John F. Watt)	Spawn of the Void	1951	Futuristic Science Stories #04	02-Science Fiction
Edward Ward(Barney Ward)	Aftermath	1951	Tales of Tomorrow #02	02-Science Fiction
Elton T. Neef(R. L. Fanthorpe)	Stranger In the Shadow	1966	Supernatural Series #103	03-Supernatural/Fantasy
Elton T. Neef(R. L. Fanthorpe)	The Manhattan Warlock	1964	Supernatural Series #091	03-Supernatural/Fantasy
Elton T. Neef(R. L. Fanthorpe)	The Paint Box	1965	Supernatural Series #099	03-Supernatural/Fantasy
Elton T. Neefe(R. L.	Uncle Julian's Typewriter	1966	Supernatural Series #105	03-Supernatural/Fantasy
Eric Lamont()	The Star Ship	1951	Tales of Tomorrow #02	02-Science Fiction
Erle Barton(R. L. Fanthorpe)	The Planet Seekers	1964	Science Fiction Series #099	02-Science Fiction
Erle Barton(R. L. Fanthorpe)	The Zombie	1963	Supernatural Series #077	03-Supernatural/Fantasy
Erle Van Loden(Ernest Lister Hale(Lisle) Willis)	Demons of Daavol	1952	Wonders of the Spaceways #05	02-Science Fiction
Erle Van Loden(Ernest Lister Hale(Lisle) Willis)	Outpost on Orbit 097	1953	Futuristic Science Stories #10	02-Science Fiction
Erle Van Loden(Ernest Lister Hale(Lisle) Willis)	Synthesis of Knowledge	1952	Wonders of the Spaceways #03	02-Science Fiction
Everet Rigby()	Treachery From Venus	1951	Worlds of Fantasy #03	02-Science Fiction

Psuedo/(Author)	Story Name	Date	Serie No./ Title	Section
Frank C. Kneller(John F. Watt)	Danger Out of Space	1953	Tales of Tomorrow #09	02-Science Fiction
Frank C. Kneller(John F. Watt)	Death Ships	1950	Futuristic Science Stories #02	02-Science Fiction
Frank C. Kneller(John F. Watt)	Journey into Tomorrow	1953	Futuristic Science Stories #09	02-Science Fiction
Frank C. Kneller(John F. Watt)	Lunar Revolt	1950	Worlds of Fantasy #02	02-Science Fiction
Frank C. Kneller(John F. Watt)	Lust for conquest	1951	Wonders of the Spaceways #01	02-Science Fiction
Frank C. Kneller(John F. Watt)	Rebels of Venus	1952	Futuristic Science Stories #07	02-Science Fiction
Frank C. Kneller(John F. Watt)	Sillisian Menace	1953	Wonders of the Spaceways #07	02-Science Fiction
Frank C. Kneller(John F. Watt)	Spacemen's Luck	1953	Futuristic Science Stories #12	02-Science Fiction
Frank C. Kneller(John F. Watt)	The Last Chance	1954	Tales of Tomorrow #11	02-Science Fiction
Frank C. Kneller(John F. Watt)	The World Beyond	1953	Worlds of Fantasy #11	02-Science Fiction
Frank C. Kneller(John F. Watt)	Threat from Mars	1952	Worlds of Fantasy #06	02-Science Fiction
Frank C. Kneller(John F. Watt)	Vandal of the Void	1950	Worlds of Fantasy #01	02-Science Fiction
Frank C. Kneller(John F. Watt)	World of Dread	1954	Futuristic Science Stories #14	02-Science Fiction
H. J. Merak(John Glasby)	House of Unreason	1954	Supernatural Series #004	03-Supernatural/Fantasy
H. K. Lennard(John Glasby)	The Cloak of Darkness	1957	Supernatural Series #010	03-Supernatural/Fantasy
Hamilton Donne(John F. Watt)	Fire-Ray Invaders	1951	Tales of Tomorrow #02	02-Science Fiction
Hamilton Donne(John F. Watt)	Martian Terror	1950	Worlds of Fantasy #01	02-Science Fiction
Hamilton Donne(John F. Watt)	One Million Years Ago	1950	Futuristic Science Stories #02	02-Science Fiction
Hamilton Donne(John F. Watt)	Space Pirates	1950	Worlds of Fantasy #02	02-Science Fiction
Hamilton Downe(John F. Watt)	Terror From the Skies	1951	Futuristic Science Stories #04	02-Science Fiction
Ian Bruce(John F. Watt)	Death From the Swamps	1954	Futuristic Science Stories #14	02-Science Fiction
J. Austin Jackson(Norman Lazenby)	Conquerors of the Moon	1950	Worlds of Fantasy #01	02-Science Fiction
J. Austin Jackson(Norman Lazenby)	Worlds of Fear	1950	Futuristic Science Stories #01	02-Science Fiction
J. B. Dexter(John Glasby)	The Time Kings	1958	Science Fiction Series #006	02-Science Fiction
J. J. Hansby(John Glasby)	Mr Pilkington's Ghost	1957	Supernatural Series #010	03-Supernatural/Fantasy
J. J. Hansby(John Glasby)	The Creature in the Depths	1959	Supernatural Series #028	03-Supernatural/Fantasy
J. J. Hansby(John Glasby)	The Night-Comer	1967	Supernatural Series #109	03-Supernatural/Fantasy
J. J. Hansby(John Glasby)	The Tunnel of Fear	1958	Supernatural Series #018	03-Supernatural/Fantasy
J. J. Hansby(John Glasby)	The Visitors	1967	Supernatural Series #107	03-Supernatural/Fantasy
J. J. Hansley(John Glasby)	The Crimson Evil	1959	Supernatural Series #026	03-Supernatural/Fantasy
J. L. Powers(John Glasby)	Black Abyss	1960	Science Fiction Series #032	02-Science Fiction
Jack Lawson(Jack Lawson)	Space Patrol	1951	Futuristic Science Stories #05	02-Science Fiction
James Elton(John F. Watt)	Perilous Expedition	1951	Worlds of Fantasy #04	02-Science Fiction
James Elton(W. H. Fear)	The Quest of the Seeker	1958	Science Fiction Series #010	02-Science Fiction
James Robertson(John F. Watt)	Space Warning	1953	Wonders of the Spaceways #06	02-Science Fiction
James Ross(Sydney J. Bounds)	Invaders From the Stars	1950	Tales of Tomorrow #01	02-Science Fiction

Psuedo/(Author)	Story Name	Date	Serie No./ Title	Section
James S. Stanton/ Edward Richards(E. C. Tubb)	The Devil's Dictionary	1957	Supernatural Series #009	03-Supernatural/Fantasy
James Stanfield(Tom W. Wade)	The Encompassed Globe	1951	Tales of Tomorrow #03	02-Science Fiction
James Williams(Tom W. Wade)	Objective Venus	1958	Science Fiction Series #004	02-Science Fiction
Jerome Strickland(Lionel Wright)	The Legacy	1952	Futuristic Science Stories #06	02-Science Fiction
John Adams(John Glasby)	When The Gods Came	1960	Science Fiction Series #031	02-Science Fiction
John C. Maxwell(John Glasby)	The World Makers	1958	Science Fiction Series #003	02-Science Fiction
John Crawford(John Glasby)	Dark Legion	1967	Supernatural Series #106	03-Supernatural/Fantasy
John E. Muller()	In The Beginning	1962	Science Fiction Series #076	02-Science Fiction
John E. Muller(A. A. Glynn)	Search the Dark Stars	1961	Science Fiction Series #048	02-Science Fiction
John E. Muller(John Glasby)	Alien	1961	Science Fiction Series #061	02-Science Fiction
John E. Muller(John Glasby)	Day of the Beasts	1961	Science Fiction Series #051	02-Science Fiction
John E. Muller(John Glasby)	Edge of Eternity	1962	Science Fiction Series #065	02-Science Fiction
John E. Muller(John Glasby)	Night of The Big Fire	1962	Science Fiction Series #075	02-Science Fiction
John E. Muller(John Glasby)	Space Void	1960	Science Fiction Series #034	02-Science Fiction
John E. Muller(John Glasby)	The Unpossessed	1961	Supernatural Series #042	03-Supernatural/Fantasy
John E. Muller(John Glasby)	The Unpossessed	1978	Weird Fantasy #101	Misc Series -1
John E. Muller(R. L. Fanthorpe)	A 1000 Years On	1961	Science Fiction Series #050	02-Science Fiction
John E. Muller(R. L. Fanthorpe)	Beyond the Void	1965	Science Fiction Series #112	02-Science Fiction
John E. Muller(R. L. Fanthorpe)	Beyond Time	1962	Science Fiction Series #071	02-Science Fiction
John E. Muller(R. L. Fanthorpe)	Crimson Planet	1961	Science Fiction Series #060	02-Science Fiction
John E. Muller(R. L. Fanthorpe)	Dark Continuum	1964	Science Fiction Series #104	02-Science Fiction
John E. Muller(R. L. Fanthorpe)	Forbidden Planet	1961	Science Fiction Series #063	02-Science Fiction
John E. Muller(R. L. Fanthorpe)	Infinity Machine	1962	Science Fiction Series #072	02-Science Fiction
John E. Muller(R. L. Fanthorpe)	Mark of The Beast	1964	Science Fiction Series #105	02-Science Fiction
John E. Muller(R. L. Fanthorpe)	Micro Infinity	1962	Science Fiction Series #070	02-Science Fiction
John E. Muller(R. L. Fanthorpe)	Negative Ones	1965	Science Fiction Series #109	02-Science Fiction
John E. Muller(R. L. Fanthorpe)	Orbit One	1962	Science Fiction Series #069	02-Science Fiction
John E. Muller(R. L. Fanthorpe)	Perilous Galaxy	1962	Science Fiction Series #066	02-Science Fiction
John E. Muller(R. L. Fanthorpe)	Phenomena X	1966	Science Fiction Series #116	02-Science Fiction
John E. Muller(R. L. Fanthorpe)	Reactor Xk9	1963	Science Fiction Series #096	02-Science Fiction
John E. Muller(R. L. Fanthorpe)	Special Mission	1963	Science Fiction Series #097	02-Science Fiction
John E. Muller(R. L. Fanthorpe)	Survival Project	1966	Science Fiction Series #117	02-Science Fiction
John E. Muller(R. L. Fanthorpe)	The Day the World Died	1962	Science Fiction Series #073	02-Science Fiction
John E. Muller(R. L. Fanthorpe)	The Man From Beyond	1965	Science Fiction Series #111	02-Science Fiction
John E. Muller(R. L. Fanthorpe)	The Man Who Conquered Time	1962	Science Fiction Series #068	02-Science Fiction
John E. Muller(R. L. Fanthorpe)	The Mind Makers	1961	Science Fiction Series #058	02-Science Fiction

Checklist 2 - Story Title by Author

Psuedo/(Author)	Story Name	Date	Serie No./ Title	Section
John E. Muller(R. L. Fanthorpe)	The Uninvited	1961	Science Fiction Series #057	02-Science Fiction
John E. Muller(R. L. Fanthorpe)	The Venus Venture	1961	Science Fiction Series #062	02-Science Fiction
John E. Muller(R. L. Fanthorpe)	Ultimate Man	1961	Science Fiction Series #056	02-Science Fiction
John E. Muller(R. L. Fanthorpe)	Uranium 235	1962	Science Fiction Series #067	02-Science Fiction
John E. Muller(R. L. Fanthorpe)	X-Machine	1962	Science Fiction Series #074	02-Science Fiction
John E. Muller(R. L. Fanthorpe)	Out of the Night	1965	Supernatural Series #100	03-Supernatural/Fantasy
John E. Muller(R. L. Fanthorpe)	Return of Zeus	1962	Supernatural Series #052	03-Supernatural/Fantasy
John E. Muller(R. L. Fanthorpe)	Spectre of the Darkness	1965	Supernatural Series #098	03-Supernatural/Fantasy
John E. Muller(R. L. Fanthorpe)	The Exorcists	1965	Supernatural Series #094	03-Supernatural/Fantasy
John E. Muller(R. L. Fanthorpe)	The Eye of Karnack	1962	Supernatural Series #056	03-Supernatural/Fantasy
John E. Muller(R. L. Fanthorpe)	Vengeance of Siva	1962	Supernatural Series #060	03-Supernatural/Fantasy
John Ellis(John F. Watt)	Forgotten World	1951	Tales of Tomorrow #03	02-Science Fiction
John Evans()	Dangerous Moon	1950	Tales of Tomorrow #01	02-Science Fiction
John F. Manders(Laurence Sandfield)	Colonist	1952	Worlds of Fantasy #06	02-Science Fiction
John Mason(E. C. Tubb)	The Ancient Alchemist	1957	Supernatural Series #009	03-Supernatural/Fantasy
John Morton(John Glasby)	The Sea Thing	1960	Supernatural Series #034	03-Supernatural/Fantasy
John Poole()	Station Neptune	1951	Futuristic Science Stories #05	02-Science Fiction
John R. Martin(Tom W. Wade)	Last Throw From Ganymede	1952	Futuristic Science Stories #08	02-Science Fiction
John Raymond(R. L. Fanthorpe)	The Incredulist	1954	Supernatural Series #002	03-Supernatural/Fantasy
John Renolds()	Black Pirate	1951	Tales of Tomorrow #02	02-Science Fiction
John Robertson(John F. Watt)	Satellite in Space	1954	Wonders of the Spaceways #09	02-Science Fiction
John Robertson(John F. Watt)	The Final Threat	1954	Wonders of the Spaceways #10	02-Science Fiction
John Robertson(John F. Watt)	The Green Cloud	1951	Wonders of the Spaceways #01	02-Science Fiction
John Robertson(John F. Watt)	The Purple Sun	1953	Wonders of the Spaceways #08	02-Science Fiction
John Sloan(Tom W. Wade)	The Elder Race	1951	Worlds of Fantasy #03	02-Science Fiction
John Toucan(William Henry Fleming Bird)	Genesis	1954	Worlds of Fantasy #13	02-Science Fiction
John Toucan(William Henry Fleming Bird)	Point in Time	1952	Wonders of the Spaceways #05	02-Science Fiction
John Toucan(William Henry Fleming Bird)	Repercussions	1953	Tales of Tomorrow #08	02-Science Fiction
John Toucan(William Henry Fleming Bird)	War Potential	1952	Tales of Tomorrow #05	02-Science Fiction
Karl Ziegfried(John F. Watt)	Beyond the Galaxy	1953	Beyond The Galaxy	02-Science Fiction
Karl Ziegfried(John Glasby)	Dark Centauri	1954	Dark Centauri	02-Science Fiction
Karl Ziegfried(John Glasby)	The Uranium Seekers	1953	The Uranium Seekers	02-Science Fiction
Karl Ziegfried(R. L. Fanthorpe)	Android	1962	Science Fiction Series #079	02-Science Fiction
Karl Ziegfried(R. L. Fanthorpe)	Atomic Nemesis	1962	Science Fiction Series #080	02-Science Fiction

Psuedo/(Author)	Story Name	Date	Serie No./ Title	Section
Karl Ziegfried(R. L. Fanthorpe)	Barrier 346	1965	Science Fiction Series #113	02-Science Fiction
Karl Ziegfried(R. L. Fanthorpe)	Escape To Infinity	1963	Science Fiction Series #082	02-Science Fiction
Karl Ziegfried(R. L. Fanthorpe)	Girl From Tomorrow	1965	Science Fiction Series #114	02-Science Fiction
Karl Ziegfried(R. L. Fanthorpe)	No Way Back	1964	Science Fiction Series #107	02-Science Fiction
Karl Ziegfried(R. L. Fanthorpe)	Projection Infinity	1964	Science Fiction Series #103	02-Science Fiction
Karl Ziegfried(R. L. Fanthorpe)	Radar Alert	1963	Science Fiction Series #083	02-Science Fiction
Karl Ziegfried(R. L. Fanthorpe)	The World That Never Was	1963	Science Fiction Series #085	02-Science Fiction
Karl Ziegfried(R. L. Fanthorpe)	Walk Through Tomorrow	1962	Science Fiction Series #078	02-Science Fiction
Karl Ziegfried(R. L. Fanthorpe)	World of Tomorrow	1963	Science Fiction Series #084	02-Science Fiction
Karl Ziegfried(R. L. Fanthorpe)	Zero Minus	1962	Science Fiction Series #081	02-Science Fiction
Karl Ziegfried(R. L. Fanthorpe)	Gods of Darkness	1962	Supernatural Series #064	03-Supernatural/Fantasy
Karl Ziegfried(Tom W. Wade)	Chaos In Arcturus	1953	Chaos In Arcturus	02-Science Fiction
Karl Ziegfried(Tom W. Wade)	Chariot Into Time	1953	Chariot Into Time	02-Science Fiction
Kenneth Boyce(John F. Watt)	Robot Threat	1953	Wonders of the Spaceways #06	02-Science Fiction
Kenneth Boyea(John F. Watt)	No Tomorrow	1954	Futuristic Science Stories #14	02-Science Fiction
Kenneth Boyea(John F. Watt)	Project Survival	1953	Tales of Tomorrow #08	02-Science Fiction
Kenneth Boyea(John F. Watt)	Renegades of the Void	1954	Wonders of the Spaceways #10	02-Science Fiction
Kenneth Boyea(John F. Watt)	Riddle of the Robots	1954	Worlds of Fantasy #12	02-Science Fiction
Kenneth Boyea(John F. Watt)	The Lethal Mist	1954	Tales of Tomorrow #11	02-Science Fiction
L. C. Powers(E. C. Tubb)	The Witch of Peronia	1957	Supernatural Series #009	03-Supernatural/Fantasy
L. P. Kenton(R. L. Fanthorpe)	Destination Moon	1959	Science Fiction Series #014	02-Science Fiction
L. S. Johnson(Tom W. Wade)	Struggle For Calisto	1952	Wonders of the Spaceways #02	02-Science Fiction
L. T. Bronson(E. C. Tubb)	First Effort	1952	Worlds of Fantasy #07	02-Science Fiction
Lan Wright(Lionel Wright)	Heritage	1952	Futuristic Science Stories #06	02-Science Fiction
Lan Wright(Lionel Wright)	No Moon Tonight	1953	Tales of Tomorrow #09	02-Science Fiction
Lan Wright(Lionel Wright)	The Long Trek	1953	Futuristic Science Stories #13	02-Science Fiction
Lan Wright(Lionel Wright)	We're Human Too	1953	Worlds of Fantasy #09	02-Science Fiction
Lawrence Smith(Sydney J. Bounds)	The Outlaw of Space	1950	Worlds of Fantasy #02	02-Science Fiction
Lee Barton(R. L. Fanthorpe)	Corporal Death	1966	Supernatural Series #103	03-Supernatural/Fantasy
Lee Barton(R. L. Fanthorpe)	Dark Staircase	1964	Supernatural Series #085	03-Supernatural/Fantasy
Lee Barton(R. L. Fanthorpe)	The Phantom Galleon	1964	Supernatural Series #089	03-Supernatural/Fantasy
Lee Barton(R. L. Fanthorpe)	The Return of Albertus	1965	Supernatural Series #095	03-Supernatural/Fantasy
Lee Barton(R. L. Fanthorpe)	The Shadow Man	1966	Supernatural Series #104	03-Supernatural/Fantasy
Lee Barton(R. L. Fanthorpe)	The Unseen	1963	Supernatural Series #078	03-Supernatural/Fantasy
Lee Barton(R. L. Fanthorpe)	Time Out of Mind	1964	Supernatural Series #093	03-Supernatural/Fantasy
Lee Barton(R. L. Fanthorpe)	Vengeance From the Past	1964	Supernatural Series #087	03-Supernatural/Fantasy

Psuedo/(Author)	Story Name	Date	Serie No./ Title	Section
Leo Brett(Harry Mansfield)	The Clubmen	1963	Supernatural Series #083	03-Supernatural/Fantasy
Leo Brett(Harry Mansfield)	The Golem	1965	Supernatural Series #095	03-Supernatural/Fantasy
Leo Brett(Harry Mansfield)	The Grip of Time Unending	1963	Supernatural Series #077	03-Supernatural/Fantasy
Leo Brett(R. L. Fanthorpe)	Exit Humanity	1960	Science Fiction Series #040	02-Science Fiction
Leo Brett(R. L. Fanthorpe)	Faceless Planet	1961	Science Fiction Series #047	02-Science Fiction
Leo Brett(R. L. Fanthorpe)	March of The Robots	1961	Science Fiction Series #053	02-Science Fiction
Leo Brett(R. L. Fanthorpe)	Mind Force	1961	Science Fiction Series #054	02-Science Fiction
Leo Brett(R. L. Fanthorpe)	Power Sphere	1963	Science Fiction Series #095	02-Science Fiction
Leo Brett(R. L. Fanthorpe)	The Alien Ones	1963	Science Fiction Series #094	02-Science Fiction
Leo Brett(R. L. Fanthorpe)	The Microscopic Ones	1960	Science Fiction Series #043	02-Science Fiction
Leo Brett(R. L. Fanthorpe)	Before the Beginning	1961	Supernatural Series #041	03-Supernatural/Fantasy
Leo Brett(R. L. Fanthorpe)	Black Infinity	1961	Supernatural Series #044	03-Supernatural/Fantasy
Leo Brett(R. L. Fanthorpe)	Contact with Satan	1961	Supernatural Series #049	03-Supernatural/Fantasy
Leo Brett(R. L. Fanthorpe)	Face In the Night	1962	Supernatural Series #058	03-Supernatural/Fantasy
Leo Brett(R. L. Fanthorpe)	Fly, Witch, Fly	1962	Supernatural Series #053	03-Supernatural/Fantasy
Leo Brett(R. L. Fanthorpe)	From Realms Beyond	1960	Supernatural Series #037	03-Supernatural/Fantasy
Leo Brett(R. L. Fanthorpe)	From Realms Beyond	1963	Supernatural Series #074	03-Supernatural/Fantasy
Leo Brett(R. L. Fanthorpe)	House of Despair	1963	Supernatural Series #073	03-Supernatural/Fantasy
Leo Brett(R. L. Fanthorpe)	I've Been Here Before	1957	Supernatural Series #012	03-Supernatural/Fantasy
Leo Brett(R. L. Fanthorpe)	Land of the Living Dead	1961	Supernatural Series #039	03-Supernatural/Fantasy
Leo Brett(R. L. Fanthorpe)	Moonlight Island	1962	Supernatural Series #055	03-Supernatural/Fantasy
Leo Brett(R. L. Fanthorpe)	Mustapha	1961	Supernatural Series #051	03-Supernatural/Fantasy
Leo Brett(R. L. Fanthorpe)	Nightmare	1962	Supernatural Series #054	03-Supernatural/Fantasy
Leo Brett(R. L. Fanthorpe)	Rusalka and the Vodyanol	1961	Supernatural Series #047	03-Supernatural/Fantasy
Leo Brett(R. L. Fanthorpe)	Temple of Quetzalcoatl	1962	Supernatural Series #059	03-Supernatural/Fantasy
Leo Brett(R. L. Fanthorpe)	The Bevelled Casket	1962	Supernatural Series #061	03-Supernatural/Fantasy
Leo Brett(R. L. Fanthorpe)	The Carnival Horror	1961	Supernatural Series #038	03-Supernatural/Fantasy
Leo Brett(R. L. Fanthorpe)	The Drud	1959	Supernatural Series #024	03-Supernatural/Fantasy
Leo Brett(R. L. Fanthorpe)	The Effigy	1958	Supernatural Series #016	03-Supernatural/Fantasy
Leo Brett(R. L. Fanthorpe)	The Forbidden	1963	Supernatural Series #072	03-Supernatural/Fantasy
Leo Brett(R. L. Fanthorpe)	The Frozen Tomb	1962	Supernatural Series #067	03-Supernatural/Fantasy
Leo Brett(R. L. Fanthorpe)	The Gliding Wraith	1963	Supernatural Series #071	03-Supernatural/Fantasy
Leo Brett(R. L. Fanthorpe)	The Immortals	1962	Supernatural Series #062	03-Supernatural/Fantasy
Leo Brett(R. L. Fanthorpe)	The Kraken	1958	Supernatural Series #019	03-Supernatural/Fantasy
Leo Brett(R. L. Fanthorpe)	The Lamia	1959	Supernatural Series #021	03-Supernatural/Fantasy
Leo Brett(R. L. Fanthorpe)	The Midnight Museum	1960	Supernatural Series #033	03-Supernatural/Fantasy
Leo Brett(R. L. Fanthorpe)	The Phantom Crusader	1963	Supernatural Series #075	03-Supernatural/Fantasy

Psuedo/(Author)	Story Name	Date	Serie No./ Title	Section
Leo Brett(R. L. Fanthorpe)	The Phantom Schooner	1962	Supernatural Series #057	03-Supernatural/Fantasy
Leo Brett(R. L. Fanthorpe)	The Return	1959	Supernatural Series #025	03-Supernatural/Fantasy
Leo Brett(R. L. Fanthorpe)	The Silent Fleet	1963	Supernatural Series #069	03-Supernatural/Fantasy
Leo Brett(R. L. Fanthorpe)	The Spawn of Satan	1958	Supernatural Series #020	03-Supernatural/Fantasy
Leo Brett(R. L. Fanthorpe)	The Unrealistic Theatre	1959	Supernatural Series #023	03-Supernatural/Fantasy
Leo Brett(R. L. Fanthorpe)	They Flew by Night	1961	Supernatural Series #043	03-Supernatural/Fantasy
Leo Brett(R. L. Fanthorpe)	They Never Came Back	1963	Supernatural Series #068	03-Supernatural/Fantasy
Leo Brett(R. L. Fanthorpe)	Vengeance of Thor	1962	Supernatural Series #065	03-Supernatural/Fantasy
Leo Brett(R. L. Fanthorpe)	White Wolf	1959	Supernatural Series #027	03-Supernatural/Fantasy
Lionel Roberts(R. L. Fanthorpe)	Cyclops In the Sky	1960	Science Fiction Series #026	02-Science Fiction
Lionel Roberts(R. L. Fanthorpe)	Dawn of the Mutants	1959	Science Fiction Series #018	02-Science Fiction
Lionel Roberts(R. L. Fanthorpe)	Discovery	1952	Futuristic Science Stories #07	02-Science Fiction
Lionel Roberts(R. L. Fanthorpe)	Last Command	1953	Worlds of Fantasy #10	02-Science Fiction
Lionel Roberts(R. L. Fanthorpe)	Marauders of the Void	1954	Wonders of the Spaceways #10	02-Science Fiction
Lionel Roberts(R. L. Fanthorpe)	Martian Bonanza	1954	Worlds of Fantasy #12	02-Science Fiction
Lionel Roberts(R. L. Fanthorpe)	Raw Material	1953	Futuristic Science Stories #11	02-Science Fiction
Lionel Roberts(R. L. Fanthorpe)	The Face of X	1960	Science Fiction Series #039	02-Science Fiction
Lionel Roberts(R. L. Fanthorpe)	The In-World	1960	Science Fiction Series #037	02-Science Fiction
Lionel Roberts(R. L. Fanthorpe)	The Synthetic Ones	1961	Science Fiction Series #052	02-Science Fiction
Lionel Roberts(R. L. Fanthorpe)	Time Echo	1959	Science Fiction Series #023	02-Science Fiction
Lionel Roberts(R. L. Fanthorpe)	Time Triangle	1953	Futuristic Science Stories #13	02-Science Fiction
Lionel Roberts(R. L. Fanthorpe)	Vengeance of Trelko	1952	Worlds of Fantasy #05	02-Science Fiction
Lionel Roberts(R. L. Fanthorpe)	Worlds Without End	1952	Futuristic Science Stories #06	02-Science Fiction
Lionel Roberts(R. L. Fanthorpe)	Flame Goddess	1961	Supernatural Series #046	03-Supernatural/Fantasy
Lionel Roberts(R. L. Fanthorpe)	Gestalt	1959	Supernatural Series #027	03-Supernatural/Fantasy
Lionel Roberts(R. L. Fanthorpe)	Guardians of the Tomb	1958	Supernatural Series #016	03-Supernatural/Fantasy
Lionel Roberts(R. L. Fanthorpe)	Out of the Vault	1958	Supernatural Series #015	03-Supernatural/Fantasy
Lionel Roberts(R. L. Fanthorpe)	Sinister Stranger	1958	Supernatural Series #020	03-Supernatural/Fantasy
Lionel Roberts(R. L. Fanthorpe)	The Dancing Wraiths	1958	Supernatural Series #017	03-Supernatural/Fantasy
Lionel Roberts(R. L. Fanthorpe)	The Golden Warrior	1958	Supernatural Series #019	03-Supernatural/Fantasy
Lionel Roberts(R. L. Fanthorpe)	The Hypnotist	1959	Supernatural Series #024	03-Supernatural/Fantasy
Lionel Roberts(R. L. Fanthorpe)	The Last Valkyrie	1961	Supernatural Series #040	03-Supernatural/Fantasy
Lionel Roberts(R. L. Fanthorpe)	The Old House	1958	Supernatural Series #014	03-Supernatural/Fantasy
Lionel Roberts(R. L. Fanthorpe)	The Spectre of the Tower	1957	Supernatural Series #013	03-Supernatural/Fantasy
Lionel Roberts(R. L. Fanthorpe)	The Swan Mea	1959	Supernatural Series #023	03-Supernatural/Fantasy
Lionel Roberts(R. L. Fanthorpe)	The Uncanny Affair at Greycove	1957	Supernatural Series #012	03-Supernatural/Fantasy
Lionel Roberts(R. L. Fanthorpe)	Unknown Realm	1959	Supernatural Series #021	03-Supernatural/Fantasy

Psuedo/(Author)	Story Name	Date	Serie No./ Title	Section
Lionel Roberts(R. L. Fanthorpe)	Vault of Terror	1960	Supernatural Series #030	03-Supernatural/Fantasy
M. B. Stone()	Beast Men of Mars	1951	Futuristic Science Stories #04	02-Science Fiction
Mack James(John F. Watt)	Suicide Mission	1952	Tales of Tomorrow #04	02-Science Fiction
Mack James(John F. Watt)	Wreckers of Space	1952	Worlds of Fantasy #06	02-Science Fiction
Mack Jones(John F. Watt)	Alien Threat	1954	Tales of Tomorrow #10	02-Science Fiction
Martin Gulliver(Norman Lazenby)	The Worm of Venus	1950	Futuristic Science Stories #01	02-Science Fiction
Martin L. Baker(Sydney J. Bounds)	The Planeteer	1950	Worlds of Fantasy #02	02-Science Fiction
Max Chartair(John Glasby)	Chronolel	1954	Wonders of the Spaceways #09	02-Science Fiction
Max Chartair(John Glasby)	Edge of Darkness	1954	Worlds of Fantasy #14	02-Science Fiction
Max Chartair(John Glasby)	Paradise Planet	1954	Worlds of Fantasy #13	02-Science Fiction
Max Chartair(John Glasby)	Point of No Return	1953	Tales of Tomorrow #06	02-Science Fiction
Max Chartair(John Glasby)	Point of No Return	1959	Science Fiction Series #013	02-Science Fiction
Max Chartair(John Glasby)	Star's End	1953	Wonders of the Spaceways #08	02-Science Fiction
Max Chartair(John Glasby)	The Road to Anywhere	1954	Tales of Tomorrow #11	02-Science Fiction
Max Chartair(John Glasby)	The Saviour	1954	Tales of Tomorrow #10	02-Science Fiction
Max Chartair(John Glasby)	A little Devil Dancing	1954	Out of this World #2	03-Supernatural/Fantasy
Max Chartair(John Glasby)	A little Devil Dancing	1960	Supernatural Series #036	03-Supernatural/Fantasy
Max Chartair(John Glasby)	Dust	1967	Supernatural Series #107	03-Supernatural/Fantasy
Max Chartair(John Glasby)	Ebb Tide	1959	Supernatural Series #026	03-Supernatural/Fantasy
Max Chartair(John Glasby)	Frog	1954	Supernatural Series #002	03-Supernatural/Fantasy
Max Chartair(John Glasby)	Haunt of the Vampire	1954	Supernatural Series #003	03-Supernatural/Fantasy
Max Chartair(John Glasby)	Lord of the Necromancers	1957	Supernatural Series #011	03-Supernatural/Fantasy
Max Chartair(John Glasby)	Lurani	1955	Supernatural Series #005	03-Supernatural/Fantasy
Max Chartair(John Glasby)	Mask of Asmodeus	1955	Supernatural Series #007	03-Supernatural/Fantasy
Max Chartair(John Glasby)	Mythos	1961	Supernatural Series #045	03-Supernatural/Fantasy
Max Chartair(John Glasby)	Nightmare on Ice	1963	Supernatural Series #079	03-Supernatural/Fantasy
Max Chartair(John Glasby)	The Beckoning Shade	1962	Supernatural Series #063	03-Supernatural/Fantasy
Max Chartair(John Glasby)	The Cloak of Darkness	1954	Supernatural Series #001	03-Supernatural/Fantasy
Max Chartair(John Glasby)	The Devil at My Elbow	1954	Out of this World #1	03-Supernatural/Fantasy
Max Chartair(John Glasby)	The Devil at My Elbow	1960	Supernatural Series #034	03-Supernatural/Fantasy
Max Chartair(John Glasby)	The Lady Labyrinth	1959	Supernatural Series #028	03-Supernatural/Fantasy
Max Chartair(John Glasby)	The Phantom Wakes	1960	Supernatural Series #031	03-Supernatural/Fantasy
Max Chartair(John Glasby)	The Serpent Ring	1959	Supernatural Series #022	03-Supernatural/Fantasy
Max Chartair(John Glasby)	The Thing In the Mist	1967	Supernatural Series #109	03-Supernatural/Fantasy
Max Chartair(John Glasby)	The Ugly Ones	1955	Supernatural Series #008	03-Supernatural/Fantasy
Max Chartair(John Glasby)	The Zegrembi Bracelet	1954	Supernatural Series #004	03-Supernatural/Fantasy

Psuedo/(Author)	Story Name	Date	Serie No./ Title	Section
Max Chartair(John Glasby)	Witch-Water	1957	Supernatural Series #010	03-Supernatural/Fantasy
Max Chartair(John Glasby)	Without a Shadow of a Doubt	1955	Supernatural Series #006	03-Supernatural/Fantasy
Meryl St. John Montague(Laurence Sandfield)	Mission Venus	1953	Wonders of the Spaceways #07	02-Science Fiction
Michael Hamilton(John Glasby)	Computer insane	1954	Tales of Tomorrow #11	02-Science Fiction
Michael Hamilton(John Glasby)	Pyramid Problem	1958	Futuristic Science Stories Vol 2 #16	02-Science Fiction
Michael Hamilton(John Glasby)	The Laughter of Space	1954	Wonders of the Spaceways #09	02-Science Fiction
Michael Hamilton(John Glasby)	Time Pit	1953	Futuristic Science Stories #10	02-Science Fiction
Michael Hamilton(John Glasby)	Zerzuran Plague	1953	Worlds of Fantasy #11	02-Science Fiction
Michael Hamilton(John Glasby)	A Place of Meeting	1955	Supernatural Series #008	03-Supernatural/Fantasy
Michael Hamilton(John Glasby)	And Midnight Falls	1962	Supernatural Series #063	03-Supernatural/Fantasy
Michael Hamilton(John Glasby)	Angel of the Bottomless Pit	1954	Out of this World #1	03-Supernatural/Fantasy
Michael Hamilton(John Glasby)	Angel of the Bottomless Pit	1960	Supernatural Series #034	03-Supernatural/Fantasy
Michael Hamilton(John Glasby)	Coven of Thirteen	1954	Out of this World #2	03-Supernatural/Fantasy
Michael Hamilton(John Glasby)	Coven of Thirteen	1960	Supernatural Series #036	03-Supernatural/Fantasy
Michael Hamilton(John Glasby)	Hexerei	1959	Supernatural Series #022	03-Supernatural/Fantasy
Michael Hamilton(John Glasby)	Never Look Behind You	1960	Supernatural Series #031	03-Supernatural/Fantasy
Michael Hamilton(John Glasby)	Solitude	1963	Supernatural Series #079	03-Supernatural/Fantasy
Michael Hamilton(John Glasby)	Somewhere in the Moonlight	1955	Supernatural Series #005	03-Supernatural/Fantasy
Michael Hamilton(John Glasby)	The Crystal Fear	1955	Supernatural Series #007	03-Supernatural/Fantasy
Michael Hamilton(John Glasby)	The Dark Possessed	1959	Supernatural Series #026	03-Supernatural/Fantasy
Michael Hamilton(John Glasby)	The Haunting of Charles Quintain	1967	Supernatural Series #109	03-Supernatural/Fantasy
Michael Hamilton(John Glasby)	The Hungry Ones	1958	Supernatural Series #018	03-Supernatural/Fantasy
Michael Hamilton(John Glasby)	The Keeper of Dark Point	1967	Supernatural Series #107	03-Supernatural/Fantasy
Michael Hamilton(John Glasby)	The Midnight Walkers	1957	Supernatural Series #010	03-Supernatural/Fantasy
Michael Hamilton(John Glasby)	The Night Creatures	1957	Supernatural Series #011	03-Supernatural/Fantasy
Michael Hamilton(John Glasby)	The Other Séance	1954	Supernatural Series #003	03-Supernatural/Fantasy
Michael Hamilton(John Glasby)	The Pipes of Pan	1959	Supernatural Series #028	03-Supernatural/Fantasy
Michael Hamilton(John Glasby)	Vengeance of Set	1954	Supernatural Series #001	03-Supernatural/Fantasy
Michael Hamilton(John Glasby)	Voice of the Drum	1955	Supernatural Series #006	03-Supernatural/Fantasy
Michael Hamilton(John Glasby)	When Darkness Falls	1961	Supernatural Series #045	03-Supernatural/Fantasy
Murray Leinster(Will F. Jenkins)	The Brain Stealers	1960	Science Fiction Series #033	02-Science Fiction
Neil Balfort(R. L. Fanthorpe)	The Laird	1964	Supernatural Series #093	03-Supernatural/Fantasy
Neil Balfort(R. L. Fanthorpe)	Trouble in Mind	1965	Supernatural Series #101	03-Supernatural/Fantasy
Neil J. Spalding(John F. Watt)	Martian Outcast	1952	Wonders of the Spaceways #03	02-Science Fiction
Neil J. Spaulding(John F. Watt)	Last Survivor	1954	Worlds of Fantasy #12	02-Science Fiction
Neil Thanet(R. L. Fanthorpe)	Beyond the Veil	1964	Supernatural Series #086	03-Supernatural/Fantasy

Psuedo/(Author)	Story Name	Date	Serie No./ Title	Section
Neil Thanet(R. L. Fanthorpe)	Old Man of the Snow	1963	Supernatural Series #077	03-Supernatural/Fantasy
Neil Thanet(R. L. Fanthorpe)	Return of the Hag	1963	Supernatural Series #081	03-Supernatural/Fantasy
Neil Thanet(R. L. Fanthorpe)	The Man Who Came Back	1964	Supernatural Series #088	03-Supernatural/Fantasy
Neil Thanet(R. L. Fanthorpe)	The Stone Tablet	1963	Supernatural Series #075	03-Supernatural/Fantasy
Neil Thanet(R. L. Fanthorpe)	The Man Who Came Back	1974	The Man Who Came Back	Unverified - 1
Nicky Shelly(Comic Strip)	Power Mad	1966	Macabre Stories #1	01-Comic
Noel Bartram(Noel Boston)	Bump in the Night	1960	Supernatural Series #037	03-Supernatural/Fantasy
Noel Bartram(Noel Boston)	The Brass Tombstone	1961	Supernatural Series #051	03-Supernatural/Fantasy
Noel Bertram(Noel Boston)	Right Through My Hair	1960	Supernatural Series #030	03-Supernatural/Fantasy
Noel Bertram(Noel Boston)	Scraping the Barrel	1962	Supernatural Series #061	03-Supernatural/Fantasy
Noel Bertram(Noel Boston)	The Audit Chamber	1960	Supernatural Series #033	03-Supernatural/Fantasy
Noel Bertram(Noel Boston)	The Barrier	1962	Supernatural Series #057	03-Supernatural/Fantasy
Noel Bertram(Noel Boston)	The Bellarmine Jars	1961	Supernatural Series #041	03-Supernatural/Fantasy
Noel Bertram(Noel Boston)	The Face at the Window	1961	Supernatural Series #043	03-Supernatural/Fantasy
Noel Bertram(Noel Boston)	The Half Legs	1961	Supernatural Series #049	03-Supernatural/Fantasy
Noel Bertram(Noel Boston)	The North Cloister	1962	Supernatural Series #053	03-Supernatural/Fantasy
Oben Lerteth(R. L. Fanthorpe)	Lord of the Black Valley	1964	Supernatural Series #087	03-Supernatural/Fantasy
Oben Lerteth(R. L. Fanthorpe)	Lord of the Crags	1966	Supernatural Series #105	03-Supernatural/Fantasy
Oben Lerteth(R. L. Fanthorpe)	Reading Room	1965	Supernatural Series #099	03-Supernatural/Fantasy
Oben Lerteth(R. L. Fanthorpe)	The Border Raider	1965	Supernatural Series #097	03-Supernatural/Fantasy
Olaf Trent(R. L. Fanthorpe)	Roman Twilight	1963	Supernatural Series #083	03-Supernatural/Fantasy
Olaf Trent(R. L. Fanthorpe)	The Tunnel	1963	Supernatural Series #075	03-Supernatural/Fantasy
Olaf Trent(R. L. Fanthorpe)	Valley of the Kings	1964	Supernatural Series #085	03-Supernatural/Fantasy
Othello Baron(R. L. Fanthorpe)	The Bow and the Bugle	1964	Supernatural Series #091	03-Supernatural/Fantasy
Othello Baron(R. L. Fanthorpe)	The Unconfined	1965	Supernatural Series #101	03-Supernatural/Fantasy
P. L. Manning(John Glasby)	The Destroyers	1958	Science Fiction Series #011	02-Science Fiction
Paul Hammond(Sydney J. Bounds)	Exiles in Time	1950	Tales of Tomorrow #01	02-Science Fiction
Pel Torro(Harry Mansfield)	The Zoologist	1965	Supernatural Series #097	03-Supernatural/Fantasy
Pel Torro(R. L. Fanthorpe)	Force 97X	1965	Science Fiction Series #110	02-Science Fiction
Pel Torro(R. L. Fanthorpe)	Formula 29X	1963	Science Fiction Series #087	02-Science Fiction
Pel Torro(R. L. Fanthorpe)	Frozen Planet	1960	Science Fiction Series #042	02-Science Fiction
Pel Torro(R. L. Fanthorpe)	Galaxy 666	1963	Science Fiction Series #086	02-Science Fiction
Pel Torro(R. L. Fanthorpe)	Space No Barrier	1964	Science Fiction Series #106	02-Science Fiction
Pel Torro(R. L. Fanthorpe)	The Green Hell of Venus	1954	Futuristic Science Stories #15	02-Science Fiction
Pel Torro(R. L. Fanthorpe)	The Last Astronaut	1963	Science Fiction Series #093	02-Science Fiction
Pel Torro(R. L. Fanthorpe)	The Return	1964	Science Fiction Series #101	02-Science Fiction

Psuedo/(Author)	Story Name	Date	Serie No./ Title	Section
Pel Torro(R. L. Fanthorpe)	Through The Barrier	1963	Science Fiction Series #091	02-Science Fiction
Pel Torro(R. L. Fanthorpe)	World of the Gods	1960	Science Fiction Series #045	02-Science Fiction
Pel Torro(R. L. Fanthorpe)	Black River Mill	1958	Supernatural Series #015	03-Supernatural/Fantasy
Pel Torro(R. L. Fanthorpe)	Charlatan	1959	Supernatural Series #025	03-Supernatural/Fantasy
Pel Torro(R. L. Fanthorpe)	Fang	1957	Supernatural Series #012	03-Supernatural/Fantasy
Pel Torro(R. L. Fanthorpe)	Fangs in the Night	1963	Supernatural Series #071	03-Supernatural/Fantasy
Pel Torro(R. L. Fanthorpe)	Footprints in the Sand	1963	Supernatural Series #075	03-Supernatural/Fantasy
Pel Torro(R. L. Fanthorpe)	Graven in the Rock	1961	Supernatural Series #047	03-Supernatural/Fantasy
Pel Torro(R. L. Fanthorpe)	Last Bus to Llangery	1958	Supernatural Series #016	03-Supernatural/Fantasy
Pel Torro(R. L. Fanthorpe)	Legion of the Lost	1962	Supernatural Series #066	03-Supernatural/Fantasy
Pel Torro(R. L. Fanthorpe)	The Black Hound	1957	Supernatural Series #013	03-Supernatural/Fantasy
Pel Torro(R. L. Fanthorpe)	The Creature	1958	Supernatural Series #014	03-Supernatural/Fantasy
Pel Torro(R. L. Fanthorpe)	The Face of Fear	1963	Supernatural Series #082	03-Supernatural/Fantasy
Pel Torro(R. L. Fanthorpe)	The Face of Stone	1961	Supernatural Series #038	03-Supernatural/Fantasy
Pel Torro(R. L. Fanthorpe)	The Friendly Stranger	1963	Supernatural Series #073	03-Supernatural/Fantasy
Pel Torro(R. L. Fanthorpe)	The Frozen Claw	1962	Supernatural Series #057	03-Supernatural/Fantasy
Pel Torro(R. L. Fanthorpe)	The Lake Thing	1964	Supernatural Series #093	03-Supernatural/Fantasy
Pel Torro(R. L. Fanthorpe)	The Other Driver	1958	Supernatural Series #020	03-Supernatural/Fantasy
Pel Torro(R. L. Fanthorpe)	The Phantom Ones	1961	Supernatural Series #048	03-Supernatural/Fantasy
Pel Torro(R. L. Fanthorpe)	The Poltergeist	1959	Supernatural Series #024	03-Supernatural/Fantasy
Pel Torro(R. L. Fanthorpe)	The Room With the Broken Floor	1962	Supernatural Series #053	03-Supernatural/Fantasy
Pel Torro(R. L. Fanthorpe)	The Screaming Skull	1958	Supernatural Series #017	03-Supernatural/Fantasy
Pel Torro(R. L. Fanthorpe)	The Secret of Dr. Stark	1961	Supernatural Series #051	03-Supernatural/Fantasy
Pel Torro(R. L. Fanthorpe)	The Strange Ones	1963	Supernatural Series #070	03-Supernatural/Fantasy
Pel Torro(R. L. Fanthorpe)	The Thing from Boulter's Cavern	1962	Supernatural Series #067	03-Supernatural/Fantasy
Pel Torro(R. L. Fanthorpe)	The Timeless Ones	1963	Supernatural Series #076	03-Supernatural/Fantasy
Pel Torro(R. L. Fanthorpe)	The Twisted Track	1961	Supernatural Series #049	03-Supernatural/Fantasy
Pel Torro(R. L. Fanthorpe)	The Unfinished Chapter	1962	Supernatural Series #061	03-Supernatural/Fantasy
Pel Torro(R. L. Fanthorpe)	The Voice	1962	Supernatural Series #059	03-Supernatural/Fantasy
Pel Torro(R. L. Fanthorpe)	Vampire Castle	1962	Supernatural Series #055	03-Supernatural/Fantasy
Pel Torro(R. L. Fanthorpe)	Ventriloquist	1963	Supernatural Series #069	03-Supernatural/Fantasy
Pel Torro(R. L. Fanthorpe)	Wokolo	1962	Supernatural Series #065	03-Supernatural/Fantasy
Pel Torro(R. L. Fanthorpe)	Wolf Man's Vengeance	1961	Supernatural Series #039	03-Supernatural/Fantasy
Peter Laynham(John Glasby)	The Things That are Mars	1958	Futuristic Science Stories Vol 2 #16	02-Science Fiction
Peter Laynham(John Glasby)	Dark Kith and Kin	1958	Supernatural Series #018	03-Supernatural/Fantasy
Peter Laynham(John Glasby)	In the Midst of Night	1963	Supernatural Series #079	03-Supernatural/Fantasy

Psuedo/(Author)	Story Name	Date	Serie No./ Title	Section
Peter Laynham(John Glasby)	Refugee	1961	Supernatural Series #045	03-Supernatural/Fantasy
Peter Laynham(John Glasby)	Something Old	1960	Supernatural Series #031	03-Supernatural/Fantasy
Peter Laynham(John Glasby)	Somewhere the Devil Hides	1959	Supernatural Series #022	03-Supernatural/Fantasy
Peter Laynham(John Glasby)	The Dark Time	1967	Supernatural Series #109	03-Supernatural/Fantasy
Peter Laynham(John Glasby)	The Lonely Things	1957	Supernatural Series #011	03-Supernatural/Fantasy
Peter Laynham(John Glasby)	To Suffer a Witch	1962	Supernatural Series #063	03-Supernatural/Fantasy
Peter Laynham(John Glasby)	Where Dead Men Dream	1967	Supernatural Series #107	03-Supernatural/Fantasy
Peter O'Flinn(R. L. Fanthorpe)	Chimney Piece	1966	Supernatural Series #105	03-Supernatural/Fantasy
Peter O'Flinn(R. L. Fanthorpe)	Forgotten Country	1963	Supernatural Series #081	03-Supernatural/Fantasy
Peter O'Flinn(R. L. Fanthorpe)	Land of the Green Shadows	1963	Supernatural Series #083	03-Supernatural/Fantasy
Peter O'Flinn(R. L. Fanthorpe)	Return of the Banshee	1964	Supernatural Series #089	03-Supernatural/Fantasy
Peter O'Flynn(R. L. Fanthorpe)	Isles of the Blessed	1965	Supernatural Series #097	03-Supernatural/Fantasy
Peter O'Flynn(R. L. Fanthorpe)	The Wanderer	1965	Supernatural Series #101	03-Supernatural/Fantasy
Phil Nobel(R. L. Fanthorpe)	Hand From Gehanna	1964	Supernatural Series #091	03-Supernatural/Fantasy
Phil Noble(Harry Mansfield)	I'll Never Leave You	1964	Supernatural Series #089	03-Supernatural/Fantasy
Phil Noble(Harry Mansfield)	The Chinese Lustre Vase	1964	Supernatural Series #087	03-Supernatural/Fantasy
Phil Noble(R. L. Fanthorpe)	Blurred Horizon	1963	Supernatural Series #077	03-Supernatural/Fantasy
R. Brothwell(R. Brothwell)	Agent of Earth	1952	Worlds of Fantasy #05	02-Science Fiction
R. Brothwell(R. Brothwell)	Power Politics	1953	Futuristic Science Stories #09	02-Science Fiction
R. Brothwell(R. Brothwell)	Space Trader	1951	Futuristic Science Stories #04	02-Science Fiction
R. Brothwell(R. Brothwell)	The Isolationists	1952	Wonders of the Spaceways #02	02-Science Fiction
R. C. Kerwood()	Machine-Men of Avaion	1952	Wonders of the Spaceways #04	02-Science Fiction
R. G. Lomax(Tom W. Wade)	The Menace of the Discoids	1952	Wonders of the Spaceways #03	02-Science Fiction
R. J. Norton()	Soldiers of Space	1951	Tales of Tomorrow #02	02-Science Fiction
R. L. Bowers(John Glasby)	This Second Earth	1957	Science (Fiction) Series #1	02-Science Fiction
Randall Conway(John Glasby)	The Aphesian Riddle	1954	Futuristic Science Stories #15	02-Science Fiction
Randall Conway(John Glasby)	The City	1953	Tales of Tomorrow #07	02-Science Fiction
Randall Conway(John Glasby)	The Entropists	1958	Futuristic Science Stories Vol 2 #16	02-Science Fiction
Randall Conway(John Glasby)	Time Trouble	1954	Worlds of Fantasy #13	02-Science Fiction
Randall Conway(John Glasby)	A Place of Shadows	1963	Supernatural Series #079	03-Supernatural/Fantasy
Randall Conway(John Glasby)	Body And Soul	1967	Supernatural Series #107	03-Supernatural/Fantasy
Randall Conway(John Glasby)	Dark Conquest	1962	Supernatural Series #063	03-Supernatural/Fantasy
Randall Conway(John Glasby)	Dark of the Dawn	1959	Supernatural Series #028	03-Supernatural/Fantasy
Randall Conway(John Glasby)	Hunter's Moon	1954	Supernatural Series #002	03-Supernatural/Fantasy
Randall Conway(John Glasby)	It Came by Appointment	1957	Supernatural Series #011	03-Supernatural/Fantasy
Randall Conway(John Glasby)	Nightmare	1957	Supernatural Series #010	03-Supernatural/Fantasy
Randall Conway(John Glasby)	Not Without Sorcery	1961	Supernatural Series #045	03-Supernatural/Fantasy

Psuedo/(Author)	Story Name	Date	Serie No./ Title	Section
Randall Conway(John Glasby)	Out of The Shadows	1959	Supernatural Series #022	03-Supernatural/Fantasy
Randall Conway(John Glasby)	Something About Gargoyles	1958	Supernatural Series #018	03-Supernatural/Fantasy
Randall Conway(John Glasby)	Strange Company	1960	Supernatural Series #031	03-Supernatural/Fantasy
Randall Conway(John Glasby)	The Black Mirror	1967	Supernatural Series #109	03-Supernatural/Fantasy
Randall Conway(John Glasby)	The Gods of Fear	1954	Supernatural Series #001	03-Supernatural/Fantasy
Randall Conway(John Glasby)	The Hungry Gods	1955	Supernatural Series #007	03-Supernatural/Fantasy
Randall Conway(John Glasby)	The Hungry House	1955	Supernatural Series #006	03-Supernatural/Fantasy
Randall Conway(John Glasby)	The Man Who Lost Thursday	1955	Supernatural Series #008	03-Supernatural/Fantasy
Randall Conway(John Glasby)	The Seventh Image	1954	Out of this World #1	03-Supernatural/Fantasy
Randall Conway(John Glasby)	The Seventh Image	1960	Supernatural Series #034	03-Supernatural/Fantasy
Randall Conway(John Glasby)	The Shadow of Terror	1959	Supernatural Series #026	03-Supernatural/Fantasy
Randall Conway(John Glasby)	The Whisper of the Wind	1955	Supernatural Series #005	03-Supernatural/Fantasy
Randall Conway(John Glasby)	They Fly by Night	1954	Supernatural Series #004	03-Supernatural/Fantasy
Randall Conway(John Glasby)	Time To Die	1954	Out of this World #2	03-Supernatural/Fantasy
Randall Conway(John Glasby)	Time To Die	1960	Supernatural Series #036	03-Supernatural/Fantasy
Randall Conway(John Glasby)	Will O' the Wisp	1954	Supernatural Series #003	03-Supernatural/Fantasy
Ray Cosmic(John Glasby)	A Matter of Concealment	1953	Tales of Tomorrow #09	02-Science Fiction
Ray Cosmic(John Glasby)	Allomorph	1953	Wonders of the Spaceways #08	02-Science Fiction
Ray Cosmic(John Glasby)	Final Answer	1958	Futuristic Science Stories Vol 2 #16	02-Science Fiction
Ray Cosmic(John Glasby)	Ghost Moon	1952	Worlds of Fantasy #07	02-Science Fiction
Ray Cosmic(John Glasby)	Void Warp	1953	Wonders of the Spaceways #07	02-Science Fiction
Ray Cosmic(John Glasby)	World of Tomorrow	1954	Futuristic Science Stories #15	02-Science Fiction
Ray Cosmic(John Glasby)	Lorelei	1955	Supernatural Series #006	03-Supernatural/Fantasy
Ray Cosmic(John Glasby)	Lycanthrope	1954	Supernatural Series #001	03-Supernatural/Fantasy
Ray Cosmic(John Glasby)	Shadow Over Endor	1955	Supernatural Series #007	03-Supernatural/Fantasy
Ray Cosmic(John Glasby)	Something from the Sea	1954	Supernatural Series #003	03-Supernatural/Fantasy
Ray Cosmic(John Glasby)	The Chair	1954	Supernatural Series #004	03-Supernatural/Fantasy
Ray Cosmic(John Glasby)	The Dark Ones	1955	Supernatural Series #005	03-Supernatural/Fantasy
Ray Cosmic(John Glasby)	The Golden Scarab	1955	Supernatural Series #008	03-Supernatural/Fantasy
Ray Cosmic(John Glasby)	The Nightmare Road	1954	Out of this World #1	03-Supernatural/Fantasy
Ray Cosmic(John Glasby)	The Nightmare Road	1960	Supernatural Series #034	03-Supernatural/Fantasy
Ray Cosmic(John Glasby)	The Stairway	1954	Out of this World #2	03-Supernatural/Fantasy
Ray Cosmic(John Glasby)	The Stairway	1960	Supernatural Series #036	03-Supernatural/Fantasy
Ray Mason(John F. Watt)	Captives of Vesta	1954	Wonders of the Spaceways #10	02-Science Fiction
Ray Mason(John F. Watt)	Death From the Swamps	1952	Worlds of Fantasy #06	02-Science Fiction
Ray Mason(John F. Watt)	Doomed World	1951	Worlds of Fantasy #04	02-Science Fiction
Ray Mason(John F. Watt)	Martian Terror	1952	Worlds of Fantasy #08	02-Science Fiction

Psuedo/(Author)	Story Name	Date	Serie No./ Title	Section
Ray Mason(John F. Watt)	Slave Ships	1952	Tales of Tomorrow #04	02-Science Fiction
Ray Mason(John F. Watt)	Spawn of Space	1953	Wonders of the Spaceways #07	02-Science Fiction
Ray Mason(John F. Watt)	The Devil's Weed	1953	Futuristic Science Stories #13	02-Science Fiction
Ray Mason(John F. Watt)	The Green Ray	1950	Futuristic Science Stories #01	02-Science Fiction
Ray Mason(John F. Watt)	The Thought Machine	1953	Tales of Tomorrow #06	02-Science Fiction
Raymond L. Burton(E. C. Tubb)	The Dolmen	1957	Supernatural Series #009	03-Supernatural/Fantasy
Raymond Leroyd(Tom W. Wade)	The Aquatic Piracy	1952	Worlds of Fantasy #05	02-Science Fiction
Rene Rolant(Harry Mansfield)	Shadow of Fear	1965	Supernatural Series #099	03-Supernatural/Fantasy
Rene Rolant(R. L. Fanthorpe)	Au Pair	1966	Supernatural Series #103	03-Supernatural/Fantasy
Rene Rolant(R. L. Fanthorpe)	The Reluctant Corpse	1963	Supernatural Series #083	03-Supernatural/Fantasy
Rene Rolant(R. L. Fanthorpe)	Vampire's Moon	1964	Supernatural Series #089	03-Supernatural/Fantasy
Robert D. Ennis(E. C. Tubb)	The Artist's Model	1957	Supernatural Series #009	03-Supernatural/Fantasy
Robin Tate(Harry Mansfield)	God's Sin Eater	1965	Supernatural Series #101	03-Supernatural/Fantasy
Robin Tate(Harry Mansfield)	In a Glass Darkly	1964	Supernatural Series #093	03-Supernatural/Fantasy
Robin Tate(Harry Mansfield)	Spring Fever	1965	Supernatural Series #095	03-Supernatural/Fantasy
Robin Tate(Harry Mansfield)	The Abbot's Ring	1964	Supernatural Series #085	03-Supernatural/Fantasy
Robin Tate(R. L. Fanthorpe)	Curse of the Incas	1964	Supernatural Series #089	03-Supernatural/Fantasy
Robin Tate(R. L. Fanthorpe)	Midnight Ghoul	1963	Supernatural Series #081	03-Supernatural/Fantasy
Robin Tate(R. L. Fanthorpe)	The Devil's Brood	1964	Supernatural Series #091	03-Supernatural/Fantasy
Robin Tate(R. L. Fanthorpe)	The Eldritch Guide	1964	Supernatural Series #087	03-Supernatural/Fantasy
Robin Tate(R. L. Fanthorpe)	The House That Wouldn't Die	1966	Supernatural Series #103	03-Supernatural/Fantasy
Rod Patterson(John F. Watt)	Crimson Terror	1953	Futuristic Science Stories #10	02-Science Fiction
Rod Patterson(John F. Watt)	Destination - Infinity	1954	Wonders of the Spaceways #10	02-Science Fiction
Rod Patterson(John F. Watt)	Destination - Infinity	1959	Science Fiction Series #020	02-Science Fiction
Roger Carne(Sydney J. Bounds)	Prison Planet	1950	Futuristic Science Stories #03	02-Science Fiction
Ronald Adison()	Revolt!	1951	Worlds of Fantasy #03	02-Science Fiction
Roy Arnold(Tom W. Watt)	Cano Sapiens	1952	Futuristic Science Stories #07	02-Science Fiction
Stephen James()	The Purple Flower	1951	Wonders of the Spaceways #01	02-Science Fiction
Thomas Rochdale(Alfred E. Hind)	Reaction	1951	Tales of Tomorrow #03	02-Science Fiction
Thornton Bell(Harry Mansfield)	The Lady Loves Cats	1964	Supernatural Series #091	03-Supernatural/Fantasy
Thornton Bell(R. L. Fanthorpe)	Space Trap	1964	Science Fiction Series #098	02-Science Fiction
Thornton Bell(R. L. Fanthorpe)	Bell Book and Candle	1964	Supernatural Series #087	03-Supernatural/Fantasy
Thornton Bell(R. L. Fanthorpe)	Chaos	1964	Supernatural Series #092	03-Supernatural/Fantasy
Thornton Bell(R. L. Fanthorpe)	Endor's Daughter	1964	Supernatural Series #085	03-Supernatural/Fantasy
Thornton Bell(R. L. Fanthorpe)	Grimoir	1965	Supernatural Series #095	03-Supernatural/Fantasy

Psuedo/(Author)	Story Name	Date	Serie No./ Title	Section
Trebor Thorpe(Ernest Kemp)	Traveller's Rest	1963	Supernatural Series #083	03-Supernatural/Fantasy
Trebor Thorpe(R. L. Fanthorpe)	Galactic Twin	1954	Worlds of Fantasy #14	02-Science Fiction
Trebor Thorpe(R. L. Fanthorpe)	Lightning World	1960	Science Fiction Series #038	02-Science Fiction
Trebor Thorpe(R. L. Fanthorpe)	Princess in a Bubble	1953	Worlds of Fantasy #10	02-Science Fiction
Trebor Thorpe(R. L. Fanthorpe)	Saucers From Space	1954	Futuristic Science Stories #14	02-Science Fiction
Trebor Thorpe(R. L. Fanthorpe)	An Eye for an Eye	1963	Supernatural Series #071	03-Supernatural/Fantasy
Trebor Thorpe(R. L. Fanthorpe)	Bardell's Wild Talent	1960	Supernatural Series #037	03-Supernatural/Fantasy
Trebor Thorpe(R. L. Fanthorpe)	Black Marsh Mill	1961	Supernatural Series #038	03-Supernatural/Fantasy
Trebor Thorpe(R. L. Fanthorpe)	Dragon's Blood Mountain	1965	Supernatural Series #095	03-Supernatural/Fantasy
Trebor Thorpe(R. L. Fanthorpe)	Dungeon Castle	1964	Supernatural Series #093	03-Supernatural/Fantasy
Trebor Thorpe(R. L. Fanthorpe)	Excalibur	1960	Supernatural Series #030	03-Supernatural/Fantasy
Trebor Thorpe(R. L. Fanthorpe)	Five Faces of Fear	1960	Supernatural Series #032	03-Supernatural/Fantasy
Trebor Thorpe(R. L. Fanthorpe)	Forest of Evil	1961	Supernatural Series #047	03-Supernatural/Fantasy
Trebor Thorpe(R. L. Fanthorpe)	Ghost Ship	1957	Supernatural Series #013	03-Supernatural/Fantasy
Trebor Thorpe(R. L. Fanthorpe)	Lost Land of Lemuria	1961	Supernatural Series #041	03-Supernatural/Fantasy
Trebor Thorpe(R. L. Fanthorpe)	Return of Lilith	1962	Supernatural Series #055	03-Supernatural/Fantasy
Trebor Thorpe(R. L. Fanthorpe)	Secret of the Shamen	1962	Supernatural Series #065	03-Supernatural/Fantasy
Trebor Thorpe(R. L. Fanthorpe)	Song of the Banshee	1958	Supernatural Series #014	03-Supernatural/Fantasy
Trebor Thorpe(R. L. Fanthorpe)	Spirit of Darkness	1963	Supernatural Series #073	03-Supernatural/Fantasy
Trebor Thorpe(R. L. Fanthorpe)	Strange Country	1962	Supernatural Series #067	03-Supernatural/Fantasy
Trebor Thorpe(R. L. Fanthorpe)	Stranger in the Skull	1963	Supernatural Series #075	03-Supernatural/Fantasy
Trebor Thorpe(R. L. Fanthorpe)	Swamp Thing	1961	Supernatural Series #043	03-Supernatural/Fantasy
Trebor Thorpe(R. L. Fanthorpe)	The Clock That Struck Thirteen	1959	Supernatural Series #023	03-Supernatural/Fantasy
Trebor Thorpe(R. L. Fanthorpe)	The Dream of Camelot	1962	Supernatural Series #059	03-Supernatural/Fantasy
Trebor Thorpe(R. L. Fanthorpe)	The Earthen Vessel	1958	Supernatural Series #015	03-Supernatural/Fantasy
Trebor Thorpe(R. L. Fanthorpe)	The Eight Immortals	1961	Supernatural Series #051	03-Supernatural/Fantasy
Trebor Thorpe(R. L. Fanthorpe)	The Eldritch Chair	1962	Supernatural Series #057	03-Supernatural/Fantasy
Trebor Thorpe(R. L. Fanthorpe)	The House of Dreams	1961	Supernatural Series #049	03-Supernatural/Fantasy
Trebor Thorpe(R. L. Fanthorpe)	The Iron Oven	1958	Supernatural Series #016	03-Supernatural/Fantasy
Trebor Thorpe(R. L. Fanthorpe)	The Man Who Was Nothing	1959	Supernatural Series #027	03-Supernatural/Fantasy
Trebor Thorpe(R. L. Fanthorpe)	The Man Within	1959	Supernatural Series #025	03-Supernatural/Fantasy
Trebor Thorpe(R. L. Fanthorpe)	The Phantom Hand	1958	Supernatural Series #017	03-Supernatural/Fantasy
Trebor Thorpe(R. L. Fanthorpe)	The Phantom of the Goodwins	1958	Supernatural Series #019	03-Supernatural/Fantasy
Trebor Thorpe(R. L. Fanthorpe)	The Sinister Circle	1960	Supernatural Series #033	03-Supernatural/Fantasy
Trebor Thorpe(R. L. Fanthorpe)	The Snarling Shadow	1962	Supernatural Series #061	03-Supernatural/Fantasy
Trebor Thorpe(R. L. Fanthorpe)	The Sorcerer's Cave	1957	Supernatural Series #012	03-Supernatural/Fantasy
Trebor Thorpe(R. L. Fanthorpe)	The Swing of the Pendulum	1963	Supernatural Series #069	03-Supernatural/Fantasy

Checklist 2 - Story Title by Author

Psuedo/(Author)	Story Name	Date	Serie No./ Title	Section
Trebor Thorpe(R. L. Fanthorpe)	The Sword and the Statue	1964	Supernatural Series #085	03-Supernatural/Fantasy
Trebor Thorpe(R. L. Fanthorpe)	Voodoo Hell Drums	1961	Supernatural Series #039	03-Supernatural/Fantasy
Trevor Thorpe(R. L. Fanthorpe)	The Haunted Pool	1959	Supernatural Series #021	03-Supernatural/Fantasy
Uncredited()	The Forgotten days	1950	Tales of Tomorrow #01	02-Science Fiction
Uncredited()	Treasure in Space	1950	Futuristic Science Stories #03	02-Science Fiction
Uncredited(Barney Ward)	Space Adventurer	1952	Worlds of Fantasy #08	02-Science Fiction
Uncredited(Leonard G. Fish)	The Visitors	1950	Worlds of Fantasy #02	02-Science Fiction
Victor La Salle(Gerald Evans)	The Black Sphere	1952	The Black Sphere	02-Science Fiction
Victor La Salle(John Glasby)	Dawn of the Half-Gods	1953	Dawn Of The Half-Gods	02-Science Fiction
Victor La Salle(John Glasby)	Twilight Zone	1954	Twilight Zone	02-Science Fiction
Victor La Salle(John Glasby)	Twilight Zone	1959	Science Fiction Series #013	02-Science Fiction
Victor La Salle(Leonard G. Fish)	After the Atom	1953	After The Atom	02-Science Fiction
Victor La Salle(R. L. Fanthorpe)	Menace From Mercury	1954	Menace From Mercury	02-Science Fiction
Victor La Salle(Tom W. Wade)	Assault From Infinity	1953	Assault From Infinity	02-Science Fiction
Victor La Salle(Tom W. Wade)	Suns in Duo	1953	Suns In Duo	02-Science Fiction
Victor La Salle(Tom W. Wade)	The 7th Dimension	1953	The 7th Dimension	02-Science Fiction
Victor LaSalle(Tom W. Wade)	More Than Mortal	1954	Menace From Mercury	02-Science Fiction
Vincent Robertson(Tom W. Wade)	The Crystalline World	1952	Tales of Tomorrow #05	02-Science Fiction
Vincent Robertson(Tom W. Wade)	The Moment in Time	1953	Tales of Tomorrow #09	02-Science Fiction
W. B. Clarke(Norman Lazenby)	Stratoship X9	1951	Worlds of Fantasy #03	02-Science Fiction
W. E. Clarkson(Sydney J. Bounds)	Martian Apemen	1950	Futuristic Science Stories #03	02-Science Fiction
W. E. Clarkson(Sydney J. Bounds)	Menace from the Atom	1950	Futuristic Science Stories #03	02-Science Fiction
Willi Deinhardt()	Galactic Interlude	1953	Tales of Tomorrow #06	02-Science Fiction
Willi Deinhardt()	Laughing Gas	1953	Tales of Tomorrow #07	02-Science Fiction
Willi Deinhardt()	Mad Heritage	1953	Futuristic Science Stories #11	02-Science Fiction
William Bird(William Henry Fleming Bird)	Critical Age	1953	Futuristic Science Stories #12	02-Science Fiction

Psuedo/(Author)	Story Name	Date	Serie No./ Title	Section
(Charlie Coombs)	Survival in the Sky	1959	Science Series #2	02-Science Fiction
(Gray Barker)	The Unidentified	1960	Science Series #3	02-Science Fiction
(M. Vassiliev/ V. V. Dobronravov)	Sputnik Into Space	1959	Science Series #1	02-Science Fiction
(Willy Ley /Wernher Von Braun)	Project Mars	1962	Science Series #4	02-Science Fiction

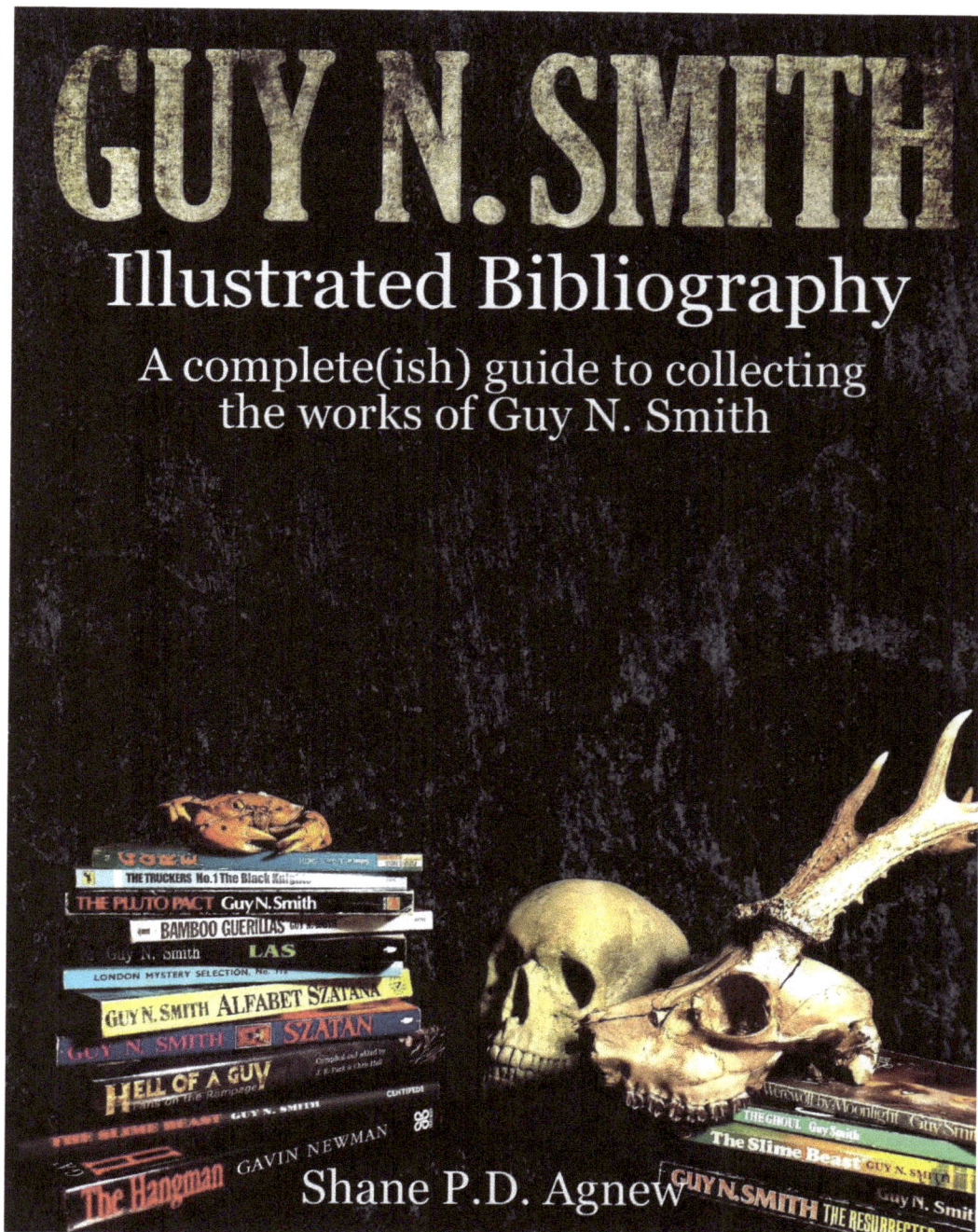

GUY N. SMITH

Illustrated Bibliography

A complete(ish) guide to collecting the works of Guy N. Smith

Shane P.D. Agnew

Also available by the Author from Amazon

A4/Letter sized, 341-page full colour Deluxe Edition with over 950 images and title information with additional space for recording and tracking your collection.

https://amzn.to/2uRf0pm